Revisiting the Philosophical Foundations of Trademarks in the US and UK

Revisiting the Philosophical Foundations of Trademarks in the US and UK

By

Mohammad Amin Naser

CAMBRIDGE
SCHOLARS
PUBLISHING

Revisiting the Philosophical Foundations of Trademarks in the US and UK,
by Mohammad Amin Naser

This book first published 2010

Cambridge Scholars Publishing

12 Back Chapman Street, Newcastle upon Tyne, NE6 2XX, UK

British Library Cataloguing in Publication Data
A catalogue record for this book is available from the British Library

ISBN (10): 1-4438-1779-1, ISBN (13): 978-1-4438-1779-0

To the soul of my late father

TABLE OF CONTENTS

PREFACE

DR ANDREAS RAHMATIAN, UNIVERSITY OF GLASGOW, UK

Until recently, the area of trademark law has not been subject to much rigorous theoretical and philosophical examination when compared with copyright or patent law. This has changed somewhat, but it has mainly been US-American scholarship which has looked into questions such as: What are the foundations of trademark systems? In which way can trademarks be justified? What is the function and purpose of trademarks? How is this function reflected in the practical application of the law by the courts? Stimulating as these debates are, they have inevitably focused on US-American trademark law and US-American legal culture.

Dr Mohammad Naser has undertaken to put the findings of US-scholarship into a broader perspective, and, by taking UK trademark law as the paradigmatic jurisdiction besides US law, he has adapted US trademark theory successfully to a European outlook and European trademark systems. In his work, the author discusses first the various philosophical theories justifying trademarks (utilitarian, economic and labour-based theories, and personality-based theories), and then develops an "economic-social planning theory" which posits that trademark systems should be formulated in a manner that helps fostering free and fair competition in the marketplace: this can only be achieved if one is aware of the fact that it is not only the trademark owner, who, by creating and using his trademark, establishes the goodwill the sign denotes, but it is also the consuming public who reacts to the sign and thereby "co-authors" the trademark. The public grants the degree of association and everything the mark stands for, thus ownership of the trademark proprietor must be qualified in the light of the (cultural) contribution of the consumers in creating the trademark.

The strength of Dr Naser's work lies in the theoretical discussion of the foundation of trademarks as well as in the detailed examination of the eminent practical implications of his theory. He highlights that current trade mark legislation has departed from the dual protection of owners and the public to the sole protection of trade mark owners, especially through widening the notion of "confusion" and introducing the idea of "dilution" within trademark infringement. Furthermore, the overemphasis on the trademark owner's rights impacts upon freedom of speech, and the author illustrates this problem with the attitude of the courts, especially the US courts, to trademark parody. The author proposes a new principle of trademark protection which permits non-confusing uses and thus protects fair competition. This principle also takes account of the right of free speech and the development of cultural and expressive uses of trademarks, in line with the economic-social planning theory. Dr Naser's work is therefore not only a major contribution to the academic debate in this area, but also relevant to the work of practitioners of trademark law.

ACKNOWLEDGEMENTS

I would like to thank and acknowledge with deep gratitude, the extraordinary effort and support of a number of people without whom this work would not have been possible.

I have to begin with my father, Qassem Al-Nasser, who shared this dream with me, but unfortunately did not live to see it come true. His unconditional love and support until the last day of his life have given me the strong base from which to rise. It is to his soul that I dedicate this work, and to his generosity and affection that I shall forever be indebted.

My mother, Shahira, whose patience and selflessness taught me that no goal is impossible to achieve. My wife, Dana and my children, Wafa and Qassem, who put up patiently with my constant preoccupations, and sacrificed valuable family time in order to see this work through. My eldest brother, Sami, who stepped up as a second father to me, and whose insight and advice I value and admire. My sisters, Rania and Rula and the rest of my brothers and sisters, who all gave me emotional stability.

My supervisor during my PhD studies, Dr. Andreas Rahamatian, deserves a special mention for his assistance and feedback. His help was indispensible in the accomplishment of this work, and his meticulous efforts in helping and guiding me towards my end goal, shall always be warmly remembered and appreciated.

Special thanks to Dr. Lior Zemer, who provided me with a steady flow of comments and invaluable suggestions, and enlightened me with his wisdom and knowledge, and for his endless support whenever my spirits were flagging. I thank him for his friendship which I value and treasure. It has made a world of difference.

I want to express as well, my gratitude to Professor Panu Minkkinen, Professor Mark Bell, Dr. Camilla Baasch Andersen, Professor Paul Torremans, Dr. Sirko Harder and Professor Spyros Maniatis. The same goes to the University of Leicester, and the University of Nottingham which have both embraced my work and extended bridges of knowledge through their faculty and grounds, without which I could not have accomplished this.

Special thanks and appreciation to the distinguished law firm, Khalaf Masadeh & Partners, to whom I owe my practical experience, and to His

Excellency Khalaf Masadeh in person for providing me with his wisdom and for believing in my capabilities.

My mentors at the University of Jordan, Dr. Tariq Hammouri, Dr. Fayad Al-Quadah, Dr. Ahamd Masadeh, Dr. Abdul-Rahman Jum'a, Dr. Bassam Talhouni and Dr. Qais Mahafzah, to whom I owe my first peek into the world of law. They are the ones who instilled in me the love of knowledge and the thrill in its pursuit. Each and every one of them was an inspiration.

I would also like to extend my deep gratitude and sincere appreciation to Dr. Aymen Masadeh, the Dean of the Faculty of Law at Yarmouk University, for his diligence and continuous support until this day.

To all of them, I offer my heartfelt thanks, for their generosity and guidance I remain indebted and humbled.

Parts of chapter two were published in 'Rethinking the Foundations of Trademarks' (2007) 5 *Buffalo Intellectual Property Law Journal* (1-49); parts of chapter three appeared in 'Re-examining the Functions of Trademark Law' (2008) 8 *Chicago-Kent Journal of Intellectual Property* (99-110); chapter four is an expanded version of 'The Lanham Act and the Trade Mark Monopoly Phobia' (2009) 4(5) *Oxford Journal of Intellectual Property Law & Practice*, (365-375); an earlier version of chapter six appeared in 'Trademarks and Freedom of Expression' (2009) 40(2) *The International Review of Intellectual Property & Competition Law (IIC)*, (188-205).

LIST OF CASES

(Case C-10/89) *S.A. Cnl-Sucal NV v Hag GF AG* [1990] 3 CMLR 571 (ECJ).

(Case C-191/01) *OHIM v Wm Wrigley Jr Co (Doublemint)* [2003] ECR I-12447 (ECJ).

(Case C-206/01) *Arsenal Football Club Plc v Reed* [2003] 1 CMLR 12 (ECJ).

(Case C-251/95) *Sabel BV v Puma AG* [1998] RPC 199 (ECJ).

(Case C-252/07) *Intel Corp Inc v CPM UK Ltd* [2008] ECR 00 (ECJ).

(Case C-291/00) *LTJ Diffusion SA v Sadas Vertbaudet SA* [2003] FSR 608 (ECJ).

(Case C-292/00) *Davidoff v Gofkid Ltd* [2003] 1 CMLR 35 (ECJ).

(Case C-292/00) *Davidoff v Gofkid Ltd* [2003] ETMR 42 (ECJ).

(Case C-299/99) *Koninklijke Philips Electronics NV v Remington Consumer Products Ltd* [2002] ECR I-5475 (ECJ).

(Case C-321/03) *Dyson Ltd v Registrar of Trade Marks* [2007] 2 CMLR 14 (ECJ).

(Case C-337/95) *Parfums Christian Dior v Evora* [1997] ECR I-6013 (ECJ).

(Case C-375/97) *General Motors Corp v Yplon Sa* [1999] 3 CMLR 427 (ECJ).

(Case C-375/97) *General Motors Corp v Yplon Sa* [2000] RPC 572 (ECJ).

(Case C-39/97) *Canon Kabushiki Kaisha v Metro-Goldwyn-Mayer Inc* [1999] RPC 117 (ECJ).

(Case C-408/01) *Adidas-Salomon AG v Fitnessworld Trading Ltd* [2004] ETMR 10 (ECJ).

(Case C-517/99) *Merz & Krell GmbH & Co* [2001] ECR I-6959 (ECJ).

(Case R 10/1998-2) *International Business Machine Corp's Application* [1998] ETMR 642 (ECJ).

24 Hour Fitness USA Inc v 24/7 Tribeca Fitness LLC 447 F.Supp.2d 266 (2006) USA.

AD2000 Trade Mark [1997] RPC 168.

Alan Kenneth McKenzie Clark v Associated Newspapers Ltd [1998] RPC 261 (Ch).

American Family Life Insurance Co v Timothy Hagan 266 F.Supp.2d 682 (2002) USA.

AMF Inc v Sleekcraft Boats 599 F.2d 341 (1979) USA.

Aunt Jemima Mills Co v Rigney & Co 247 F. 407 (1917) USA.

Avery Dennison Corp v Jerry Sumpton 189 F.3d 868 (1999) USA.

Avrick et al. v Rockmont Envelope Co 155 F.2d 568, 69 U.S.P.Q. 431 (1946) USA.

Bach and Bach Flower Remedies Trade Marks [2000] RPC 513 (CA).

Barbecue Marx Inc v 551 Ogden Inc 110 F.Supp.2d 689 (2000) USA.

Barbecue Marx Inc v 551 Ogden Inc 235 F.3d 1041 (2000) USA.

BASF Plc v CEP (U.K.) Plc [1996] ETMR 51 (Ch).

Basic Trademark SA's Application [2006] ETMR 24.

Bayer Co Inc v United Drug Co 272 F. 505 (1921) USA.

Baywatch Production Co Inc v The Home Video Channel [1997] FSR 22 (Ch).

Black Dog Tavern Co Inc v Hall 823 F.Supp. 48 (1993) USA.

Board of Supervisors of the Louisiana State University and Agricultural and Mechanical College v Smack Apparel Co 438 F.Supp.2d 653 (2006) USA.

Bond Stores v Bone Stores 104 F.2d 124 (1939) USA.

Boston Athletic Association v Mark Sullivan 867 F.2d 22 (1989) USA.

British Sugar Plc v James Robertson & Sons Ltd [1996] RPC 281 (Ch).

British Telecommunications Plc v One In A Million Ltd [1999] FSR 1 (CA).

C. A. Sheimer (M.) Sdn Bhd's Trade Mark Application [2000] RPC 484.

Cable News Network L.P. v CNNews.com 177 F.Supp.2d 506 (2001) USA.

Canal Company v Clark 80 U.S. 311 (1871) USA.

Central Hudson Gas & Elec. Corp v Public Service Commission of New York 447 U.S. 557, 100 S.Ct. 2343 (1980) USA.

Checkpoint Systems Inc v Check Point Software Technologies Inc 269 F.3d 270 (2001) USA.

Chester Barrie Ltd v The Chester Laurie Ltd 189 F.Supp. 98 (1960) USA.

Citizen Financial Group Inc v The Citizens National Bank of Evans City and Citizens Inc WL 32808575 (W.D.Pa.) (2002) USA.

Clinique Laboratories Inc v Dep Corp 945 F.Supp. 547 (1996) USA.

Coca-Cola Co v Gemini Rising Inc 346 F.Supp. 1183 (1972) USA.

Corgi Trade Mark Application [1999] RPC 549.

Dallas Cowboys Cheerleaders Inc v Pussycat Cinema 604 F.2d 200 (1979) USA.

Dart Drug Corp v Schering Corp 320 F.2d 745, 116 U.S.App.D.C. 23 (1963) USA.

Deere & Co v MTD Products Inc 41 F.3d 39 (1994) USA.

Design Solange Ltd Inc v Lane Bryant Inc WL 599552 (S.D.N.Y.) (1997) USA.

Diane Von Furstenberg Studio v Catherine Snyder and Richard Snyder 2007 WL 2688184 (E.D.Va.) USA.

Dorr-Oliver Inc v Fluid-Quip Inc 94 F.3d 376 (1996) USA.

Dr. Seuss Enterprises L.P. v Penguin Books USA Inc 924 F.Supp. 1559 (1996) USA.

Duluth News-Tribune v Mesabi Publishing Co 84 F.3d 1093 (1996) USA.

Electrocoin Automatics Ltd v Coinworld Ltd [2005] FSR 7 (Ch).

Eli Lilly & Co v Natural Answers Inc 233 F.3d 456 (2000) USA.

Elvis Presley Enterprises Inc v Barry Capece 950 F.Supp. 783 (1996) USA.

Elvis Presley Enterprises Inc v Capece 141 F.3d 188 (1998) USA.

Estate of P. D. Beckwith Inc v Comr of Patents 252 U.S. 538, 40 S.Ct. 414 (1920) USA.

Farberware Inc v Mr. Coffee Inc 740 F.Supp. 291 (1990) USA.

Feathercombs Inc v Solo Products Co 306 F.2d 251 (1962) USA.

Fisons Horticulture Inc v Vigoro Industries Inc 30 F.3d 466 (1994) USA.

Freedom Savings and Loan Association v Vernon Waw Jr. d/b/a Freedom Realty 757 F.2d 1176 (1985) USA.

French Connection Ltd's Trade Mark Application [2007] ETMR 8.

Giant Food Inc v Nation's Foodservice Inc 710 F.2d 1565 (1983) USA.

Gilbert/Robinson Inc v Carrie Beverage-Missouri Inc 758 F.Supp. 512 (1991) USA.

Girl Scouts of the US of America v Personality Posters Mfg Co 304 F.Supp. 1228 (1969) USA.

Hanover Star Milling Co v Metcalf 240 US 403 (1916) USA.

Hyde Park Clothes Inc v Hyde Park Fashions Inc 204 F.2d 223 (1953) USA.

Intel Corp Inc v CPM UK Ltd [2007] ETMR 59 (CA).

International Bancorp L.L.C. v Societe Des Bains De Mer Et Du Cercle Des Etrangers A Monaco 192 F.Supp.2d 467 (2002) USA.

J.M. Huber Corp v Lowery Wellheads Inc 778 F.2d 146 (1985) USA.

Javar Coffee Co Inc v Jos Martinson & Co Inc 142 F.Supp. 423 (1956) USA.

Jews For Jesus v Steven C. Brodsky 993 F.Supp. 282 (1998) USA.

Jordache Enterprises Inc v Hogg Wyld Ltd 828 F.2d 1482 (1987) USA.

Jordache Enterprises Inc v Levi Strauss & Co 841 F.Supp. 506 (1993) USA.

King-Seeley Thermos Co v Aladdin Industries Inc 321 F.2d 577 (1963) USA.

Knight v Beyond Properties Pty Ltd [2007] FCR 34 (Ch).
Kraft Foods Holdings Inc v Helm 205 F.Supp.2d 942 (2002) USA.
L.L. Bean Inc v Drake Publishers Inc 811 F.2d 26 (1987) USA.
L'Oreal SA v Bellure NV [2008] ETMR 1 (CA).
Lawrence Manuf'g Co v Tennessee Manuf'g Co 138 U.S. 537, 11 S.Ct. 396 (1891) USA.
Linkin Park LLC's Application [2006] ETMR 74.
Lois Sportswear U.S.A. Inc v Levi Strauss & Co 799 F.2d 867 (1986) USA.
Lone Star Steakhouse & Saloon Inc v Alpha of Virginia Inc 43 F.3d 922 (1995) USA.
Louis Vuitton Malletier v Haute Diggity Dog 507 F.3d 252 (2007) USA.
Major League Baseball Properties Inc v Sed Non Olet Denarius Ltd 817 F.Supp. 1103 (1993) USA.
Manufacturing Co v Trainer 101 U.S. 51 (1879) USA.
McDonald'S Corp v McBagel's Inc 649 F.Supp. 1268 (1986) USA.
McGregor-Doniger Inc v Drizzle Inc 599 F.2d 1126 (1979) USA.
McLean v Fleming 96 U.S. 245, 6 Otto 245 (1877) USA.
Miles Shoes Inc v R. H. Macy & Co Inc 199 F.2d 602 (1952) USA.
Miller Brewing Co v Carling O'Keefe Breweries of Canada Ltd 452 F.Supp. 429 (1978) USA.
Miss World Ltd v Channel Four Television Corp [2007] ETMR 66.
Montblanc-Simplo GmbH v Aurora Due S.R.L. 363 F.Supp.2d 467 (2005) USA.
Mushroom Maker Inc v R. G. Barry Corp 441 F.Supp. 1220 (1977) USA.
Mutual of Omaha Ins. Co v Novak 836 F.2d 397 (1987) USA.
Nabisco Inc v PF Brands Inc 191 F.3d 208 (1999) USA.
Nike Inc v Just Did It Enterprises 6 F.3d 1225 (1993) USA.
Nike Inc v Nikepal International Inc 2007 WL 2688499 (E.D.Cal.) USA.
O2 Holdings Ltd v Hutchison 3G Ltd [2006] RPC 29 (Ch).
Origins Natural Resources Inc v Origin Clothing Ltd [1995] FSR 280 (Ch).
Ortho Pharmaceutical Corp v American Cyanamid Co 361 F.Supp. 1032 (1973) USA.
Pepsico Inc v #1 Wholesale LLC 2007 WL 2142294 (N.D.Ga.) USA.
Perkins School for the Blind v Maxi-Aids Inc 274 F.Supp.2d 319 (2003) USA.
Pet Silk Inc v Maria Jackson 481 F.Supp.2d 824 (2007) USA.
Pfizer Ltd v Eurofood Link (U.K.) Ltd [2001] FSR 3 (Ch).
Phones 4u Ltd v Phone4u.co.uk. Internet Ltd [2007] RPC 5 (CA).
Planetary Motion Inc v Techsplosion Inc 261 F.3d 1188 (2001) USA.
Polaroid Corp v Polarad Electronics Corp 287 F.2d 492 (1961) USA.

Polymer Technology Corp v Emile Mimran 37 F.3d 74 (1994) USA.
Premier Brands UK Ltd v Typhoon Europe Ltd [2000] ETMR 1071 (Ch).
R. v Besnier S.A.'s Trade Mark Application [2002] RPC 6.
R. v IDG Communications Ltd's Trade Mark Application [2002] RPC 10.
Reckitt & Colman Products Ltd v Borden Inc [1990] RPC 341 (HL).
Ringling Bros.-Barnum v Utah Division of Travel Development 170 F.3d 449 (1999) USA.
Sally Beauty Co Inc v Beautyco Inc 304 F.3d 964 (2002) USA.
San Francisco Arts & Athletics Inc v US Olympic Committee 483 US 522, 107 S Ct 2971 (1987) USA.
Scott Paper Co v Scott's Liquid Gold Inc 589 F.2d 1225 (1978) USA.
Stop the Olympic Prison v US Olympic Committee 489 F.Supp. 1112 (1980) USA.
Surfvivor Media Inc v Survivor Productions 406 F.3d 625 (2005) USA.
Syntex Laboratories Inc v The Norwich Pharmacal Co 437 F.2d 566 (1971) USA.
Taittinger SA v Allbev Ltd [1993] FSR 641 (CA).
The Earth Technology Corp v Environmental Research & Technology Inc WL 877 (C.D.Cal.) (1983) USA.
The New West Corp v NYM Co of California Inc 595 F.2d 1194 (1979) USA.
Times Mirror Magazines Inc v Las Vegas Sports News LLC 212 F.3d 157 (2000) USA.
Tommy Hilfiger Licensing Inc v Nature Labs LLC 221 F.Supp.2d 410 (2002) USA.
Trade-Mark Cases 100 US 82 (1879) USA.
Trans Union LLC v Credit Research Inc 142 F.Supp.2d 1029 (2001) USA.
Two Pesos Inc v Taco Cabana Inc 505 U.S. 763, 112 S.Ct. 2753 (1992) USA.
U.S. Structures Inc v J.P. Structures Inc 130 F.3d 1185 (1997) USA.
Universal City Studios Inc v Nintendo Co Ltd 746 F.2d 112 (1984) USA.
V Secret Catalogue Inc v Victor Moseley 2000 WL 370525 (W.D.Ky.) (2000) USA.
V Secret Catalogue Inc v Victor Moseley 259 F.3d 464 (2001) USA.
V Secret Catalogues Inc v Victor Moseley 558 F.Supp.2d 734 (2008) USA.
Victor Moseley v V Secret Catalogue Inc 537 U.S. 418, 123 S.Ct. 1115 (2003) USA.
W.W.W. Pharmaceutical Co Inc v The Gillette Co 984 F.2d 567 (1993) USA.
Wagamama Ltd v City Centre Restaurants Plc [1995] FSR 713 (Ch).
Westchester Media v PRL USA Holdings Inc 214 F.3d 658 (2000) USA.

Western Publishing Co Inc v Rose Art Industries Inc 910 F.2d 57 (1990) USA.

WHS Entertainment Ventures v United Paperworkers International Union 997 F.Supp. 946 (1998) USA.

Worthington Foods Inc v Kellogg Co 732 F.Supp. 1417 (1990) USA.

Yale Electric Corp v Robertson Comr of Patents 26 F.2d 972 (2d Cir. 1928) USA.

CHAPTER ONE

INTRODUCTION

This book starts with the observation that the rights of trademark owners have recently expanded to extreme levels.[1] This has happened to the detriment of the rights of the consuming public and other traders and rivals.[2] The assessment of trademark infringement has departed from "confusion" to a new standard, which does not take into consideration the state of mind of the consuming public: "dilution". This expansion in favour of trademark owners threatens to hinder the ability of the public to use trademarks in cultural and expressive uses.[3] In addition, the rights of other traders and rivals would also be affected. Other traders and rivals are prevented from using registered marks, even if such uses are not likely to confuse the public as to "source and origin".[4] This could create barriers against new entrants, and eventually might result in obstructing free and fair competition.

Arguments attempting to justify the expansion of the rights of trademark owners have relied upon utilitarian and economic justifications. This justification considers that trademarks reduce consumer search costs.[5] According to this utilitarian and economic theory, trademark owners should be ensured the maximum protection possible.[6] This aims to provide owners with the proper incentives to produce high quality products,[7] and

---

[1] See *infra* pp 4-5.

[2] ibid.

[3] See *infra* p 11.

[4] In this book, the terms "source" and "origin" hold the same meaning; they are used to denote the identification function of trademarks.

[5] WM Landes and RA Posner 'The Economics of Trademark Law' (1988) 78 Trademark Reporter 270. See also, SL Carter 'The Trouble with Trademark' (1989-1990) 99 Yale L J 762. See also, N Economides 'The Economics of Trademarks' (1988) 78 Trademark Reporter 526. See also, ch 2 pp 17-23.

[6] See ch 2 pp 17-23.

[7] PS Menell 'Intellectual Property: General Theories' in B Bouckaert and G de Geest (eds) *Encyclopedia of Law & economics* (Edward Elgar Cheltenham UK 2000) Vol 2, 149. See also, A Kozinski 'Trademarks Unplugged' (1994) 84

to ensure the maximization of wealth.[8] The book holds that the incentive argument is subjective, and differs on an individual basis.[9] It is also suggested that the wealth maximization argument is artificial,[10] and focuses solely on trademark owners. As such, the utilitarian and economic justification is responsible for this expansion of rights in favour of trademark owners. However, the reduction of consumer search costs is a valid argument, because it proves the need for the existence of trademark systems. Nevertheless, this could only be a starting point in the process of justifying trademarks, but falls short in providing a full justification, because it does not provide boundaries for the rights of trademark owners.

Since a theoretical approach is deployed for the maximization of trademark owners' rights, it seems that revisiting the philosophical foundations of current trademark systems is essential. In addition, it is vital to provide a further theoretical framework, which could set out boundaries to protect trademark owners, and would be able to provide justice to trademark owners, the consuming public and other traders and rivals. In search of more theoretical clarity, this book examines Locke's labour theory,[11] and Hegel's personhood approach.[12] However, it is suggested that the premises of these theories are not applicable to trademarks.[13]

The case of the Social-Planning theory is different. This theory considers that trademark systems should be formulated in a manner which helps to foster a "just and attractive culture".[14] In this culture monopoly is prohibited,[15] and an environment of free and fair competition is

---

Trademark Reporter 451. See also, AD Moore 'Intellectual property, Innovation, and Social Progress: The Case Against Incentive Based Arguments' (2003) Vol 26:3 Hamline L Rev 607. See also, EC Hettinger 'Justifying Intellectual Property' (1989) Vol 18 No 1 Philosophy and Public Affairs 47-48. See also, ch 2 pp 17-23.

[8] NS Kinsella 'Against Intellectual Property' (2001) Vol 15 No 2 J of Libertarian Studies 11, available at <http://www.mises.org/journals/jls/15_2/15_2_1.pdf> (26 August 2009). See also, ch 2 pp 17-23.

[9] See ch 2 pp 25-27.

[10] ibid pp 23-24.

[11] ibid pp 30-34.

[12] ibid pp 40-44.

[13] ibid pp 34-30, 44-47.

[14] W Fisher 'Theories of Intellectual Property' in S Munzer (ed) *New Essays in the Legal and Political Theory of Property* (1st edn Cambridge University Press Cambridge 2001) 172. See also, *infra* p 10. See also, ch 2 pp 57-59.

[15] WJ Gordon 'On Owning Information: Intellectual Property and the Restitutionary Impulse' (1992) Virginia L Rev 157.

promoted.[16] The Public Authorship Model, which is a sub-theory, helps to clarify the claims of the Social-Planning theory.[17] It considers that the process of creating a trademark passes through two stages, in the first stage the trademark owner affixes a sign over his/her products,[18] while in the second stage the consuming public attribute an association between the mark and the products on which the mark is affixed.[19] Thus, trademarks are jointly "authored" and owned by trademark owners and the consuming public.[20]

As such, this book develops what could be called the Economic-Social Planning theory, which is not merely a conjuncture of parts of the economic and social theories, but rather builds upon these theories in order to provide proper solutions to the current troubles with trademarks.[21] In an attempt to combine theory with practice, the Economic-Social Planning theory provides new arguments regarding the functions of trademarks. Accordingly, the source and origin function is considered as the only *primary* function of trademarks,[22] and owners of well-known trademarks are provided with extra protection.[23] A major theme that stems from the theoretical and practical propositions developed by book consider that the consuming public should enjoy the right not to be confused in regards to trademarks, and shall also be able to use trademarks for cultural and expressive purposes. In addition, the trademark owner should be able to offer his/her products, and compete with other traders, by ensuring product differentiation in the marketplace. However, other traders and rivals should enjoy the right to use trademarks when such uses are not likely to affect the product differentiation.

The US and UK are used as case studies[24] which will assist in proving the merits of the suggested theoretical approach and the need to revisit the philosophical foundations of current trademark systems. After this general outline of the book, the next section clarifies in more clarity the trouble with current trademark systems.

---

[16] See *infra* p 10.

[17] See ch 2 pp 50-52.

[18] S Wilf 'Who Authors Trademarks?' (1999) 17 Cardozo Arts & Entertainment L J 8. See also, ch 2 pp 57-59.

[19] Wilf (n18) 8. See also, ch 2 pp 57-59.

[20] See ch 2 pp 57-59. See also, *infra* p 10.

[21] See *infra* pp 6-8.

[22] ibid. See also, ch 3 pp 75-78.

[23] See *infra* pp 6-8. See also, ch 3 pp 78-80.

[24] See generally chs 4, 5 and 6.

The Trouble with Trademarks

As has been outlined above, current trademark systems have widened the scope of the rights of trademark owners. Today, words, designs, devices, shapes and packaging of goods are registrable, amongst others.[25] In respect of this wide range of registrable marks, the scope of the confusion test for trademark infringement has been widened,[26] in addition to the introduction of the dilution test which aims to preserve the uniqueness and singularity of trademarks.[27] Some scholars have cited this expansion of the rights of trademark owners. For example, Assaf argues that:

> '[T]h[e] extensive protection [of trademarks] is primarily due to two factors: (1) a very broad interpretation of the term "consumer confusion" and (2) the dilution doctrine, which protects famous trademarks from non-confusing uses.'[28]

This expansion in the rights of trademark owners has happened to the detriment of the rights of the consuming public. The consuming public are affected in two main respects, amongst others. Firstly, as has been argued above, the confusion test for trademark infringement is interpreted widely,[29] and the dilution concept is directed towards the non-confusion

---

[25] See for example, Trade Marks Act 1994 (UK) c 26 s 1(1), providing that: 'A trade mark may, in particular, consist of words (including personal names), designs, letters, numerals or the shape of goods or their packaging.' See also, Trademarks Act 1946- Lanham Act (USA) 15 U.S.C. § 1127 (Section 45), providing that: 'The term "trademark" includes any word, name, symbol, or device, or any combination thereof'.

[26] For example, section 32(a) of the Lanham Act does not require that confusion should be as to the source of origin of goods or services. See- Trademarks Act 1946- Lanham Act (USA) 15 U.S.C. § 1114 (Section 32(a)). This open the way for concepts such as subliminal confusion. See- M Leaffer 'Sixty Years of the Lanham Act: The Decline and Demise of Monopoly Phobia' in H Hansen (ed) *U.S. Intellectual Property Law and Policy* (1st edn Edward Elgar Cheltenham 2006) 131. See also, ch 4 pp 102-106.

[27] FI Schechter 'The Rational Basis of Trademark Protection' (Reprint in 1970 of the 1927 text) 60 Trademark Reporter 339. See also, ch 3 pp 64-67 and ch 4 pp 125-128.

[28] K Assaf 'The Dilution of Culture and the Law of Trademarks' (2008) 49 IDEA: The Intellectual Property L Rev 4.

[29] See ch 4 pp 96-113. See also, ch 5 pp 162-174.

uses.[30] Therefore, the state of mind of the public is not considered as *the* test trademark infringement, this undermines the role of the public in trademarks. Secondly, the right of the consuming public to use trademarks to express their ideas and communicate their thoughts is put at serious possible risk.[31] Some jurisdictions have totally ignored the right of the public to use trademarks in cultural contexts,[32] while other jurisdictions have treated this right of the public as an exception to the rights of the trademark owner.[33] It is suggested that treating the right of the public to use trademarks in cultural and expressive uses as an exception is not satisfactory.[34] After having identified the research problem, it is important to discuss the scope and objectives of this book.

Scope and Objectives

In the light of the above-mentioned troubles with trademarks, this book aims to deal with the following questions: Is there a real need to revisit the philosophical foundations of trademarks? If so, how could the protection of trademarks be formulated in a manner that ensures the rights of the parties in the trademark formula?

As such, the scope of this book is not to provide definite answers to the technicalities of trademark protection. Rather, its purpose is to underline a new theoretical justification which forms a just and equitable approach to trademarks. In particular, the book focuses on the process of the creation of marks, giving more emphasis to the usually ignored role of the public in this regard. The book aims to establish a justification for a system which allows more public access to trademarks, namely in cultural and expressive contexts.[35] This also forms the premise of this book; namely that a reform in the current systems of trademarks is crucial in seeking to overcome the weaknesses they are encountering. Policy should be driven

---

[30] See ch 4 pp 115-139. See also, ch 5 pp 174-187.

[31] RC Dreyfuss 'Expressive Genericity: Trademarks as Language in the Pepsi Generation' (1989-1990) 65 Notre Dame L Rev 416. See also, ch 2 pp 52-56.

[32] For example, in the UK no freedom of expression defence is provided. See- SM Maniatis and E Gredley 'Parody: A Fatal Attraction? Part 2: Trade Mark Parodies' (1997) 19(8) EIPR 420.

[33] For example, see- Trademark Dilution Revision Act 2005 (USA) § 2 – Trademarks Act 1946- Lanham Act (USA) 15 U.S.C. § 1125 (Section 43(c) (3)).

[34] See *infra* pp 6-8. See also, ch 6 pp 196-199.

[35] Parody is taken as an example of the relevance of the Economic-Social Planning theory which is developed by this book. See *infra* p 11.

to ensure justice amongst all the parties in the trademark context,[36] because trademarks should not turn into monopolies, but rather, should be beneficial to all parts of the community.

It should be noted that the scope of the justification sought in this book is only considered from the perspective of trademark law. Therefore, the role of other laws lies beyond the ambit of this book. For example, the right of trademark owners to contest uses affecting the reputation of their marks by the law of defamation, and the rights of the consuming public under contract and consumer protection, laws are irrelevant for the purposes of this book.

Tools of Evaluation

In regards to testing the premises, the evaluation of theory will be the main methodological tool. Different theoretical approaches are deployed in order to revisit the philosophical foundations of trademark protection. In this assessment, the cases of the USA and UK will be examined to outline the problem and assert its existence. The US deploys a theory which forms the extreme end for trademark protection in the world, where monopolistic rights are enjoyed by trademark owners, and the rights of the public are almost diminished. Thus, this serves as a good model for this book. Such a study will clearly show the negative effects of such a theoretical approach, and prove the need to revisit the foundations of current trademark systems. The case of the UK is also significant; it represents a model of the majority of trademark systems in the world today, because of its implementation of European and international frameworks. As such, the UK Trade Marks Act (TMA) represents an interesting case for study.

Having defined the scope and objectives of this book, and the tools for evaluating its premises, it seems beneficial to outline the main features of the Economic-Social Planning theory, as developed by this book.

The Economic-Social Planning Theory

In dealing with the above-mentioned troubles with current trademark systems,[37] this book develops the Economic-Social Planning theory. This theory adopts the economic aspect that trademarks reduce consumer search costs,[38] in addition to the Social-Planning theory and its sub-theory:

---

[36] See ch 7 p 223.
[37] See *supra* pp 4-5.
[38] See ch 2 pp 27-30.

the Public Authorship Model.[39] However, the Economic-Social Planning theory is not confined to picking and mixing a number of theoretical approaches. It develops a coherent argument by building upon, and altering, the premises of these approaches. As such, the Economic-Social Planning theory contributes to existing theoretical approaches in a number of aspects, such as, amongst others:

Firstly, as regards the right of the public, this book develops an argument which considers that the consuming public should enjoy the right in having their state of mind as the sole test for trademark infringement.[40] Accordingly, the confusion test should be the only standard for assessing infringement of trademarks. This derives from the premise of the Economic-Social Planning theory that trademarks are "co-authored" by the public and trademark owners.

Here, it seems essential to define "why" and "how" the "co-authorship" is a critical issue. The "co-authorship" of trademarks is critical because it provides boundaries to the rights of trademark owners. Owners are not considered as the only player in the context of trademarks. As such, the "co-authorship" of trademarks justifies the right of trademark owners to offer their goods and/or services in the marketplace, and to compete with other traders and rivals. In addition, this "co-authorship" creates competing interests in favour of the consuming public; this means that the proprietary rights of trademark owners are limited *ab initio*.[41] As regards the manner of obtaining such rights, the "co-authorship" explains the manner of creating trademarks. The Economic-Social Planning theory does not aim to extinguish the rights of trademark owners. Therefore, the rights of owners are taken into consideration because of their role in "co-authoring" trademarks. This role is manifested by the initiative taken by a trademark owner in affixing a sign over his/her goods and/or services. However, without the association that the consuming public attribute between the mark and the products, the mark will not get any value. Therefore, the "co-authorship" is obtained through the roles of the owners and consuming public in creating trademarks.

Secondly, this book develops an argument in relation to the functions of trademarks.[42] The merit of the offered approach towards the functions of trademarks is that it acknowledges all the functions thereof, unlike other

---

[39] ibid pp 42-53.
[40] ibid pp 51-53. See also, ch 3 p 81.
[41] Wilf (n18) 3-5.
[42] See ch 3 pp 75-80.

approaches.[43] As such, trademarks denote the source and origin of products. They also resemble quality to consumers; this quality varies amongst individual consumers according to their tastes and preferences.[44] In addition, trademarks assist in advertising and conveying information to consumers.

The Economic-Social Planning theory considers that the source and origin function should be the only *primary* function.[45] This is because protection of trademarks should be based upon this function. This accords with the presumption that the state of mind of the public (confusion) should be the standard for trademark infringement. This does not aim to cancel other functions; rather, these should be considered as secondary functions. They are considered secondary because the quality function differs amongst individuals. Therefore, protection cannot be built upon this function. Regarding the advertising and informative functions, these could be assessed through the confusion test.[46] As such, these functions are acknowledged by this book, but only as secondary functions, upon which trademark systems could not be based. By contrast, the source and origin function, being the only *primary* function, forms the basis upon which trademark systems should be based.

Thirdly, the Economic-Social Planning theory develops a new vision regarding the protection of well-known trademarks. It is suggested that owners of well-known trademarks should enjoy more protection than owners of ordinary trademarks.[47] However, this book considers that this extra protection should extend to cover dissimilar goods and/or services, provided that the use of the well-known mark is likely to confuse the public as to source and origin. This proves that the source and origin function, as the only *primary* function, has been developed by the Economic-Social Planning theory to deal with the problem of extending the protection of well-known marks.

---

[43] For example, Schechter disregards the origin function of trademarks, he argues that: 'Four hundred years ago a trademark indicated either the origin or ownership of the goods to which it was affixed. To what extent does the trademark of today really function as either? Actually, not in the least!' See- Schechter (n27) 335. See also, ch 3 pp 64-67.

[44] See ch 3 pp 70-72.

[45] ibid pp 75-78.

[46] Some scholars considered the advertising and informative functions are indirectly included under the source function. See- PLC Torremans 'The Likelihood of Association of Trade Marks: An Assessment in the Light of the Recent Case Law of the Court of Justice' (1998) 3 Intellectual Property Q 307.

[47] See ch 3 pp 78-80.

Fourthly, the Economic-Social Planning theory develops new orientations regarding the right of the public to use trademarks in cultural and expressive uses.[48] Accordingly, the consuming public should be able to use trademarks for such purposes provided that such uses are non-confusing. Similarly, other traders should be able to use trademarks if such uses are not likely to confuse the consuming public. This creates a new formula for trademarks which includes trademark owners, the consuming public and other traders and rivals.[49]

In the light of the above-mentioned conceptions, a number of terms have been introduced. These terms shall be defined below in accordance with the premises of the Economic-Social Planning theory.

Definition 1: Trademarks

For the purposes of this book, the word "trademarks" will be used to refer to any sign which is adopted by an undertaking, who attaches this sign to the goods and/or services which he/she produces or provides, and to which the consuming public attribute an association between this sign and the products. The amount of association provided by the public is ordinary: as such, the word "trademarks" is the equivalent of the term "ordinary trademarks". The effectiveness and use of "trademarks" in the marketplace is thus straightforward: They mainly refer to the source and origin of the products to which the "trademark" is affixed. They need not denote the producers *per se*; however, they should refer to a certain source and origin, which could be anonymous.

Definition 2: Well-Known Trademarks

The term "well-known trademarks" refers to signs which were originally "ordinary trademarks", but to which the consuming public attribute a higher degree of association than other ordinary trademarks. The ability of "well-known trademarks" to fulfill the primary function as source and origin identifiers is also higher. Thus, in order to protect the validity of such signs as source identifiers, there should be a distinct mode of protection for "well-known trademarks". This should provide extra protection, to the extent that it ensures the protection of the public and the owner in cases of any use by others, which might affect the "well-known"

[48] See ch 2 pp 57-59. See also, ch 6 pp 196-205.

[49] See *infra* p 11.

mark's ability to denote the source and origin of the products to which they are affixed.

Definition 3: Co-Authorship of Trademarks

As may be inferred from definitions 1 and 2 above, the creation of trademarks depends upon a two step process; first, the owner adopts a sign and affixes it to his/her products, second, the public create an association between the sign and the products. The case of well-known trademarks includes a further third step where the public provide higher level of association. This process of trademarks' creation is referred to as the "co-authorship of trademarks" by the owner and the consuming public. It shall be argued that the process of "co-authorship" entitles the owner and the public to the "co-ownership" of such marks.

Definition 4: Trademark Owners

In accordance with the view that trademarks are "co-authored" by the public and the owner, and due to the nature of trademarks, this book holds the view that trademarks are not the sole property rights of owners, but are, rather, a bundle of rights in favour of the owner *and* the consuming public. Therefore, rights in trademarks should be mutually enjoyed and exercised by the public and the owner; such rights reside in the entitlements that should be conveyed to those parties. As such, the public and owners are both the real owners of the rights in trademarks; this means that reference to the owner does not mean ownership *per se*, but rather, refers to the trademark registrant. The use of the term "owner" of the trademark refers to the user or registrant of the trademark, who affixes the sign over his/her products, and retains ownership of certain rights in the mark.

Definition 5: Just and Attractive Culture

The Economic-Social Planning theory considers that trademark systems should be formulated in a manner which helps to foster a "just and attractive culture". This term will be used in this book to refer to a culture where monopoly of trademarks on the part of owners is not permitted. In this "just and attractive culture", the use of trademarks should promote an environment of free and fair competition in the marketplace.

Definition 6: Trademark Formula

To achieve a "just and attractive culture", there exists the need to recognize the parties involved in the context of trademarks. Plainly, the owner and also the public are parties to the trademarks. However, they are not the only parties; other traders and rivals are suggested to be another third party, which retains the right to use the mark in cases where such use shall not affect the ability of the mark to denote the source and origin of the goods and/or services to which they are attached.[50] Consequently, the owner, consuming public and other traders and rivals are the parties involved in a trademark context; this phenomenon will be referred to as the "trademark formula".

Definition 7: Cultural and Expressive Uses

The Economic-Social Planning theory argues in favour of ensuring the right of the consuming public to use trademarks for cultural and expressive uses.[51] The forms of cultural and expressive uses are manifold, from amongst of which are parodistic uses and uses for comparative advertising. These uses, as part of the fundamental human right of free speech, aim to protect the speaker's interest in communicating ideas and information, and/or safeguarding the audience's interest in receiving ideas and information, and/or ensuring the public's interest in speech.[52]

In this book, parody, in particular, is taken as an example of the relevance of the Economic-Social Planning theory, for many reasons. For instance, parody is an example which involves the right of the speaker,[53] and the public interest.[54] In any case, parody also maintains the right of the public to receive the information. By contrast, the case of comparative advertising, for example, focuses mainly on the right of rivals to use trademarks of others to explain the features of their products, therefore, the rights of the public are less apparent in this case.

---

[50] CDG Pickering *Trade Marks in Theory and Practice* (1st edn Hart Publishing Oxford 1998) 97-98.

[51] See ch 2 pp 52-56.

[52] E Barendt *Freedom of Speech* (2nd edn Oxford University Press Oxford 2005) 23-30.

[53] When the parody is done by an individual.

[54] When a group of people use the mark to express their ideas.

The Road Map

The purpose of Chapter Two is to discuss the different ideologies justifying trademarks. It starts with the utilitarian and economic justification for trademarks, which forms the grounds for the current expansion in trademark owners' rights. It will be argued that the premises of this theory are not based on solid ground. However, this chapter supports partial adherence to the utilitarian and economic justification, on the grounds that trademarks do reduce and lower consumer search costs. Nevertheless, this necessitates other theoretical frameworks, in order to define the protectable parties and the scope for their protection. In the search for more theoretical clarity, the validity of Locke's labour theory and Hegel's personhood approach will be evaluated. It will be argued that the labour theory, which was designed to cover tangible property, over-compensates trademark owners. Similarly, the Hegelian approach fails to justify trademarks. The main argument for rejecting this theory is that it presupposes that any piece of property is part of its owner's will, and is thus inalienable. This theory fails to justify the alienability of trademarks from one owner to the other. However, the intervention of the last theory, the Social-Planning theory, is essential in providing the limits and boundaries of the trademark owner's rights. It admits the role of the public in the creation of the mark and draws a balance between the rights of the owner and the public, by granting the public the entitlement to cultural and expressive uses, because they contribute to the creation of trademarks. The conclusion of this second chapter lies in the adoption of the suggested framework, which is the Economic-Social Planning for the justification of trademarks.

The third chapter develops an argument as to the functions of trademarks, in the light of the suggested theoretical framework in chapter two. It argues that the source and origin function is the only *primary* function of trademarks, and forms the real rational basis for trademark protection. As such, the proper implementation of this function is to adopt the confusion concept as the test for assessing trademark infringement. The adoption of the confusion test fulfils the moral claims of the suggested theory. It ensures proper protection to all parties in the trademark formula. More importantly, this argument is capable of providing extra protection for owners of well-known trademarks, namely in prohibiting any use of the well-known mark over dissimilar products, if such a use causes any confusion to the public. As such, this chapter provides a practical application to the suggested theoretical framework, attempting to combine theory with practice.

Chapter Four looks extensively at the US trademark system (Lanham Act). It examines the theoretical foundations of the Act, and cites the shift in the aims and purposes of this Act, because when it was first enacted it aimed to protect the owners and the public, whereas today there exists an extreme shift towards exclusive proprietary rights for owners, at the expense of other parties as set out in the trademark formula. Furthermore, this chapter examines two forms of trademark infringement: the confusion doctrine and the dilution doctrine. It will be argued that the adoption of dilution, on the basis of the utilitarian theory, is the real harm in the field of trademarks. This is based on the premise that trademarks are quality identifiers and should provide wide scope of protection for trademark owners to ensure them the proper incentives to maintain the production of quality products. This chapter aims to prove that the protection afforded currently under the Lanham Act assists in the assessment and proof of the premise that current trademark systems are not based on real and solid theoretical grounds, and that they do not comply with the standards of the suggested theoretical framework, thus revisiting the philosophical foundations of trademarks is evident.

Chapter Five examines the UK TMA in the light of the EC approach. It considers whether the UK TMA has also shifted towards the dilution doctrine favouring trademark owners. This chapter tackles the foundations of this system; it is suggested that this Act does not rely on a clear theoretical basis. This is, in particular, due to the fact that this Act came to fulfill regional and international obligations. However, it seems that the utilitarian aspects are prevalent through the adoption of "semi-dilution" concept and granting property rights solely to trademark owners. Accordingly, this chapter contributes in the estimation and assessment of the premises of this book.

Chapter Six examines the right of the public in using trademarks in cultural and expressive contexts. It takes the case of trademark parody as an example of the relevance of the suggested theoretical framework. This chapter aims to support the argument for a wide public access to trademarks. The process of "meaning-making" of trademarks entitles the public to be protected in using trademarks as means of ensuring their fundamental human right in free expression. This chapter argues that the utilitarian justification for trademarks harms extensively the use of cultural signs and symbols for the purposes of parody, satire, criticism which the public attribute to the mark. The right of the public in freedom of speech is supported by the premises of the Economic-Social Planning theory, and also constitutes a fundamental human right which is usually ignored by current trademark systems. This contradicts the US Constitution and the

UK Human Rights Act, which aim to secure the public this fundamental right.

The concluding chapter reemphasises the premises of the Economic-Social Planning theory, in order to recollect the solutions which this book aims to provide to current trademark systems.

CHAPTER TWO

THE PHILOSOPHICAL FOUNDATIONS OF TRADEMARKS

Introduction

Trademarks are social and legal entities.[1] This derives from the fact that misallocation of property rights in trademarks might have significant effects on society.[2] Trademarks are, thus, jointly "authored" and owned by trademark owners and the consuming public.[3] However, current trademark legislation, as well as a wide range of scholarship, fails to recognize this joint authorship of trademarks. Therefore, it seems essential to revisit the current philosophical foundations of trademarks. This requires investigating the many arguments that justify and confer property rights on trademark.

Legal scholarship is divided as regards the importance of theory to intellectual property rights. Some scholars argue that, from a practical point of view, it is not necessary to tackle the appropriate justification for trademarks or intellectual property rights in general.[4] Yet such justifications are in fact an extreme necessity, because such philosophical foundations are crucial to the understanding of the policy behind any piece of legislation. Indeed, they form guidelines determining the rights granted

---

[1] L Zemer *The Idea of Authorship in Copyright* (1st edn Ashgate Publishing Limited England 2007) 1, Zemer's argument concerns copyright, but the same rationale applies to trademarks.

[2] SM Maniatis 'Trade Mark Rights– A Justification Based on Property' (2002) 2 Intellectual Property Q 130, Maniatis argues that property is both a legal and social institution, and as such, 'the biases of property systems, and the resulting allocation of power … are of social significance.'

[3] *The Idea of Authorship in Copyright* (n1) 25.

[4] A Rahmatian 'Copyright and Commodification' (2005) 27(10) EIPR 374. Rahmatian argues that '[f]rom a strictly positivist view, these justifications of [intellectual property] as a property right are not (or no longer) necessary. One could say that [an intellectual property right] is a property right because Parliament said so'.

and to legitimize their grant, as well as determining the obligations imposed, and the reason thereof. In the context of trademarks, such philosophical justifications are vital to admit the right of the public, which has been an ignored right for a long period of time, and to provide the balance between the right holders rights and interests.

From amongst the theories that justify trademarks are theories that have been formulated some time ago.[5] It could be questioned whether it is appropriate to justify current and modern trademark systems on the basis of such ancient theoretical frameworks. It is suggested that historical backgrounds and theories are relevant to trademark justification for two reasons. First, studying the inadequacies of such outmoded justifications is important, in that it opens up a way for further theoretical arguments which in turn enrich the discussion, leading to further arguments regarding trademarks, which shall result in finding the appropriate justification thereof. Second, 'history may be useful in the study of intellectual property law-related topics',[6] because when any study of the history is tackled, it emphasizes the points that are uncovered in a particular theory. This strengthens the argument because it supports the reasons why the adopted framework is most appropriate.

Scholars have failed to agree on a suitable theoretical framework for intellectual property justification. Some scholars argue that 'intellectual property is either labor or personality, *or* it is theft.'[7] Others divide intellectual property justification in accordance with their own criteria. For example, Menell divides intellectual property theories into utilitarian and non-utilitarian theories; in the latter, he provides a list of eight theories of intellectual property.[8] Others find it appropriate to provide an open-ended list, essentially naming and discussing six major theories.[9]

The theories discussed here are the utilitarian and economic theory; the labour theory; the personality theory; and finally, the Social-Planning theory. The assessment of the capability of this theoretical background of justifying trademarks shall be lead to the Economic-Social Planning

[5] Such as Locke's labour theory, and Hegel's personality theory.

[6] J Phillips and I Simon 'Going Down in History: Does History Have Anything to Offer Today's Intellectual Property Lawyer' (2005) 3 Intellectual Property Q 233.

[7] J Hughes 'The Philosophy of Intellectual Property' (1988-1989) 77 The Georgetown L J 290.

[8] PS Menell 'Intellectual Property: General Theories' in B Bouckaert and G de Geest (eds) *Encyclopedia of Law & economics* (Edward Elgar Cheltenham UK 2000) Vol 2, 156-163.

[9] L Zemer 'On the Value of Copyright Theory' (2006) 1 Intellectual Property Q 56.

theory, which is developed and defended by this book. This theory builds upon the economic and social models, and alters their premises in order to contribute in achieving a proper justification for trademark systems.[10]

Utilitarian and Economic Based Theory

Unlike other intellectual property rights,[11] trademark laws did not embody any sign of utilitarian grounds for its justification. Utilitarian grounds could be found in the Constitution of the United States of America, in the context of providing the logical backgrounds for both patents and copyrights systems. The Constitution provides that:

> '[t]he Congress shall have Power … To promote the Progress of Science and useful Arts, by securing for limited Times to Authors and Inventors the exclusive Right to their respective Writings and Discoveries.'[12]

Accordingly, the first US Trademark Act of 1870 was regarded as unconstitutional, because trademark protection was not mentioned in this constitutional clause.[13]

In the United Kingdom, trademark legislations did not refer to utilitarian grounds, whereas the case of copyright legislation is different. For example, the Statute of Anne, the first Copyright Act provided explicitly in its preamble that this Act is: 'for the Encouragement of Learning, by Vesting the Copies of Printed Books in the Author's or Purchasers of Such Copies.'[14] It is also stated that its purpose is to prevent the practices of printing and reprinting books and other writings, without the consent of the authors or proprietors of such books and writings, and 'for the encouragement of learned men to compose and write useful books.'[15]

However, the lack of reference to utilitarian and economic grounds in trademark legislations does not mean that trademarks could not be justified

[10] See ch 1 pp 6-8. See also, *infra* pp 57-59.

[11] Such as patents and copyrights.

[12] The United States Constitution art 1 s 8.

[13] K Aoki 'Authors, Inventors, and Trademark Owners: Private Intellectual Property and the Public Domain Part 2' (1993-1994) 18 Columbia-VLA J of L & the Arts 235-236.

[14] Statute of Anne 1709 (UK) 8 Anne c 19.

[15] ibid.

on such grounds. A number of scholars[16] adhered to the utilitarian theory to justify trademarks and intellectual property systems. Menell, for example, argues that utilitarianism is the principal theory to be applied to such works and systems.[17] He asserts that trademarks particularly are justifiable in utilitarian terms. In his words: '[t]rademark law is principally concerned with ensuring that consumers are not misled in the marketplace and hence is principally amenable to economic analysis.'[18]

The utilitarian argument provides that trademarks should be accorded protection on the basis that such protection shall result in the maximizing of wealth. The main idea is that more protection and enforcement of trademark legislations will lead to the increase of wealth to its optimal levels. 'Thus, wealth is optimized, or at least increased, by granting [trademark] monopolies'.[19]

Utilitarian theorists start their argument by studying the benefits and advantages of protecting intellectual creations and trademarks, as the basis for justifying their protection and existence. They emphasise that the economic role such creations play is sufficient grounds for the existence of systems protecting them.

The first and most considered benefit of trademarks is that brand names reduce consumers' search costs.[20] This is apt, because trademarks 'facilitate and enhance consumer decisions'[21] in choosing the product they wish to consume. Consumers will be able to identify the product bearing the mark and distinguish it from amongst other products of the same class of goods.[22] In this sense, customers will be able to recognize the goods they require in future purchases without being obliged to differentiate between the products and trying to stipulate which product identifies and

---

[16] Such as William Landes, Richard Posner, Peter Menell, Nicholas Economides, WR Cornish, Jennifer Phillips and others. See below for references.

[17] Menell (n8) Vol 2, 130.

[18] ibid.

[19] NS Kinsella 'Against Intellectual Property' (2001) Vol 15 No 2 J of Libertarian Studies 11, available at
<http://www.mises.org/journals/jls/15_2/15_2_1.pdf> (26 August 2009).

[20] WM Landes and RA Posner 'The Economics of Trademark Law' (1988) 78 Trademark Reporter 270. See also, SL Carter 'The Trouble with Trademark' (1989-1990) 99 Yale L J 762.

[21] N Economides 'The Economics of Trademarks' (1988) 78 Trademark Reporter 526.

[22] Carter (n20) 762. Carter argues that '[i]f goods were not marked, potential purchasers, unable to rely on any brand name … or distinctive appearance of the packaging … to identify the producer, would need a means of testing the products directly.'

fulfills their needs and preferences.[23] This is because a trademark 'is easier to recognize and remember; and it is often easier to physically mark on the goods themselves rather [than] provide the producer's full name and address.'[24]

A second benefit of trademarks –from this theory perspective– is that they play 'an unusual ancillary social benefit',[25] according to which '[a]n entirely different benefit of trademark protection derives from the incentives that such protection creates to invest resources … in inventing new words'.[26] Trademarks enrich the language and improve it by increasing the stock of words used in everyday life by inventing totally new words that were not used before which shall result in 'economizing on communication and information costs'.[27] Moreover, trademarks may, in certain circumstances, turn into generic words used by people to identify the whole class of goods, and 'represent the name of a category of products'[28] rather than identifying a certain product produced by a certain firm.[29] Finally, it is claimed that trademarks 'enrich the language, by creating words or phrases that people value for their intrinsic pleasingness as well as their information value'.[30]

---

[23] Landes and Posner provide an example of a consumer who prefers decaffeinated coffee bearing the brand name SANKA, which is manufactured and produced by General Foods. They argue that it would be easier for the consumer to ask for "SANKA coffee" rather than asking 'the decaffeinated coffee made by General Foods.' See- Landes and Posner (n20) 270.

[24] DM Higgins and TJ James 'The Economic Importance of Trade Marks in the UK (1973-1992) A Preliminary Investigation' (1996) The Intellectual Property Institute 4.

[25] W Fisher 'Theories of Intellectual Property' in S Munzer (ed) *New Essays in the Legal and Political Theory of Property* (1st edn Cambridge University Press Cambridge 2001) 170.

[26] Landes and Posner (n20) 272-273. Landes and Posner also provide a similar utilitarian justification for copyrights. See- W Landes and R Posner 'An Economic Analysis of Copyright Law' (1989) 18 J of Legal Studies (325-363).

[27] Landes and Posner (n20) 273.

[28] J Jacoby 'The Psychological Foundations of Trademark Law: Secondary Meaning, Genericism, Fame, Confusion and Dilution' (2001) 91 Trademark Reporter 1031. See also, Higgins and James (n24) 5.

[29] Port points out that, '[w]hen a trademark stops denoting the source of a product but rather the product itself, it becomes' a generic trademark. See- KL Port 'Foreword: Symposium on Intellectual Property Law Theory' (1992-1993) 68 Chicago-Kent L Rev 597.

[30] After the argument that was provided by Landes and Posner regarding the benefits of trademarks, they only hold their defence for the first benefit, whereas they provided that the advantages of the second benefit are small. They argue that

The heart of the utilitarian justification focuses on the idea that

> '[t]he primary justifications for trademark law are "to facilitate and enhance consumer decisions" and "to create incentives for firms to produce products of desirable qualities even when these are not observable before purchase".'[31]

If a number of guarantees were not provided, producers of intellectual creations would be reluctant to produce intellectual property, especially given that imitators will free-ride such works without bearing any costs.[32] 'This possibility would reduce the incentive for a successful firm to mark its goods and would thereby raise consumer search costs.'[33] However, as will be shown below, this incentive argument does not stand as a means of justifying trademarks.

It is argued that '[u]tilitarian theorists endorse the creation of intellectual property rights in order to induce innovation and intellectual productivity.'[34] Such an argument suggests that if trademark systems did not exist, or if those systems existed but did not sufficiently protect trademarks, then producers would not have the *incentive* to produce high quality products. Accordingly, trademark systems should provide appropriate incentives by 'eliminating the risk that competitors will free-ride upon such investments.'[35] If someone has goods and/or services of

---

the goal of the language 'is to minimize the sum of the costs of avoiding misunderstanding and the costs of communicating', this goal is not satisfied by trademarks because of the distortions that could result from them. They further argue that 'we do not need trademark protection just to be sure of having enough words'. Landes and Posner compare trademarks to patents and copyrights, and provide that 'we may need patent protection to be sure of having enough inventions, or copyright protection to be having enough books, movies and musical compositions.' See- Landes and Posner (n20) 273, 275.

[31] Menell (n8) Vol 2, 149. See also, A Kozinski 'Trademarks Unplugged' (1994) 84 Trademark Reporter 451, Kozinki provides that 'a utilitarian would argue for [trademark] laws with the best incentives for creative output and wealth maximization.' Adam Moore argues that the utilitarian theory is based upon the premise that granting control to creators of intellectual creations 'provides incentives necessary for social progress', and the aim of this theory is to 'maximize social utility'. See- AD Moore 'Intellectual Property, Innovation, and Social Progress: The Case Against Incentive Based Arguments' (2003) Vol 26:3 Hamline L Rev 607.

[32] Moore (n31) 611.

[33] Carter (n20) 763.

[34] Zemer (n9) 57.

[35] Menell (n8) Vol 2, 149.

high and superior quality, he/she will be deterred from putting his/her products or services on the market, because this lack of trademark protection will make him/her unable to inform consumers of the qualities of such products or services.[36]

According to the utilitarian justification, 'promoting the creation of valuable intellectual works requires that intellectual laborers be granted property rights in those works', without which 'adequate incentives for the creation of a socially optimal output of intellectual products would not exist.'[37] Thus, property rights are granted to intellectual creators

> 'not because they deserve such rights or have mixed their labor in an appropriate way, but because this is the only way to ensure that an optimal amount of intellectual products will be available for society.'[38]

Utilitarian theorists argue that the economic justification of trademarks does not recognize the rights of the trademark proprietor only. They claim that subject to economic terms, the impact of the protection of trademark owner's rights would result in the benefit and good of society as a whole and for others, otherwise trademark protection should not exist. This is because

> '[t]he key concept of the economic theory of property rights is that of externality. An externality is an economic situation in which an individual's pursuit of his self-interest has spillover effects on the utility or welfare of others.'[39]

In this sense, utilitarian theorists try to draw a balance between the trademark owner's economic rights and the interests of the consuming

---

[36] WR Cornish and J Phillips 'The Economic Function of Trade Marks: An Analysis with Special Reference to Developing Countries' (1982) Vol 13 No 1 Intl Rev of Industrial Property and Copyright L 46.

[37] EC Hettinger 'Justifying Intellectual Property' (1989) Vol 18 No 1 Philosophy and Public Affairs 47-48.

[38] Moore (n31) 612.

[39] HM Spector 'An Outline of a Theory Justifying Intellectual and Industrial Property Rights' (1989) 11 EIPR 271. Spector's argument is that externality could be either negative or positive. And by applying trademarks to his argument, one may conclude that trademarks should enjoy protection if such protection is not only in favour of its proprietor, but also in the benefit of the society, and this is the positive externality. Whereas if the trademark protection would result in harmful effects due to its owner's exploitation, then such protection should be prevented. This is the notion of negative externality.

public.[40] Fisher points out that the utilitarian argument should be construed as a beacon for 'the maximization of net social welfare.'[41] He argues that to achieve this goal, a balance should be drawn between the powers and entitlements granted to trademark proprietors in order to stimulate the creation of trademarks and to ensure consistent quality control over goods and/or services on the one hand, and on the other hand 'the partially offsetting tendency of such rights to curtail widespread public enjoyment of those creations.'[42] However, it shall be argued that this theory fails to draw the balance that it alleges, because 'the utility gains from increased incentives … must be weighed against the utility losses incurred from monopolization'.[43]

Landes and Posner suggest a model based on economic premises for the justification of trademarks. They define the "full price" of a good or service as the monetary price of the good or service plus 'the search costs incurred by the buyer in obtaining information about the relevant attributes of the good [or service].'[44] According to them, the more a trademark reduces consumers' search costs by providing more information, the more a producer may raise the price of his/her product, without exceeding the "full price" which the customer is willing to pay for the good or service. They argue that

> '[t]he more resources the firm spends developing and promoting its mark, the stronger will its mark be and the lower, therefore, consumer search costs will be; so the firm will be able to charge a higher price.'[45]

According to Economides, products have some features which are unobservable. He argues that trademarks simply play an economic role in helping and assisting consumers in identifying those features. Such an identification could not be achieved without trademarks, and the absence of trademark systems in the light of the fact that consumers will have the choice with other identical goods will result in a number of disadvantages.[46]

Economides argues that in the absence of trademarks 'the consumer will only by chance pick the one with the desirable unobservable

[40] Zemer (n9) 57.
[41] Fisher (n25) 169.
[42] ibid.
[43] TG Palmer 'Are Patents and Copyrights Morally Justified? The Philosophy of Property Rights and Ideal Objects' (1990) 13 Harvard J of L & Public Policy 849.
[44] Landes and Posner (n20) 277.
[45] ibid.
[46] Economides (n21) 526.

qualities.'[47] Moreover, producers will not invest in improving their products or services; they

> 'would produce products with the cheapest possible unobservable qualities, because high levels of unobservable qualities would not add to a firm's ability to sell at a higher price'.[48]

Economides concludes that a number of aspects participate in the success of trademarks. The ability of consumers to memorize and recall the trademark, and the inability of other rivals to use similar or identical trademarks, all serve to ensure the efficiency of trademark systems.[49] Economides argues that this economic background legitimizes and presupposes the existence of trademarks. Landes and Posner also agree with this argument, stressing that trademarks should not be duplicated to achieve their goals.[50]

It could be concluded that utilitarian and economic justifications call for monopolistic rights to be enjoyed by trademark owners. The main grounds for this monopoly are the reduction of search costs, in addition to providing the proper incentives to trademark owners. Focus shall, thus, be directed to those grounds, to assess whether they are suitable in justifying such a granting of monopoly.

Criticism of the utility and economic model

Although many scholars regard the utilitarian argument as an ideal theory to justify the existence of trademark systems, it is clear that the utilitarian justification faces a number of problems. The rationale upon which this argument is based is untenable. Moreover, economic theory cannot stand alone in justifying trademarks. The inadequacies in this theory are manifold, starting from wealth maximization, incentive and quality products arguments, amongst others.

- Artificiality of the utilitarian argument

The arguments of the utilitarian and economic justification lead to artificial results. They neither justify, nor legitimize the entitlements over trademarks. This justification relies upon the economic results emerging

[47] ibid.
[48] ibid.
[49] ibid 526-527.
[50] Landes and Posner (n20) 270.

from the protection of trademarks, which is not capable of the justification thereof. The artificiality of the utilitarian argument derives from the fact that one could not bring economic principles into legal theory. A theory that justifies trademarks should find real grounds for legitimizing the existence of trademark rights, and seek justice in granting the rights and imposing obligations amongst the parties in a trademark formula.[51] For example, the presumption that trademarks protection shall provide an incentive to producers is subject to economic and market considerations, but does not constitute grounds for justifying why trademarks should exist.

The economic theory presupposes that providing efficient systems for the protection of trademarks shall result in maximizing the wealth to its optimal levels. This argument, at first glance, could appear intuitive. However, it is a further manifestation of the artificiality of this theory; thus, the question of crucial importance is to determine to whom wealth is maximized. As this theory argues in favour of trademarks proprietors, they are hence the party holding the advantages, and their wealth is maximized. Thus, this theory, unlike the claim of its proponents, does not draw a balance between the trademark owners' interests on the one hand and those of the consuming public. Thus, '[s]triking an appropriate balance between private and public … cannot be fully realised under the auspices of utilitarian justification.'[52]

Moreover, it is a matter of debate as to whether the policy of legislations should aim to maximize wealth or to achieve certain utility ends or achievements. Rather, trademark systems should not aim at maximizing wealth; and policy-makers should strive to provide a fair legal system assuring justice to all involved parties within the trademark formula.[53] After all, '[w]ealth maximization is not the goal of law; rather, the goal is justice– giving each man his due.'[54] Even if trademarks do result in maximizing wealth, this does not justify 'the unethical violation of some individuals' rights to use their own property as they see fit.'[55] Therefore, wealth maximization is an economic argument, and could not be applied to legal theory. In addition, this theory suffers from the inadequacy of the premises of its incentive argument.

---

[51] See ch 1 p 11.
[52] Zemer (n9) 60.
[53] See ch 1 p 11.
[54] Kinsella (n19) 12.
[55] ibid.

- The incentive argument

The incentive rationale in this theory is divided into two arguments: the incentive to invest in a trademark and undertaking a business, and the incentive to produce quality products.

As regards the former, the incentive to use a trademark is solely based on the economics of the market, and whether someone has the incentive to undertake a business is based on individual cases and upon market rules. This is apparently distinct from any justification in law. In opposition to this incentive rationale, Aoki considers that 'the need [of trademark owners] to differentiate their product from others provides sufficient incentive to develop striking and attractive denotative marks.'[56]

This incentive argument focuses on the trademark owner and ignores the role of the consuming public in the trademark formula.[57] It also deprives them of their rights to the trademark. This argument suggests that incentive should be enhanced to trademark owners, and that to provide the necessary incentives, trademark systems should protect the aspects that the public most value and appreciate.[58] This undermines the rights of the public, and considers them to be passive in the context of trademarks. Moreover, the benefits of undertaking a business and achieving financial gain and profit is the real incentive for traders. This is, as mentioned above, subject to market strategy and economic terms. It is questionable whether 'the production of specific sorts of intellectual products depend upon'[59] trademark protection and the incentives they provide. However, '[o]ther monetary or nonmonetory rewards … would be sufficient to sustain current levels of production even in the absence of intellectual-property protection.'[60] Therefore, the incentive argument is unfounded.

In support of this argument, a number of scholars argue against the incentive rationale. Palmer totally opposes the economic theory, arguing that there is no strong evidence that intellectual property rights provide an incentive or actually 'result in an increase in innovation and creativity.'[61] Carter also argues that '[t]rademark law … provides no incentive to create

---

[56] Aoki (n13) 241. Aoki argues that 'it sounds slightly ridiculous that we would want to create incentives for trademark owners to produce and circulate new trademarked symbols by granting extremely broad rights in such marks'.

[57] See ch 1 p 11.

[58] J Litman 'The Public Domain' (1990) 39 Emory L J 997.

[59] Fisher (n25) 180.

[60] ibid. See also, Hettinger (n37) 49.

[61] TG Palmer 'Intellectual Property: A Non-Posnerian Law and Economics Approach' (1988-1989) 12 Hamline L Rev 300.

new marks.'[62] He distinguishes between trademarks on the one hand and copyrights and patents on the other, and asserts that '[o]ne might conceive of an optimal supply of copyrighted works or patented inventions, but it makes no sense to refer to an optimal supply of marks as such.'[63]

The second incentive argument, that of producing quality products, imposes another kind of hurdle. The majority of utilitarian argument focuses on an alleged fact; that trademarks provide the incentive for producers to produce high quality products and to preserve this quality.[64] This "quality argument" finds its roots in Frank Schechter's argument. In his famous 1927 article, Schechter argued that trademarks no longer function as source or origin identifiers, rather 'the true functions of the trademark are … to identify a product as satisfactory', thus a trademark is the resemblance of quality.[65]

This argument is not convincing, for a number of reasons, first and foremost because the practice in the field of trademarks shows that even though trademark systems exist, not all firms and producers are producing goods and/or services of high quality. This is a relative issue, which differs from one producer to another according to economic and market considerations.[66] For example, in the field of the automobile industry, although protection of trademark systems is available to all producers, the quality of their products considerably varies. In this respect, Akerlof argues that the preservation of *consistent* quality is the crucial issue, while the preservation of *high* quality products is uncertain.[67] Thus, it could be concluded from Akerlof's argument that the high quality argument is not practical, due to the differences amongst producers.

Secondly, even utilitarian scholars were confused regarding this quality assurance argument; some utilitarian theorists clearly argued that the function of trademarks was that of quality resemblance, such as Landes and Posner. Others were less clear regarding this issue. Economides, for example, argued that trademarks were meant to identify and distinguish the source of products or services. At the same time he argued that

---

[62] Carter (n20) 768.
[63] ibid.
[64] Landes and Posner (n20) 271. See also, Economides (n21) 525. See also, Spector (n39) 272. See also, Higgins and James (n24) 4-5.
[65] FI Schechter 'The Rational Basis of Trademark Protection' (Reprinted in 1970) 60 Trademark Reporter 337. The functions of trademarks will be the subject of further discussion. See generally ch 3.
[66] See ch 3 pp 70-72.
[67] GA Akerlof 'The Market for "Lemons": Quality Uncertainty and the Market Mechanism' (1970) 84 Q J of Economics 499.

trademarks identified the quality of the product.[68] It is apparent that there is some confusion in this regard amongst utilitarian theorists.

In addition, the incentive for producing quality products after all is a result, and a result could not justify the whole system of trademarks. A proper question could be proposed in this regard: Is the result not the purpose of a rational legal system, in the same way that the result of traffic lights is the reason for adopting them? In response to this question, it could be argued that what is far more important is to provide a justification for putting a traffic light in a certain road. It is equally important to justify the restriction over the right of cars and pedestrians to pass in certain times. By analogy, this could be applied to the case of trademarks. What is crucial is to justify the rights and limitations over the rights of trademark owners, the consuming public and other traders and rivals.

As a result, the arguments of wealth maximization and incentives are not convincing for the justification of trademark systems. However, the reduction of consumers' search costs could form the basis for such a justification.

Consumer search cost and trademarks justification

The opposition to the utilitarian theory does not mean that trademarks are not amenable to economic consideration. It is suggested that trademarks are justifiable according to the utilitarian theory, but this theory *alone* is not enough for the justification of trademark systems. A partial aspect of this theory is reliable for this purpose. However, this ground is not exhaustive, and could not on its own be sufficient to justify trademarks. This theory fails to provide a limit to the proprietor's rights; nor does it recognize the role of the public in the creation of trademarks, and thus it does not draw a balance between the proprietor's rights and the rights of the public. As such, this theory could not be exhaustive for trademark justification, and needs another theoretical framework to provide the limits and boundaries of the parties' rights, and to draw the required balance.

Trademarks, in fact, reduce consumer search costs. Trademarks are indeed a means for consumers to differentiate goods and/or services of one undertaking from those of others, without which consumers will not be able to choose the goods and/or services of their preferences. However, it is essential to define "consumer search cost" to understand how its reduction could establish a basis for trademark justification. In order to

[68] Economides (n21) 524, 527.

achieve this goal, one should imagine a world without trademarks. In this case, the consuming public would be unable to choose the articles they wish to consume. They would be unable to identify the products from amongst each other,[69] and '[t]he value of being able to choose between alternatives ... diminishes'.[70] This leads us to the fact that trademarks provide the consumer with the information necessary to make the decision of purchase. Indeed,

> '[a] trademark is a convenient way of giving the person searching in the market a great deal of information in a very small package. Trademarks are protected because they lower consumer search costs, enabling people to make quicker, cheaper decisions about what they want to buy.'[71]

A cheaper decision is one which could be based on a trademark, because this mark makes the unobservable features and those of personal preference more clear, and thus consumers are able to make this decision without huge efforts, which saves time and resources.[72]

However, it should be borne in mind that the fact that trademarks do reduce and lower consumers' search costs should not be related to any other economic considerations, because legal theory could not be based upon economic principles. As has been argued, the economic rationale is artificial in the context of the justification and theory of trademarks. Thus, unlike the argument of utilitarian scholars,[73] one could not use the fact of the reduction of consumers' search costs, to conclude that this creates an incentive to producers. Utilitarian scholarship seeks to assert such a connection, but fails to justify any link between search costs and incentive presumptions. Moreover, this does not mean that the owner of a trademark

---

[69] CDG Pickering *Trade Marks in Theory and Practice* (1st edn Hart Publishing Oxford 1998) 88.

[70] SM Maniatis *The Communicative Aspects of Trade Marks: A Legal, Functional and Economic Analysis* (PhD Thesis University of London 1998) 109.

[71] SL Carter 'Owning What Doesn't Exist' (1990) Vol 13 No 1 Harvard J of L & Public Policy 105.

[72] *Trade Marks in Theory and Practice* (n69) 88.

[73] Scholars argue that due to the fact that trademarks lower consumers search costs, this creates an incentive for consumers to produce goods or services with a certain amount of quality. Thus, '[t]rademark protection encourages the development of branding and distinctive products. Without trademark protection, companies might lack the incentive to produce quality goods, limiting commercial intercourse.' See- Zemer (n9) 59. Also, Landes and Posner argue that 'an important and widely recognized benefit of trademarks is that they give firms an incentive to improve the quality of their products.' See- Landes and Posner (n20) 279.

can impose higher prices for his/her products because that trademark lowers consumers' search costs.[74] This is due to the fact that lowering consumers' search costs is the basis for justifying a trademark system, not an economic ground for increasing the article's price. Indeed,

> 'the purpose of trademark law is not … to provide an incentive for the creation of new and better trademarks. Rather, … trademark law seeks to protect consumers by allowing product –and producer– differentiation that reduces the risk of consumer confusion and lowers search costs.'[75]

Nevertheless, the problem with this theory is that it does not provide a limit for any protection accorded for trademarks. According to utilitarianism, the more trademarks reduce consumers' search costs, the more they are worthy of protection. This leads to the conclusion that the protection of trademarks –if solely justified upon utilitarianism– could result in monopolies on the part of trademark proprietors, and will not achieve the balance which utilitarian theorists claim that this theory achieves. This leads to the important disadvantage of adhering to the utilitarian theory; according to this, no limitations are stipulated with regard to the rights granted to trademark owners, resulting in extreme control over their trademarks, which would be harmful to fair and free competition.

In conclusion, the utilitarian and economic theory cannot be seen as an exhaustive theoretical framework for trademark justification. Major aspects of this theory do not stand for this purpose.[76] However, as argued earlier, the consumer search cost rationale only forms a starting point in the process of trademark justification. Nonetheless, some fundamental questions, regarding the manner of creating trademarks and the limitations of the owner's rights, are still without clear answers, and call for explanation.

From this point, the coming sections shall tackle alternative theoretical grounds in a search for an equitable approach which recognizes the role of all parties in the trademark formula.[77] It will be argued that the labour and personhood justifications fail to justify trademarks. However, the analysis of these theories and the highlighting of their deficiencies shall lead to

---

[74] Such as the model suggested by Landes and Posner. See *supra* pp 17-23.

[75] VR Moffat 'Mutant Copyrights and Backdoor Patents: The Problem of Overlapping Intellectual Property Protection' (2004) 19 Berkeley Technology L J 1488-1489.

[76] See *supra* pp 23-27.

[77] See ch 1 p 11.

establishing a solid and clear justification. This will lead to the Social-Planning theory, which in conjunction with the economic reduction of search costs, shall form the proper justification of trademarks.

Labour-Based Justification

Locke's labour theory is part of a larger theoretical framework upon which property may be justified. Locke's theory, as well as other theories, could be labelled by the title of "Natural Rights". For example, the notion of the "Occupancy Theory" is found in the legal literature based on Roman law.[78] According to the "Occupancy Theory", the first person to physically possess and occupy an object obtains a natural right to possess it, and acquires property rights upon it, on condition that this object is in the commons and is eligible for appropriation.[79] However, the argument will be restricted to Locke's labour theory, as it is the best manifestation of natural right theories.

A labour-based justification of property rights finds its origin in John Locke's *Two Treatises of Government*, a text written over three centuries ago. When Locke stated his ideas about property, it was intended to cover only real tangible property, and was not intended in any sense to cover intellectual property rights,[80] or to be more precise, to trademarks.

Locke started his treatise of property by describing the state of nature; he believed that God had given the earth to the children of man, and this earth had been given to them in common.[81] In the commons, it is impossible for any man to have any property. However, earth has been

---

[78] H Grotius *De Jure Belli Ac Pacis Libri Tres* (Oceana Publications New York and Wildy & Sons Ltd London, FW Kelsey Translation, Reprinted 1964) Vol 2, 206-219.

[79] K Port 'The "Unnatural" Expansion of Trademark Rights: Is a Federal Dilution Statute Necessary?' (1995) 85 Trademark Reporter 559-560. However, the Occupancy theory has a major difference than Locke's labour theory, as Moulds puts it: '[I]t is not the one who sits on land [as the Occupancy theory suggests], but the one who tills it, pastures it, mines it or in some way works it who acquires a property claim.' See- H Moulds 'Private Property in John Locke's State of Nature' (1964) 23(2) The American J of Economics and Sociology 180.

[80] P Drahos *A Philosophy of Intellectual Property* (1st edn Dartmouth England 1996) 47. See also, SV Shiffrin 'Lockean Arguments for Private Intellectual Property' in S Munzer (ed) *New Essays in the Legal and Political Theory of Property* (1st edn Cambridge University Press Cambridge 2001) 154.

[81] J Locke *Two Treatises of Government, a Critical Edition with an Introduction and Apparatus Criticus by Peter Laslett* (1st edn Cambridge University Press Cambridge 1964) 304.

given to man to derive the best advantage from life, and to support and comfort their being.[82] God grants this bounty to humanity for its enjoyment, but goods held in common cannot be enjoyed in their natural state.[83] Despite the premise that no one shall posses any property, Locke argued that

> '[t]hough the earth, and all inferior Creatures be common to all Men, yet every Man has a *property* in his own *Person*. This no Body has any Right to but himself. The *Labour* of his Body, and the *Work* of his Hands, we may say are properly his. What so ever then he removes out of the State that Nature hath provided, and left it in, he hath mixed his *labour* with, and joyned to it something that is his own, and thereby makes it his *property*.'[84]

The applicability of the labour theory to intellectual property rights could be appealing. In some instances, one may say that it applies to intangible property in general, and to intellectual property rights in particular, more so than it does to real property, upon which Locke presented his theory of property.[85] Some commentators argue that the notion of owning one's self embraces the ownership of one's mind, hence, mixing labour of intellect or mind entitles the labourer to private ownership.[86] 'A person's labour and its product are inseparable, and so ownership of one can be secured only by owning the other.'[87] However, in the field of trademarks, Locke's theory of property is not applicable.

No Harm Principle

Locke's theory is subject to a number of restrictions and conditions; these are known as the "no harm principle". This principle means that after the appropriation of objects held in the commons, commoners suffer due to such acquisition.[88] This principle ensures that the natural right of acquisition through labour does not conflict with the common good.[89] The

---

[82] ibid.

[83] Hughes (n7) 297. See also, A Bell and G Parchomovsky 'A Theory of Property' (2005) Vol 90 No 3 Cornell L Rev 542.

[84] *Two Treatises of Government* (n81) 305-306.

[85] CJ Craig 'Locke, Labour and Limiting the Author's Right: A Warning Against a Lockean Approach to Copyright Law' (2002-2003) 28 Queen's L J 23. See also, Shiffrin (n80) 139.

[86] Spector (n39) 271.

[87] Hettinger (n37) 37.

[88] Fisher (n25) 188.

[89] Zemer (n9) 63.

"no harm principle" consists of two conditions: the "enough and as good condition" and the "non-waste condition".[90]

Locke's treatise of property stipulates that ownership of one's self entitles mankind to the fruits of his/her labour, and '[*a*]*s much Land* as Man Tills, Plants, Improves, Cultivates, and can use the Product of, so much is his *Property*.'[91] This view of Locke includes a natural limit to one's property, and indicates that work is a requirement and prerequisite for property and ownership.

In Locke's commons and primitive state, there are sufficient objects to satisfy the needs of all commoners.

> '[I]n this primitive state there are enough unclaimed goods so that everyone can appropriate the objects of his labour without infringing upon goods that have been appropriated by someone else.'[92]

However, if 'the appropriation of an unowned object worsens the situation of others',[93] then such an ownership is prohibited. Individual possession should not involve prejudice to other men.[94] Locke explains that a man is entitled to private property as long as there is enough and as good left to others. In Locke's words:

> '[n]or was the *appropriation* of any parcel of *Land*, by improving it, any prejudice to any other Man, since there was still enough, and as good left; and more than the yet unprovided could use.'[95]

Introducing such a restriction over the right to appropriate arose for various reasons; Locke intended to ensure that other commoners did not complain about such appropriation, because after the appropriation, there would still remain objects of similar quality and quantity, i.e. that the situation of others is not worse.[96] Locke also intended to assert that his

---

[90] *Two Treatises of Government* (n81) 309-314. See also, A Moore 'A Lockean Theory of Intellectual Property' (1997-1998) 21 Hamline L Rev 78. See also, Zemer (n9) 63. See also, Hughes (n7) 297-298.
[91] *Two Treatises of Government* (n81) 308.
[92] Hughes (n7) 297.
[93] R Nozick *Anarchy, State, and Utopia* (1st edn Blackwell Oxford 1974) 175.
[94] WH Hamilton 'Property- According to Locke' (1931-1932) 41 Yale L J 867.
[95] *Two Treatises of Government* (n81) 309. See also, *Anarchy, State, and Utopia* (n93) 175.
[96] Spector (n39) 270.

view did not embody any kind of immoral inequality,[97] and safeguarded the right of access to common materials for all individual commoners.[98]

Some commentators have regarded the non waste condition 'as an ugly step-sister of the enough and as good condition',[99] while others have questioned the need for this condition in the presence of the "enough and as good" condition.[100]

For Locke, 'no one was entitled to more than was necessary for [his/her] subsistence, because the excess would spoil before it could be consumed';[101] he considers this as an offence 'against the common Law of Nature'.[102] Hence, no person should appropriate more than the amount he/she can use. Locke demonstrates this limitation by stating that:

> '[a]s much as any one can make use of to any advantage of life before it spoils; so much he may by his labour fix a Property in. ... Nothing was made by God for Man to spoil or destroy.'[103]

This condition, if applied to trademarks, means that not using the mark is a waste, according to Locke's non-waste limitation. Thus, one shall not be able to appropriate a mark if one is not intending to use it. Although trademarks are not literally perishable and could not be spoiled, not using a mark is indeed a true waste. The trademark owner shall have monopoly rights over his/her mark, and if it is not used, then this is a waste because others could have made use of it.[104]

This condition is not intended to limit the amount which one can appropriate, since the amount of labour one is capable of expending determines his/her property. Rather, this condition provides that one can appropriate as much labour as one wishes, but that one should not 'let anything perish uselessly' in one's possession.[105] However, a spoiled object is wasted because it 'might be the Possession of any other',[106] and

---

[97] Hughes (n7) 297.

[98] G Sreenivasan *The Limits of Lockean Rights in Property* (1st edn Oxford University Press Oxford 1995) 113.

[99] Hughes (n7) 325.

[100] *Anarchy, State, and Utopia* (n93) 176.

[101] DM Byrne 'Locke, Property, and Progressive Taxes' (1999) 78 Nebraska L Rev 706.

[102] *Two Treatises of Government* (n81) 313.

[103] ibid 308.

[104] See *infra* pp 38-40.

[105] J Waldron *The Right to Private Property* (1st edn Clarendon Press Oxford 1988) 209.

[106] *Two Treatises of Government* (n81) 313.

others could have benefited from it. The solution, from a Lockean perspective, was the transformation to a money economy. Every individual could exchange whatever is more than what he can consume with money, a lasting unspoilable object.[107] By its very nature, 'money is imperishable and thus unaffected by the spoilage limitation', because it could be accumulated indefinitely, without violating the non-waste condition.[108]

Critiques of labour-based justification to trademarks

A point of crucial importance is to assess the applicability of a labour-based justification of trademarks. Clearly, Locke's theory of property relies upon exerting labour, which means that labour is the basis for ownership entitlement. It is a matter of debate whether the rationale for the labour theory of property applies to trademarks, whether producing a trademark requires any kind of labour, and whether the rights accorded to the labourer are equivalent to the amount of mental labour exerted in creating a trademark. The start will be to question Locke's notions of "commons" and "mixing labour" as related to trademark, in seeking to assess Locke's conditions or limitations. In conclusion, it will be shown that this theory falls short in terms of justifying trademarks.

- Locke's labour and trademarks

The premises that Locke started with prevent their applicability to trademarks. Locke started from the proposition that no person is entitled to any kind of property rights, but to his/her own person. Such ownership of one's body or self entitles him/her to the fruits of his/her labour; thus, the outcome of this labour is the property and the private right of the labourer. Locke's rationale is that objects in the commons 'are not useful to anyone, [thus,] an individual exerts labour upon the object and transforms it into something useful and worthy of property ownership.'[109] However, this rationale is not convincing. If the commons in the trademarks context are words, then their existence before someone labours on a mark and transforms it into property, as Locke's theory suggests, are useful as a means of communication amongst individuals.

Moreover, the premise that in the state of nature everything belongs to men and that they share everything therein seems to be undermined by the

---

[107] ibid 318-320.

[108] *The Limits of Lockean Rights in Property* (n98) 35.

[109] Port (n79) 561.

fact that if 'one takes a particular item from the common, one violates the right of other commoners, to whom this particular item also belongs',[110] because in Locke's commons everything belongs to all individuals. It seems that Locke has implicitly acknowledged this problem, and in solving it, he argues that 'taking any part of what is common … does not depend on the express consent of all the Commoners.'[111] The appropriation of objects in Locke's common in real property is different from the appropriation of ideas and cultural property in intellectual property rights, in that the former does not depend on the express consent of all commoners; in contrast, the latter do.[112] Hence, the 'appropriation of real property commons can take place without the assent of others[, whereas a]cquiring cultural property requires consent.'[113]

This book argues that Locke's theory is not applicable to trademarks *ab initio*, because the commons, as imagined by Locke, is not applicable to trademarks. However, it would be beneficial to look at the chain of links between the trademark and the marked product and its producer. Scholars defending the applicability of the labour theory to trademarks consider that this chain passes through three stages. The first stage concerns planning the creation of the mark, the second stage relates to applying the mark and putting it into the market, the third and final stage lies in the labour invested in building the goodwill of the trademark.[114]

Applying Locke's labour theory over this chain of links presumes that the labouror (the trademark owner) is the party who plans to create the mark and puts it in the market; it also presumes that the trademark owner creates the goodwill. Indeed, the trademark owner takes the initiative to choose a mark and affixes it to his/her products. This is an important role, for which trademark owners should enjoy protection. However, as regards to the goodwill, this book suggests that the goodwill derives through the association which the public attribute between the trademark and the marked product.[115] A trademark owner could use a sign and apply it over his/her products, but unless the public associate the producer with the marked object, the mark will not have any value, and will be useless. Ignoring this aspect in the chain of links between marks and marked

[110] Zemer (n9) 62. See also, Shiffrin (n80) 144-145. See also, *The Limits of Lockean Rights in Property* (n98) 24.
[111] *Two Treatises of Government* (n81) 307.
[112] S Wilf 'Who Authors Trademarks?' (1999) 17 Cardozo Arts & Entertainment L J 30.
[113] ibid.
[114] Maniatis (n2) 145.
[115] See ch 5 pp 148-151.

products renders the Lockean theory individualistic, because it considers the labouror as the only party who creates such links.

Locke has stated that property is justified when someone mixes his/her labour with objects from the commons. This argument has been a matter of criticism. First, in the context of trademarks, what is the "commons"? Is it the words already existing in the language? If this is the case, then this could not be applied to trademarks for various reasons, mainly because this "commons" as such does not exist; in many instances the trademark owner creates a word that has never existed before, such as the KODAK trademark. This example demolishes Locke's argument about the commons, simply because this word (KODAK) is an invented word and did not exist in the commons; hence, no one could labour on it and appropriate it for him/herself out of the commons because it never existed in the commons. Or could this common be any new invented word? When Locke was referring to the commons, he meant objects that already existed at least as raw materials, and in order for someone to deserve owning them he/she should mix his/her labour with them. Furthermore, it is questionable whether a trademark could be considered an object *per se*; a trademark is more a right and entitlement of rights, rather than an object, because trademarks are intangibles, and they could not be objects. Thus, trademark legislations grant the owners rights over their trademarks, such as the right of using the mark and preventing others from using it for the same class of goods and/or services.

Some scholars have sought to determine what kind of labour is necessary to satisfy the labour theory content,[116] and some have demonstrated that the production of ideas does not come from nowhere; it needs a certain amount of labour.[117] It could also be argued that in some instances, the idea occurs to the owner without any kind of labour or innovative thought; in other instances it comes by way of coincidence. This occurs, for example, when one trader uses his/her family name as a trademark, where the exertion of labour could not be really claimed, i.e. when the labour exerted in the creation of the mark is not consistent with Locke's notion of labour exertion, or when the trademark owner simply takes an existing word and uses it as a trademark without exerting labour in its creation, such as the use of a word in a different context, for instance using the word "Table" as a trademark for computers.

It could be argued that the production of trademarks does not include any kind of labour, in the sense of Locke's theory. According to such an

[116] Maniatis (n2) 143-144. See also, Hughes (n7) 300-305.
[117] Hughes (n7) 300-301.

argument, the mere act of choosing a name from the common of words or symbols and affixing it to goods and/or services does not include labour. Trademarks are examples of things that are made effortlessly.[118] Perhaps the best emphasis of the argument that trademarks lack labour in their creation is in the words of the US Supreme Court:

> 'Trademarks do not depend upon novelty, invention, discovery, or any work of the brain. It requires no fancy or imagination, no genius, no laborious thought. Trademarks are simply founded on priority of appropriation.'[119]

Contrary to this argument, the production of trademarks includes some kind of mental labour. The hurdle that faces the applicability of the Lockean approach to trademarks is that the amount of labour exerted in the production of a trademark cannot readily be compared with the extent of rights and entitlements that the proprietor of a trademark enjoys. Trademark owners have the exclusive right to enjoy a monopoly over their marks, and to exclude others from using them, a right that could potentially last forever. It is hard to imagine that such rights could be justified upon the mental effort of creating the mark according to the Lockean justification of property. However, '[a]lthough intellectual laborers often deserve rewards for their labor, [intellectual property systems] may give the labourer much more or much less than is deserved.'[120] It is suggested that the amount of rights a trademark owner holds is much more than could be justified upon the Lockean based justification. A trademark owner secures a monopoly over the mark, and thus, his/her rights are more than the rights conferred under Locke's theory.

In this context, it would be beneficial to look at the historical context in which Locke lived, which led him to envision his theory. During his lifetime, the monarch had absolute powers; to which all the property belonged.[121] In his opposition to such absolute powers, Locke considered that the ownership of private property by individuals constituted the ideal

---

[118] *Anarchy, State, and Utopia* (n93) 175.

[119] Port (n29) 594. (Citing *Trade-Mark cases* 100 US 82 (1879)). See also, W Cornish *Intellectual Property Omnipresent, Distracting, Irrelevant?* (1st edn Oxford University Press Oxford 2004) 75, providing that '[t]he right [in a mark] is not accorded for the inspiration or cleverness in deciding upon the brand.'

[120] Hettinger (n37) 51.

[121] R Ashcraft *Locke's Two Treatises of Government* (1st edn Allen & Unwin London 1987) 81.

approach to limit the monarch's absolute powers.[122] Therefore, the more property owned by individuals, the less was the power of the monarch.

Even if one were to agree with Locke's assumption that this could be the best means to limit the abuse of monarchy powers, it should be noted that the historical context in which Locke lived does not exist currently. What is actually required today is a trademark system which limits the abuse that might emerge from the expansion of trademark owners' rights. In doing so, considering the rights of the public could be one way to provide boundaries to the rights of trademark owners. It is therefore important to tackle the applicability of Locke's limitations over trademarks. This supports the conclusion that this theory fails to justify trademarks.

- Locke's limitations and trademarks

When it comes to Locke's "enough and as good condition", one might suggest that applying this condition to intellectual property rights, and in particular, to trademarks does not create any hurdle or difficulty;[123] the commons of words are infinite and inexhaustible,[124] and there will always remain enough and as good left to others.[125]

On the contrary, if Locke's condition is to be applied strictly, then if someone labours on a mark from the commons and turns it into his/her property, then he/she has a monopoly over this mark. In this sense, others would be worse off due to the fact that his/her appropriation left a loss in the commons which they could have made use of. Thus, in the field of trademarks, there will not be enough and as good for others to appropriate. Moreover, when someone appropriates a trademark then logically he/she has improved his/her situation, consequently; all other commoners are worse off. Hence, 'a person's situation is prima facie made worse by his losing the opportunity to appropriate'[126] what others have already appropriated. Lessig has provided a similar argument in the field of copyright, but also supports this idea in trademark law. He describes the situation of Walt Disney, who created a motion picture character based on a character from the commons; the commons were then open to creators to develop because legislation then did not impose restrictions on their use by

---

[122] Maniatis (n2) 139-140.

[123] Maniatis argues that 'trade marks fulfil the labour requirements and potentially can satisfy the two provisions.' See- ibid 153.

[124] Shiffrin (n80) 140.

[125] Hughes (n7) 315.

[126] *The Right to Private Property* (n105) 215.

others. Lessig then compares the situation of first comers (such as Walt Disney) and second comers; whereas the formers were free to use the commons and make considerable use of it, the second comers were not able to use the commons in the same sense that was available to first comers, thus they could not have the benefit of the commons. He argues that 'the new creators, the new Walt Disneys, must fight this system of legal regulation to find a right to speak.'[127]

This means that the "enough and as good" condition cannot be applied to trademarks, because even if ideas are inexhaustible, they are not always under the common's grasp,[128] because an idea stems from a former idea, and the new idea is the gateway for further ideas.[129] Thus, granting property rights over an idea will affect the common of marks, and will not leave as good and enough to others. This will inevitably harm the situation of second comers, because first comers have enjoyed more resources than others.

As regards Locke's limitation of "non-waste", this condition differs from the "enough and as good condition" regarding its applicability to trademarks. Trademark legislations contain rules that are similar in their content to the non-waste condition, which is the revocation of trademark registration for non-use. The revocation for non-use concept provides that if the trademark is not used in the course of trade for a certain period of time, it is subject to revocation upon request from any party with interest. Another example of applying the non-waste condition over trademarks is the prohibition of registering descriptive signs. It is suggested that allowing the registration of such marks might waste the rights of the public and other traders to use such signs. This has been manifested in the decision of the European Court of Justice (ECJ) in *Dyson Ltd v Registrar of Trade Marks*.[130] Hence, this condition, as applied to trademarks, does not conflict with Locke's argument.

In conclusion, the labour theory does not apply to, or justify, the trademark system. There is no sufficient amount of mental labour available to the granting of property rights according to Locke's notion. The high level of protection of trademarks cannot be justified on the basis of the mental labour of creating the mark. Moreover, the mental labour of creating trademarks cannot be justified on the basis of Locke's rationale and his "enough and as good proviso", because the commons of words

---

[127] L Lessig 'The Creative Commons' (2004) 65 Montana L Rev 9.

[128] Craig (n85) 24.

[129] ibid. See also, Lessig (n127) 12.

[130] (Case C-321/03) *Dyson Ltd v Registrar of Trade Marks* [2007] 2 CMLR 14. See also, ch 5 pp 156-159.

will be affected, due to the fact that if one appropriates a mark then he/she gains a monopoly that could potentially last for ever. Hence, other commoners will be worse off, which contradicts Locke's rationale. More importantly, Locke's theory fails to identify the fundamental link between a trademark and its specification. As has been shown, the focus of Locke's rationale was the justification of owning the object of property. Thus, it fails to take into consideration the link and association which the consuming public attribute between the trademark and the goods and/or services on which the marks is affixed. Since the Lockean approach fails to justify trademarks, focus should be directed towards assessing the personhood approach.

The Personhood Theory

The personhood approach to property finds its roots in the writings of Georg Wilhelm Hegel. In his work *Natural Law and Political Science in Outline; Elements of the Philosophy of Right*, Hegel embodies his treatise of property.

Hegel avoids a historical argument about the primitive state of nature.[131] Rather, the Hegelian theory derives from the premise that 'private property rights are crucial to the satisfaction of some fundamental human needs',[132] such as 'self-actualisation and recognition of an individual person'.[133] According to Hegel, '[a] person must translate his freedom into an external sphere in order to exist as Idea',[134] this freedom is best expressed and translated into the acquisition of property rights.[135] Hegel also intended to avoid a utilitarian argument for property rights, according to which property is not a means to satisfy our needs; rather, it is 'the first embodiment of freedom'.[136]

> 'The premise underlying the personhood prospective is that to achieve proper self-development –to be a *person*– an individual needs some control

[131] PG Stillman 'Hegel's Analysis of Property in the Philosophy of Right' (1988-1989) 10 Cardozo L Rev 1033.
[132] Fisher (n25) 171.
[133] Port (n79) 563. See also, Bell and Parchomovsky (n83) 542.
[134] GWF Hegel *Philosophy of Right* (1st edn Oxford University Press Oxford T M Knox Translation 1952) 40.
[135] Zemer (n9) 63-64.
[136] Palmer (43) 837.

over resources in the external environment. The necessary assurances of control take the form of property rights.'[137]

As with the Lockean approach, Hegel argues that a person has a natural possession of his/her body,[138] and such possession of one's body derives from the control of the mind or will of the person over his/her body. [139] The concept of self-possession requires

'[t]hat the body be gradually modified and turned to the will's purposes so that it becomes increasingly difficult for the agent or anyone else to view his body, especially in action, without taking into account its essentially will-governed character.'[140]

However, Locke's premise is that a person owns himself/herself as their own property, and the property of one's self entitles a person to own property, whereas Hegel's notion of one's natural possession 'is neither automatic nor easy, but a long struggle in claiming one's self and developing one's individuality.'[141]

A person should manifest their will within the external world, and this manifestation is part of one's personality, and is a reflection of it. Hence, Hegel considers the will as the core of one's existence, seeking effectiveness and self actualisation.[142] Hegel argues that anything that a person puts their will into makes it their own property, and he/she may appropriate it,[143] because 'property is the first embodiment of freedom and so is in itself a substantive end.'[144]

Unlike Locke's labour theory, 'Hegel has a much more direct approach to intellectual property.'[145] He argues that

'[m]ental aptitudes, erudition, artistic skill, even things ecclesiastical (like sermons, masses, prayers, consecration of votive objects), inventions, and

---

[137] MG Radin 'Property and Personhood' (1981-1982) 34 Stanford L Rev 957. See also, Maniatis (n2) 154.
[138] *Philosophy of Right* (n134) 40. See also, Maniatis (n2) 154. See also, Hughes (n7) 332.
[139] *The Right to Private Property* (n105) 361.
[140] ibid 363.
[141] Stillman (n131) 1040.
[142] Hughes (n7) 331. See also, W Fisher 'Property and Contract on the Internet' (1997-1998) 73 Chicago-Kent L Rev 1214.
[143] *Philosophy of Right* (n134) 41.
[144] ibid 42.
[145] Maniatis (n2) 161.

> so forth, become subjects of a contract, brought on to a parity through being bought and sold, with things recognised as things. It may be asked whether the artist, scholar, &c., is from the legal point of view in possession of his art, erudition, ability to preach a sermon, sing a mass, &c., that is, whether such attainments are 'things'...'[146]

After acknowledging the existence of intellectual creations, Hegel develops an argument as to whether such creations could be considered "things" or not.[147] He argues that they could not be "things" on the basis that they are 'owned by [the] free mind' stipulating that they 'are something internal and not external to it'.[148] He then concludes that there is no harm in calling them "things", since they should be affixed into a material support, which is something external and hence could be called "things".[149]

For Hegel, an intention to own something and make it someone's property is not enough; there should be a 'physical relation' between the proprietor and the thing.[150] He argues that

> '[s]ince property is the *embodiment* of personality, my inward idea and will that something is to be mine is not enough to make it my property; to secure this end occupancy is requisite.'[151]

Such a notion of occupancy, from a Hegelian perspective, takes one of two forms: either through taking possession of an object or through using it.[152] Taking possession of an object is initiated 'by directly grasping it physically, … by forming it, and … by merely marking it as ours.'[153] It is this last form which is related to the subject of trademarks. Hegel stipulates that marking 'is not actual but is only *representative* of my will … and the meaning of the mark is supposed to be that I have put my will into the thing.'[154]

Hegel has discussed his ideas about alienation in his treatise. According to him, anyone could freely alienate his/her property and

---

[146] *Philosophy of Right* (n134) 40.
[147] ibid.
[148] ibid 41.
[149] ibid 40-41.
[150] Maniatis (n2) 160. See also, Port (n79) 564. See also, *The Right to Private Property* (n105) 363.
[151] *Philosophy of Right* (n134) 45.
[152] ibid 46.
[153] ibid. See also, Palmer (43) 838. See also, Hughes (n7) 335.
[154] *Philosophy of Right* (n134) 49.

withdraw his/her will from the object,[155] insofar as he/she puts his/her will into it.[156] However, he argues that the 'substantive characteristics which constitute my own private personality and the universal essence of my self-consciousness are inalienable'.[157] He stresses that intellectual works, in particular, because of their connection with one's being and personality, could not be alienated. He also argues that a person's body is not alienable, by its very nature, because of its attachment to life and liberty;[158] he stipulates that intellectual works are internal and inward to their creators and hence they are inalienable. If the owner of a work of mind is entitled to alienate his/her work, then he/she will make his/her own personality and the substance of his/her being the property of another person.[159]

> '[O]n most occasions the complete alienation of intellectual property is an exercise of rights over property in an act that, by its nature, denies the personality stake necessary to justify property rights. … Abandonment of an idea is arguably alienation of personality.'[160]

Hughes considers that trademarks are justifiable as based on a Hegelian perspective. However, he argues that basing such a justification upon the rights of the consumer is weak; he contends that

> '[t]rademark is a right of expression for the manufacturer, not a right of the consumer to receive information. In fact, trademarks fulfil the recognition aspect of the personality theory of property by providing an important means of securing respect and recognition to those who originate the items bearing the trademark.'[161]

Hughes's argument focuses on one party of the trademark formula;[162] his argument gives recognition to the "manufacturer" and denies any role on the part of the consuming public. Alternatively, he could have given

---

155 *The Right to Private Property* (n105) 361, 369.
156 *Philosophy of Right* (n134) 52.
157 ibid 52-53.
158 Stillman (n131) 1042-1045.
159 *Philosophy of Right* (n134) 54.
160 Hughes (n7) 347.
161 ibid 354.
162 See ch 1 p 11.

recognition to both parties, as they are the parties involved in the creation of trademarks.[163]

After having manifested the content of Hegel's approach, it seems essential to assess it ability to justify trademarks. It shall be argued that a number of hurdles prevent its applicability to trademarks.

Critiques of the personhood justification to trademarks

In assessing the compatibility of Hegel's theory of property with trademarks, the personality theory is not applicable to trademarks. Hegel himself, when stating his comprehensive list of mental creations eligible to be property, did not discuss trademarks.[164] Palmer contends that the personality theory discusses only patents, copyright and artistic creations.[165] Hughes argues that '[i]n the field of intellectual property, the personality justification is best applied to the arts.'[166] However, the rationale of this theory and major points in it affect its justification for trademarks.

After arguing that intellectual works should be disclosed to the public to achieve their goal, Hegel stipulates that the protection of such works is vital in ensuring an advance in the field of intellectual works, and to make people interact with and understand them. Hegel discusses the situation of copyright, and argues that the book as an object is external to the creator, and hence alienable, because when someone owns a copy of the book, this copy becomes his/her 'complete and free ownership'.[167] But 'the means of expression of the idea are part of the author's mind and still belong to him.'[168] By analogy, when someone purchases an article embodying a trademark, he/she owns this article, but does not own the trademark itself, because –according to the personality theory– the trademark as a mental aptitude remains the property of its creator. Nevertheless, the personality

[163] Port (n79) 565-566. In support of this argument, Port argues that trademarks should fulfil three competing objectives: the interest of the trademark owner, the interest of consumers and the interest of innocent third parties.
[164] *Philosophy of Right* (n134) 40-41.
[165] Palmer (43) 837, 843. The personality theory is used in different jurisdictions in Europe such as France and Germany for the justification of their copyright systems. See- Fisher (n25) 174.
[166] Hughes (n7) 330. Palmer also argues that '[o]nce created, works of art are independent of their creators, as should be evident by the fact that works of art do not "die" when their creators do.' See- Palmer (43) 844.
[167] *Philosophy of Right* (n134) 55.
[168] Stillman (n131) 1045.

theory fails to justify the fact that trademarks are assets, and as such, are alienable. Hegel fails to provide any means for safeguarding and protecting the works of the intellect, and argues that this issue should be left to the individual's honours.[169]

If a trademark system is to be justified upon the personality theory, a number of questions will remain without clear answers, such as the transfer of ownership of the trademark. If a trademark is a manifestation of its proprietor's will, personality and self development, how can these facets be assigned or licensed to others? In particular, Hegel regards intellectual creations as inward and internal to the person's personality.

Although the personhood approach, unlike the Lockean approach, includes a justification as to intellectual property, two major arguments and hurdles in this theory cannot be applied to trademarks: the "marking hurdle", and the "alienability hurdle".

- The "marking hurdle"

Hegel has argued that in order to own an object, there should be occupancy to that object. By applying Hegel's occupancy argument to the case of trademarks, this occupancy is manifested in marking the object. According to Hegel, this occupancy is the entitlement to property, because this marking is the representation of the owner's will.

It could be argued that marking establishes an excellent linkage between Hegel's personality theory and trademarks,[170] because '[f]or Hegel, the marking of our animals with a personal sign will express our will to dominate the animals even when they are mixed with the animals of the neighbours.'[171]

When Hegel was considering marking as a representation of the person's will, did he mean that marking was a way of manifesting one's will to appropriate the marked object? If so, then the will's manifestation concerned the ownership of the object itself. Or, was he referring to marking as the manifesting for ownership of the mark itself? In this case, the ownership of this mark does not stand up to any real basis for justification.

Hegel's marking argument does not stand in order to justify a trademark system. It could be inferred from Hegel's argument that marking an object reflects one's will to appropriate that object. This means

[169] *Philosophy of Right* (n134) 53-56.
[170] Maniatis (n2) 160.
[171] ibid.

that marking an object entitles the person to appropriate the object, not the mark itself. Moreover, Hegel has asserted that marking, as a way of appropriating an object, is 'very indeterminate';[172] this might be because of the lack of internal or inward connection between the mark and its owner.

This hurdle imposes another question as regards the degree of personality manifested in trademarks: To what extent does the creation of a trademark reflect the owner's personality?

The creation of a trademark does not reflect the manifestation of the owner's will; nor does it 'seem to be the personal reaction of an individual upon the nature.'[173] Trademarks are usually owned by corporations and institutions. For such corporations, trademarks are neither important, nor essential, for their will and self actualization.[174] This leads to the second hurdle of applying this theory to trademarks.

- The "alienability hurdle"

This hurdle imposes a more crucial point in justifying trademark systems. According to Hegel's rationale, any piece of property, and trademarks in our case, represents a connection between the owner and the owned object, because this property is a manifestation of his/her self. If property is alienable from one owner to another, this either means that the connection between the owner and object will be harmed or that this connection never existed. It is suggested that this connection between the mark and the owner, on the basis that a trademark is a manifestation of someone's will and self, does not exist. Hence,

> '[a]lienation is the denial of th[e] personal link to an object. But if the personal link does not exist… there is no foundation for property rights over the object…[, t]hus, the justification for property is missing.'[175]

The alienability rationale is clarified in Margaret Radin's article "Property and Personhood".[176] Radin differentiates between two kinds of property.[177] The first is fungible property, which could be replaced with

[172] *Philosophy of Right* (n134) 49.
[173] Hughes (n7) 339, 341.
[174] Hettinger (n37) 45-47.
[175] Hughes (n7) 345. See also, Palmer (43) 843.
[176] Radin (n137) 966.
[177] Zemer (n9) 64.

'other goods of equal market value',[178] and such objects are alienable. The second is personal property.[179] Owners of personal property are connected with such property (i.e. there is inward and internal value of the object in its owner view) and are almost part of them, and are not alienable,[180] and this is a subjective matter that differs from one person to the other. Personal property means that 'an object or an idea is intertwined with an individual's personal identity',[181] hence it is inalienable. Trademarks fall within the ambit of the first kind of property, and are indeed fungible property, because trademarks have a market value which they might be exchanged with.

In conclusion, it seems impossible to justify trademarks on the basis of the personality theory, simply because the creation of trademarks does not reflect the personality of its creator. Even though some intellectual property rights seem to be a manifestation of their creators' personalities, others 'do not manifest any "personality" of their creators… and do not seem to be the personal reaction of an individual upon nature.'[182] Hence, the nature of trademarks and their use in industrial and commercial context does not embody an expression of the personality. Furthermore, trademarks are usually owned by corporations and institutions; this leads to the fact that trademarks are neither important nor essential for their existence and self actualization.[183]

The Social-Planning Approach

> '… *[T]he consumption of commodified representational forms is productive activity in which people engage in meaning-making to adapt signs, texts, and images to their own agendas. These practices of appropriation or "recoding" cultural forms are the essence of popular culture …*'.[184]

---

[178] Radin (n137) 960.
[179] The notion of "personal property" in this context means the property which is related to its owner's personality, not the technical notion of "personal property" in the English law, which refers to movable property.
[180] Radin (n137) 959.
[181] Menell (n8) Vol 2, 158.
[182] Hughes (n7) 340-341.
[183] Hettinger (n37) 45-47.
[184] RJ Coombe 'Objects of Property and Subjects of Politics: Intellectual Property Laws and Democratic Dialogue' (1990-1991) 69 Texas L Rev 1863-1864.

The last, and newest theory to justify trademark systems is the Social-Planning theory. The naming of this theory is not a matter of consensus among scholars. Some suggest that the "Social-Planning Theory" could be the term,[185] others suggest "Social and Institutional Planning".[186] However, the term "Social-Planning Theory" shall be used, because this title reflects the adherence of this theory to the role of the public in the creation of trademarks and the need of the society to the expressive uses of cultural signs and symbols.

Although the Social-Planning theory is 'less well known than the other [approaches]',[187] it 'is similar to utilitarianism in its teleological orientation'.[188] However, it differs from the other approaches justifying intellectual property and trademark systems. This theory is dissimilar to utilitarianism 'in its willingness to deploy visions of a desirable society richer than the conceptions of "social welfare" deployed by utilitarians.'[189] It also differs from the perspective from which it justifies trademark systems, in terms of its recognition of the public as an important factor in the trademark formula.[190] The importance of this theory derives from the balance it draws between the rights conferred upon the proprietor of the mark on the one hand, and the consuming public on the other.

This theory focuses on the reaction of the consuming public to trademarks, whether this reaction has any effect upon the legitimacy and the justification of trademark systems, and whether the association which the public attribute to marks with certain meanings shall have any effect. It shall also be crucial to assess the cultural role of trademarks, and its implications on the free will of the public, and their right to fully express themselves through social commentary.

When first enacted, trademark legislation provided protection for different purposes than those existing now. Trademarks were, in the first place, formulated to protect the consumer from any potential confusion as to the source or origin of goods and/or services, and ultimately to preserve the interests of the consuming public and trademark owners.[191] However, today trademarks 'may deprive us of the optimal *cultural* conditions for

---

[185] Fisher (n25) 173.
[186] Zemer (n9) 65.
[187] Fisher (n142) 1214.
[188] Fisher (n25) 173.
[189] ibid.
[190] See ch 1 p 11.
[191] As in the case of the Lanham Act. See ch 4 pp 85-89.

dialogic practice.'[192] They could also 'be used to prohibit access to, and use of, many cultural forms'.[193] Although

> '[o]ur intangible assets are indeed valuable, but an overbroad grant of monopoly rights to prior creators may retard the development of new intellectual products and sometimes may interfere impermissibly with the autonomy of others and with efforts by individuals to achieve cultural self-determination[,] ... impair[ing] our culture's ability to respond flexibly to future opportunities and dangers'.[194]

Indeed, such an exaggeration of protection in favour of trademark owners shall deprive the consuming public of some fundamental rights, such as the right of freedom of speech.[195] The extension of trademark protection shall have deep implications over the right of the public over trademarks, because this will put all the rights under the disposal of the trademark owner preventing the public from using it for expressive and cultural purposes. And

> '[i]f investment is dispositive of the trademark owner's right to control, then the public's ability to evoke the expressive dimension of marks is in danger of significant restriction.'[196]

Thus, it is important to discuss the arguments underlying this theory; that the public contribute in the creation of trademarks, and that trademarks are cultural and expressive tools. In this way, a proposed rationale for this

---

[192] Coombe (n184) 1866. Rosemary Coombe argues that [i]n the current climate, intellectual property laws often operate to stifle dialogic practice in the public sphere, preventing us from using the most powerful, prevalent, and accessible cultural forms to express alternative visions of social worlds.' See- RJ Coombe *The Cultural Life of Intellectual Properties* (1st edn Duke University Press Durham and London 1998) 42.

[193] J Bosland 'The Culture of Trade Marks: An Alternative Cultural Theory Perspective' (2005) Vol 10 No 2 Media & Arts L Rev 2, available at <http://www.ipria.org/publications/workingpapers/WP13.05.pdf> (26 August 2009).

[194] WJ Gordon 'On Owning Information: Intellectual Property and the Restitutionary Impulse' (1992) Virginia L Rev 157.

[195] This right embodies a number of sub-rights such as the right of parody, satire and social criticism, etc ... See- RJ Shaughnessy 'Trademark Parody: A Fair Use and First Amendment Analysis' (1986) 72 Virginia L Rev 1107-1112. See also generally ch 6.

[196] RC Dreyfuss 'Expressive Genericity: Trademarks as Language in the Pepsi Generation' (1989-1990) 65 Notre Dame L Rev 405.

theory shall be outlined, in order to suggest an ideal framework for this approach.

The creation of trademarks and the public role

The way in which trademarks are formulated is not limited to the proprietor's intellectual labour, and the fixing of the mark over the products. The point of major importance, which all other approaches ignore and fail to address, is the role the consuming public play in the creation of trademarks. As one scholar has argued, '[m]eaning is … given to trademarks by the endless stream of possible interpretations imposed by the audience/consumer/reader.'[197] In the same sense, and although discussing the author in the context of copyright, Ronald Barthes argues that the author of a work 'is always conceived of as the past of his own book', … however, '[t]he reader is the space on which all the quotations that make up a writing are inscribed without any of them being lost; a text's unity lies not in its origin but in its destination.'[198]

By analogy, in the field of trademarks, Barthes's argument could be construed in the sense that the meaning of a trademark is not constituted by its owner, but rather, through its destination; the public at large. This is evident in the way a trademark becomes a generic mark, due to the kind of recognition the consuming public attribute to the mark. The same applies to the secondary meaning doctrine, according to which the recognition of the public of the mark as a mark identifying the goods and/or services of a certain undertaking could make such marks registrable, even though it was not eligible for registration. These examples clarify the role of the consuming public in the creation of trademarks.

In his seminal work "Who Authors Trademarks?", Steven Wilf seeks to provide an answer to this question. He developed the "Public Authorship Model", which admits the role of the trademark owners, but argues that the public contribute in the creation of the trademark and are entitled to joint ownership of the mark with its proprietor.[199] As a practical model, Wilf focuses on the often ignored role of the public in creating trademarks. He argues that 'a trademark is a creature of symbolic language. Like any other symbol or text, trademarks do not simply appear

---

[197] Bosland (n193) 7.

[198] R Barthes 'The Death of the Author' in Roland Barthes, *Image, Music, Text, Essays selected and translated by Stephen Heath* (Fontana Press London 1977) 145, 148.

[199] Wilf (n112) 5.

out of whole cloth. They are authored.'[200] According to Wilf, it is us, the public, who author trademarks.[201]

In order to legitimize trademark systems, the manner of creating trademarks should be understood. The trademark owner either uses an existing word or sign or he/she develops a new word or sign. The stage of using the mark holds an extreme importance in justifying trademarks. Other theoretical approaches focused on the act of using trademarks as the source of the entitlements of the mark owner. Maniatis argues that the registration process gives the mark 'an independent externality … similar to that acquired by working on, or marking, the object of property.'[202] However, this argument focuses only on the trademark owner and his/her usage of the mark. Thus, it is important to provide a further theoretical framework which would be able to provide boundaries to the rights and entitlements of trademark owners.

Consequently, it could be argued that after the trademark is affixed to the article and is put into circulation, the public grant this mark the degree of association they find appropriate. This association is based upon consumer's consensus, through their purchasing habits. It should be noted that the amount of recognition and meaning attributed to the ordinary trademark could be very minor or minimal, and still the public shall enjoy property rights in the mark as "co-authors". This is because the public decided to grant the mark little or no recognition, and by this negative act of not granting any recognition or by limiting the recognition, the public have participated in the creation of the mark.

Wilf has designated a similar approach. He argues that a trademark is found by a process of three steps. The first step is the association stage in which 'a producer associates a sign with an object.'[203] Afterwards, this 'association is recognized and invested with meaning by the public as an interpretive community.'[204] Finally, 'the object-sign association is contextualized within a broader cultural context.'[205]

Wilf's argument is important in the way it approaches the role of the public in the creation of trademarks. However, it has some shortcomings. It seems that Wilf did not recognize that ordinary marks are different from well-known trademarks. The three step procedures do not necessarily

[200] ibid 6.
[201] In Wilf's words, 'we have met the author and he is us'. ibid 45.
[202] Maniatis (n2) 165, Maniatis's reference to "working" relates to Locke's labour theory, while the reference to "marking" related to Hegel's personhood approach.
[203] Wilf (n112) 8.
[204] ibid.
[205] ibid.

apply to ordinary trademarks, and it is apparent that Wilf did not recognize that the recognition of ordinary marks could be minimal, and hence the third step may not apply to ordinary marks. However, this does not undermine Wilf's approach, his sub-theory (The Public Authorship Model) is vitally important, because most of the literature in the field of trademarks does not grant the public any recognition in the creation of trademarks. Furthermore, Wilf's argument stresses the importance of theory in legitimizing and balancing interests in trademarks between the owner and the public.

The public contribute to the creation of trademarks. This is manifested in the association they attribute between the mark and the owner's products. The significance of the Social-Planning theory derives from the fact that it overcomes the shortcomings of all the other theories. It recognizes how a trademark is formulated, and it rewards those who contribute in its creation; the trademark owner and the public, and provides a balance between them. It follows that the public are entitled to use trademarks in cultural and expressive contexts, and this implies the need to balance rights between owner and public.

Cultural and expressive uses of trademarks

Trademarks are a means of cultural communication amongst individuals, they 'can develop into fertile sources of collective popular culture, ... by which individuals identify, translate, interpret, and critique the world around them.'[206] This means that trademarks are a way of expressing oneself in a cultural context.[207] In this context, the Social-Planning theory 'is largely devoted to discussing ways to maintain a strong civic culture that benefits from a reasonably balanced social and institutional intellectual property regime.'[208]

Trademarks are not only important in reducing consumers search costs, and helping consumers to choose the products they require. The Social-Planning theory suggests that trademarks also are culturally 'vitally important'[209] for protecting 'our social interests in freedom of speech,

---

[206] Bosland (n193) 4. See also, K Aoki 'How the World Dreams of Itself to be American: Reflections on the Relationship Between the Expanding Scope of Trademark Protection and Free Speech Norms' (1996-1997) 17 Loyola of Los Angeles Entertainment L J 528.

[207] Aoki (n206) 544.

[208] Zemer (n9) 65.

[209] Bosland (n193) 1.

[and] promoting expressive activity'.[210] This theory lies 'in the proposition that property right should be shaped so as to help foster the achievement of a just and attractive culture'.[211] In this just and attractive culture,

> 'all persons would be able to participate in the process of making cultural meaning. Instead of being merely passive consumers of images and artifacts produced by others, they would help shape the world of ideas and symbols in which they live.'[212]

This goal is achieved by recognizing the role of the public and hence, allowing them to use trademarks in cultural contexts.

Aoki argues that textual symbols play a significant role in 'both cultural and personal identity'.[213] He provides an example to illustrate this idea; the Harley-Davidson trademark.[214] This mark was first used to symbolize personal freedom, but later it was used by private entities to distinguish their products. Aoki clarifies that

> '[w]hile Harley-Davidson can generally be understood to represent personal freedom, within the Harley-Davidson subculture discrete groups interpret the core set of values associated with Harley-Davidson so as to render them consistent with their "prevailing life structures".'[215]

Another example of this was provided by Aoki, when a graphic designer group from Sarajevo named Trio used a number of postcards and depicted some western trademarks 'to convey their demand for the return of their most fundamental human right, the right to exist.'[216] Such examples illustrate how trademarks are no longer a means used in trade to perform certain functions. The public use trademarks in different social context to express their ideas, fears, thoughts, etc… Trademarks became tools to convey messages to the public.

The social theorist Coombe, starts her argument by defending the social approach to intellectual property in general, and to trademarks in particular, by discussing the difference between the objective world and the subjective self. According to her,

---

[210] *The Cultural Life of Intellectual Properties* (n192) 54.
[211] Fisher (n142) 1214. See also, Fisher (n25) 172.
[212] ibid 193.
[213] Aoki (n206) 527.
[214] This mark consists of a 'spread-winged eagle'. See- ibid.
[215] ibid 528.
[216] ibid 541.

> 'the objective world is the cultural construction of social subjects and that subjectivity itself is a product of language and cultural practice', ... [and] ... '[w]hat we experience as social reality is a constellation of cultural structures that we ourselves construct and transform in ongoing practice.'[217]

For Coombe, 'mass media imagery and commodified cultural texts provide the most important cultural resources for the articulation of identity and community in western societies.'[218] However, Coombe's concern and fear is that 'objectifying and reifying cultural forms' shall result in 'freezing the connotations of signs and symbols and fencing off fields of cultural meaning[s]',[219] thus trademark laws restrict 'certain forms of political practice[s]',[220] in particular the right of freedom of speech. This right is protected in the UK under the Human Rights Act,[221] and in the USA under the First Amendment.[222] As Dreyfuss argues, 'the essence of the first amendment claim is that there are instances in which the loss of vocabulary is, effectively, the loss of the ability to communicate.'[223]

An instructive example which is raised in the majority of the social theory literature[224] is that of the *San Francisco Arts & Athletics Inc v US Olympic Committee*.[225] This case is peculiar, because it shows that the ability to restrict the use of words and signs is simply because the registrant owns the mark; therefore, it is a sound example which proves that prohibiting the public from using a sign might seriously affect their right to free speech.[226] In this case, a Californian non-profit gay advocacy group called "San Francisco Arts and Athletics Inc." (SFAA) intended to

---

[217] Coombe (n184) 1858.
[218] ibid 1864.
[219] ibid 1866.
[220] ibid.
[221] Human Rights Act 1998 (UK) c 42 s 12.
[222] The United States Constitution Amendment I.
[223] Dreyfuss (n196) 412.
[224] Coombe (n184) 1874-1876. See also, MJ Kaplan 'Antidilution Statutes and the First Amendment' (1992) 21 Southwestern U L Rev 1145-1146. See also, Aoki (n206) 539-540. See also, Dreyfuss (n196) 398-399, 404-405. See also, T Martino *Trademark Dilution* (1st edn Clarendon Press Oxford 1996) 63. See also, Bosland (n193) 6.
[225] *San Francisco Arts & Athletics Inc v US Olympic Committee* 483 US 522, 107 S Ct 2971 (1987). Also knows as the *Gay Olympic* case.
[226] See ch 6 pp 199-204.

promote an Olympic games for gays, under the name "Gay Olympic Games". However, under the United States Amateur Sports Act of 1978, the use of the word "Olympic" is restricted to the US Olympic Committee (USOC), and it is the only party to use this mark and to enable and authorize other parties or entities to its use. The Act also entitles USOC to prohibit others from using the Olympic mark, whether such use is likely to cause confusion or not.[227] USOC filed a case requesting to restrain SFAA from using the Olympic mark. SFAA alleged that its use of this mark falls under the ambit of the first amendment, and thus, could not be prohibited,[228] because the aim of this game was 'to promote the acceptance and profile of the gay community',[229] and to 'convey a political statement about the status of homosexuals in society'.[230] The court rejected the SFAA claim, ruling that the prohibition of the use of the mark Olympic did not prohibit SFAA from conveying its message.[231] The court stressed USOC's rights because

> 'the use of the word by other entities to promote an athletic event would directly impinge on the USOC's legitimate right if exclusive right [, and] [t]he mere fact that SFAA claims an expressive, as opposed to a purely commercial, purpose does not give it a First Amendment right to appropriate the value which the USOC's efforts have given to the word.'[232]

However, Brennan J and Marshall J of the court have dissented. They argue that the court has broadened the prohibition in the Amateur Sports Act to include non-commercial speech,[233] which is unacceptable. They have pointed out that '[b]y prohibiting use of the word "Olympic," the USOC substantially infringes upon the SFAA's right to communicate ideas',[234] and its right to deliver the message it was trying to convey.

As the court in the *Gay Olympic* case has provided itself, this case is different from regular trademark cases in a number of aspects; the Olympic mark is not protected under trademark legislations; rather, it is protected under a *sui generis* system,[235] which is the Amateur Sports Act. Moreover, the USOC does not need to prove the existence of confusion or

---

227 United States Amateur Sports Act of 1978 s 110.

228 *San Francisco Arts & Athletics Inc* (n225) 523.

229 Bosland (n193) 6.

230 *San Francisco Arts & Athletics Inc* (n225) 523, 535.

231 ibid 536.

232 ibid 523, 540.

233 ibid 568.

234 ibid 570. See also, Dreyfuss (n196) 411.

235 Dreyfuss (n196) 404.

likelihood of confusion.[236] However, fears exist that this judgment could be applied to ordinary trademark cases,[237] which might have adverse effects on the cultural life of society at large, and would probably deprive individuals and entities of their essential right to express themselves through democratic dialogue. As Dreyfuss correctly points out, this judgment 'puts in jeopardy the public's ability to avail itself of the powerful rhetorical capacity of trademarks.'[238]

The *Gay Olympic* case also demonstrates another social significance of trademarks. They are socially important for democratic dialogue amongst individuals, as people are using them in their communication, because 'dialogue is always already our state of being and consciousness.'[239] A telling example has been provided by one scholar where two children from two different social and cultural backgrounds meet, and one of whom tries to communicate with the other by saying "Ninja, Ninja, Ninja Turtles", waiting for the reaction from the other child, but he/she does not respond because his/her parents have restricted their child's watching of television. Hence, the communication between the two of them fails because of the lack of communicative tools.[240]

The case of trademarks is different from other intellectual property systems, where the owner of the work of intellect is only remunerated though the selling of his/her work, and hence, the exclusivity of rights to the owner is vital, whereas in the case of trademarks, the owner is remunerated by several means: the selling power of the mark, the profits of selling the article itself, etc… The exclusivity in favour of the trademark owner is only necessary to the extent that trademarks identify the source of goods and/or services. As long as the trademark identifies the source function, there is no harm to the trademark owner from the expressive use of the mark by the public, and other meanings they might attribute to the mark in social and cultural contexts,[241] especially insofar as developing new words to substitute the expressive use of the mark is a long, complicated process.[242] In conclusion, the cultural and expressive use of the mark neither affects, nor deprives the owner of his/her proprietary rights; rather, it strikes a balance between him/her and the public.

---

[236] *San Francisco Arts & Athletics Inc* (n225) 531.
[237] Dreyfuss (n196) 404.
[238] ibid 398.
[239] *The Cultural Life of Intellectual Properties* (n192) 47.
[240] ibid 53.
[241] Dreyfuss (n196) 408.
[242] ibid 416.

Proposed rationale for the Social-Planning theory

It is important to provide a clear vision regarding the application of the Social-Planning theory for a number of reasons. First, the arguments for this theory are divided in a number of scholarly works. Second, this theory aims to provide a solution to the extreme exaggeration of the extent of proprietary rights granted to trademarks owners; thus the argument of this theory needs to be clarified in order to legitimize the need for drawing a balance in the conferred rights and the reason for recognizing the entitlement of the public in the context of trademarks.

This theory seeks to ensure that trademark systems are formulated to achieve a just and attractive culture. In this culture, trademarks are a means of democratic and civic dialogue. In order to achieve this goal, it is necessary to perceive the formulation process of trademarks.

In the first stage, the trademark owner chooses and/or invents a new word and affixes it on his/her goods and/or services, and puts the article bearing the mark into circulation in the market. In the second stage, once the trademark is in circulation, the public begin to recognize the mark. This stage is important, because the degree of recognition of the public determines the amount of protection granted to trademarks. The recognition of the public varies, and differs from one mark to the other; in this sense, the role of the public is crucial in determining the amount of recognition that a mark deserves. In some instances, the recognition of the public of a trademark is minimal, but this does not mean that the public role in recognizing the mark does not exist and hence there is no entitlement to the public in such marks. On the contrary, the role of the public is still strongly present, because the public decided to grant limited recognition to the mark. In other instances the recognition reaches a high level to the extent that renders the mark generic.[243]

Here, it could be asked: How would a trademark be protected in practice until the dialogue relationship is established? As outlined at the outset,[244] this book does not aim to provide technical solutions for the whole system of trademarks. However, one of the arguments that could tentatively be deployed to answer this question is to avoid conferring property rights to trademark owners solely.[245] Afterwards, the practical application could be left to courts, either in favour of trademark owners or the public, depending on the degree of association attributed to the mark.

---

[243] See *supra* p 19.

[244] See ch 1 p 5.

[245] As in the case of the UK Trade Marks Act 1994. See ch 5 pp 147-155.

Since the trademark owner and the public have contributed to the creation of the trademark, the owner and the public are the parties to enjoy the rights and entitlements in the mark. On the one hand, the trademark owner shall enjoy the right to use his/her trademark in the course in commerce, and to exclude others from using his/her mark in trade context and on the same class of goods and/or services to which they are registered and/or used. On the other, the public shall enjoy the right of having their state of mind (confusion) as the sole test for trademark infringement,[246] and to be able to use trademarks in cultural and expressive contexts, to express their ideas, wills and needs, amongst others.[247] The significance of this argument derives from its recognition of the rights of the public, and therefore, not being an individualistic approach. This vision towards trademark protection is not achievable under the utilitarian, Lockean and Hegelian theories. The utilitarian theory focuses on providing the incentives for trademark owners,[248] the Lockean theory focuses on the labouror,[249] while the Hegelian approach takes into consideration the self-actualization of trademark owners.[250] Thus, the rights of the public could not be justified under these approaches.

The consumption habits of the public and the recognition of trademarks lead to the use of trademarks for cultural and expressive purposes; this in turn shall result in the meaning-making of the mark. Since the public are allowed to practice their rights in the mark for cultural and expressive purposes, the mark could be attributed certain meanings which are distinct from the use of trademark by its proprietor. This whole process is the manner that makes trademarks a factor in achieving a just, attractive and proper culture. As one scholar points out, 'th[e] acceptance by the public-at-large is part of what gives trademarks their value in the first place, and part of what justifies [expressive] use[s]'.[251]

In conclusion, it will now be clear that the Social-Planning theory is devoted to achieving a just, attractive culture. The first stage to achieve this culture is by comprehending the manner by which a trademark is formulated. This occurs when a trademark owner chooses a trademark and affixes it over his/her goods. Then comes the second stage, which is the

---

[246] See generally chs 4 and 5.
[247] See generally ch 6.
[248] See *supra* pp 17-23.
[249] See *supra* pp 30-34.
[250] See *supra* pp 40-44.
[251] JA Hofrichter 'Tool of the Trademark: Brand Criticism and Free Speech Problems with the Trademark Dilution Revision Act of 2006' (2007) 28 Cardozo L Rev 1929.

role of the public through the recognition they attribute to the mark, and the association of this mark with certain cultural meanings: this is the meaning-making of a trademark. The suggested justification of trademark systems is achieved by linking the economic theory with the Social-Planning theory, according to which trademarks are justifiable in economic terms because they reduce consumer search costs. The Social-Planning theory regulates the rights and their granting to the right holders in the trademark formula.[252] This could be called the Economic-Social Planning justification.

Conclusion

This chapter has discussed the theoretical justifications for trademarks. It has departed from the employment of the utilitarian theory used, in order to justify the expansion of owners' rights. However, it has been argued that this theory fails to justify trademark systems. This is due to the fact that it is based on artificial economic grounds, which are distinct from legal theory. The incentive argument is subjective, in that it differs from person to person, and has proved to be misplaced. Therefore, in search of an equitable approach, neither Lockean nor Hegelian justifications are of much assistance. As in the case of the utilitarian theory, they are individualistic in their recognition of owners as the only party to enjoy property right. Locke's labour theory, as applied to trademarks, over-compensates the owner for the mental labour he/she exerts in the creation. Hegel's personality theory, meanwhile, fails to justify the alienability of trademarks. This is quite apart from any other hurdles in these theories.

The Economic-Social Planning theory, which is introduced and defended by this book, departs from the fact that trademarks reduce consumers' search cost.[253] It argues that trademark systems should foster the achievement of a just, attractive culture.[254] In this culture, trademark systems should recognize the rights of all parties in the trademark formula.[255] According to this, the role of the public in the creation of trademarks should be recognized,[256] in addition to the right of other traders to use the mark. If this does not affect the rights of the owners, it will result in promoting free, fair competition. This, however, does not aim to

[252] See ch 1 p 11.
[253] See *supra* pp 27-30.
[254] See *supra* pp 57-59.
[255] See ch 1 p 11.
[256] See *supra* pp 50-52, 57-59.

undermine the owners' rights. Rather, it aims to give each party his/her due.

The Way Forward

This book argues in favour of revisiting the philosophical foundations of trademarks. In proving the premises of this book, it is important first to provide a practical translation to the suggested theoretical framework. A theoretical approach is difficult to apply to the practice of current trademark systems without having the practical approach outlined. Therefore, it seems important, on the basis of the Economic-Social Planning justification, to tackle the functions of trademarks. Chapter Three considers that the source and origin function is the only primary functions of trademarks. It opens the way for the adoption of other secondary functions. It establishes that the only test for trademark infringement should be the confusion test. This criterion is the proper application of the Economic-Social Planning justification. Chapters Four and Five attempt to show that the cases of the US and the UK assist in proving the need to revisit the current philosophical foundation of trademarks. Chapter Six emphasizes that the case of trademark parody proves the relevance of the Economic-Social Planning justification, as a manifestation of the rights of the public. The negative treatment of this human right of freedom of expression proves the necessity of rethinking the foundations of current trademark systems in the US and the UK.

One of the most important conclusions stemming from these chapters is that the consuming public and trademark owners are "co-authors" of trademarks. Thus, they shall jointly own the rights in trademarks. Both parties should ensure that the public are not confused as to the source and origin of the goods and/or services. However, the outcome of this book shows that the problem lies not only in the adoption of the dilution test, but also in the expansion of the notion of confusion. Challenging the tendency to this expansion of owners' rights, the reform of trademark systems lies in the adoption of the Economic-Social Planning theory, which considers the rights of all the parties according to the trademark formula.[257]

---

[257] See ch 1 p 11.

CHAPTER THREE

THE FUNCTIONS OF TRADEMARKS

Introduction

In a world saturated with goods and/or services of different brands, trademark owners should enjoy the right to offer their goods and/or services and compete with other rivals. In addition, consumers should be assured of the right to choose from different alternatives. Such fundamental rights should be protected through trademark systems, but such protection does not emerge automatically. Rather, it depends on the ability of trademark systems to provide trademark owners with means to differentiate their products from those of others, and consumers with the necessary tools to make the enjoyment of such right available. The cornerstone of trademark systems is the ability to provide customers with the source and origin of goods and/or services; this will benefit trademark owners by ensuring product differentiation, and will also benefit consumers in exercising their right to choice, and gives them the opportunity to link their experiences of each brand to their judgment, which is, after all, based on individual decision or opinion.

The problem with the protection of trademarks is that such systems are diverted from their original function as product identifiers in favour of other functions such as the quality function. This has resulted in a broadening out of the rights of trademark owners, to the extent that they became tools in their hands to monopolize language, unfairly preventing other traders and undertakings from using the mark on different classes of goods and/or services. It has also detracted from the original purpose of protecting consumers alongside the owner of the mark. This ignores the right of consumers not to be confused by the use of the mark, and considers the use of the mark in a cultural and expressive manner as harmful to trademark owners. This might deprive the public of their right to use the mark in the context of expressing their freedom of speech.

The Economic-Social Planning theory suggests that trademark protection should be divided into two mainstream rights. The first is the right to protect trademark owners and the consuming public in maintaining product differentiation in the marketplace. The second is directed at protecting the rights of the public in cultural and expressive usage as "co-authors" of trademarks.[1]

This chapter deals with the first of these rights, concerning the functions of trademarks. It begins with the citing of the problem of basing trademark protection on the quality, rather than the confusion function. Following this, the basis of this deployment of the quality test will be discussed, assessing the credibility of this argument. Afterwards, focus will be directed on discussing the roots of the origin function, and its relation to other secondary functions, aiming to offer a modern manifestation of the source and origin function as the basis of confusion-based protection, rather than dilution-based protection.

Origin/Quality Dilemma

The rationale behind the existence of modern trademark legislations is twofold. First, it ensures that traders and undertakings can distinguish their goods and/or services from the goods and/or services of other traders and undertakings. Second, it aims to enable the consuming public to distinguish the source of goods and/or services in order to be able to choose the items they wish to obtain.[2] This rationale is based on the origin and source function of trademarks. The policy behind this function is based on protecting consumers from any confusion as to the source and origin. However, a new function of trademarks has emerged, according to which trademarks are considered as quality identifiers, in the sense that they denote the quality resembled in the article, and enable consumers to choose the same article in future purchases.

As such, and according to the quality function, trademark owners' rights are considerably widened.[3] The introduction of dilution has led to the expansion in trademark owners' rights, in addition to widening the

---

[1] See ch 2 pp 50-52, 57-59.

[2] Shanahan (n2) 234. See also, B Mahaffey-Dowd 'Famous Trademarks: Ordinary Inquiry by the Courts of Marks Entitled to an Extraordinary Remedy' (1998) 64 Brook L Rev 424, arguing that '[t]rademark law has historically served a dual purpose of consumer protection and producer protection.'

[3] See ch 1 pp 4-5.

scope of confusion.[4] In addition, the right of the public to use trademarks for cultural purposes is put at risk.[5] As one scholar comments:

> 'It may well be that no… full justification can be given for this protection in trade mark law terms. If so, the only other question is whether that matters, if the protection granted is a useful and proper weapon in the armoury of the trade marks proprietor.'[6]

This approach, which argues that the traditional protection of trademarks as origin and source identifiers is outdated and could not stand to fulfil the current needs of modern trademark systems, fails to acknowledge that the source and origin function aims to 'benefit[…] the public by preventing customer confusion,' whereas the quality function of trademarks, resembled in the dilution doctrine, is in favour of the trademark owner's rights.[7] Moreover, this argument, which defends the extreme protection of trademark owners, results in barriers to new entrants to enter markets, and demotivates them to conduct their businesses. This is because wide protection presupposes that famous marks denote the quality of the goods and/or services, and when a new competitor comes to the market, he/she will be unable to sell his/her articles because consumers will refrain from purchasing them, preferring to buy the article with quality. As such, this shall constitute a barrier to competition.[8] Consequently, such protection might result in monopoly in the hands of trademark owners. They will have the right to prevent the use of their marks even in parody and cultural expressive courses, and will enable 'big business[es] to buy ordinary words of English language as trade marks at comparatively little cost[s].'[9]

---

[4] K Assaf 'The Dilution of Culture and the Law of Trademarks' (2008) 49 IDEA: The Intellectual Property L Rev 4.
[5] See generally ch 6.
[6] A Michaels 'Confusion in and about Sections 5(3) and 10(3) of the Trade Marks Act 1994' (2000) 22(7) EIPR 339.
[7] C Brown 'A Dilution Delusion: The Unjustifiable Protection of Similar Marks' (2003-2004) 72 U of Cincinnati L Rev 1026.
[8] M Strasser 'The Rational Basis of Trademark Protection Revisited: Putting the Dilution Doctrine into Context' (1999-2000) 10 Fordham Intellectual Property, Media & Entertainment L J 430-431, Strasser argues that wide trademark protection 'creates artificial barriers to market entry.'
[9] *British Sugar Plc v James Robertson & Sons Ltd* [1996] RPC 281 (Ch) 285. See also, J Davis 'European Trade Mark Law and the Enclosure of the Commons' (2002) 4 Intellectual Property Q 342.

Under current trademark legislation in different countries, the concept of dilution is the prominent doctrine for the protection of well-known trademarks. This concept aims to protect famous marks from any use which dilutes the distinctiveness of the mark. In this manner, trademark use has deviated too far from the aims and goals which trademarks were initially designed to formulate,

> '[a]nd when trademarks are used in this way, they acquire certain functional characteristics that are different from –and sometimes inconsistent with– their traditional role as identifiers of source.'[10]

Thus, the philosophical foundations adopted to justify the current protection should be revisited and revised. This should be directed towards assessing whether this extreme amount of protection to trademark owners is appropriate, or whether it should be subject to revisiting, so as to balance the rights of parties in the trademark formula.[11]

The introduction of the dilution doctrine has led some to argue that this should form the basis of protection, and that the origin and source function no longer qualifies for trademark protection.[12] Thus, the start shall be with Schechter's argument of quality, citing the inaccuracy of this argument, and concluding that it does not really constitute the real rational basis of trademark protection. Then, focus will be directed towards the source and origin function of trademarks, arguing that it forms the primary function of trademarks, on which protection should be based.

Schechter's Argument of Quality

This section begins by discussing the quality argument, as envisioned by Schechter. Then, the focus shall be directed towards the expansion of this argument, which accords with the current trend to monopolize trademark owners' rights.

The Quality Argument

The expansion in the protection of trademarks finds its roots in the article of Frank I. Schechter *The Rational Basis of Trademark Protection*,

---

[10] A Kozinski 'Trademarks Unplugged' (1994) 84 Trademark Reporter 443.
[11] See ch 1 p 11.
[12] PK Fletcher 'Joint Registration of Trademarks and the Economic Value of a Trademark System' (1981-1982) 36 U of Miami L Rev 320.

a text written in 1927.[13] Schechter is seen as the founder of dilution,[14] even though this particular word was only mentioned once in his argument,[15] and in the course of referring to the German's court decision in the *Odol* case.[16] His ideas about the quality function of trademarks formed the basis for a utilitarian and economic justification of trademarks. They were thoroughly deployed by utilitarian theorists to justify a wide scope of protection to trademarks owners,[17] and '[b]ehind [his] model lies a utilitarian rationale.'[18] The reason that Schechter's argument is relevant and vital in the trademark context is that it is responsible for the change in

---

[13] Schechter's article was first published in 1927, it was cited as: FI Schechter 'The Rational Basis of Trademark Protection' (1926-1927) 40 Harvard L Rev (813-833). Schechter (n15)

[14] Mahaffey-Dowd (n2) 428. See also, H Carty 'Do Marks with a Reputation Merit Special Protection' (1997) 19(2) EIPR 684, arguing that it is Schechter, the American academic, is the founder of the dilution notion, 'challeng[ing] the traditional origin/information basis of trade mark protection,' and his ideas led many states in the US to adopt anti-dilution statutes.

[15] JE Moskin 'Dilution or Delusion: The Rational Limits of Trademark Protection' (1993) 83 Trademark Reporter 126. See also, S Casparie-Kerdel 'Dilution Disguised: Has the Concept of Trade Mark Dilution Made its Way into the Laws of Europe' (2001) 23(4) EIPR 185. Some scholars argue that the roots of dilution are found in the ruling of the Supreme Court of 1894 in Germany in the *Odol* case, where the court expanded trademark protection of trademarks to include non-competing goods, but the court also required the existence of the likelihood of confusion. See- T Martino *Trademark Dilution* (1st edn Clarendon Press Oxford 1996) 4. Schechter himself referred to this case in advocating his notion of quality (dilution), See- FI Schechter 'The Rational Basis of Trademark Protection' (Reprint in 1970 of the 1927 text) 60 Trademark Reporter 345-346.

[16] The term "dilution" seems to be an English translation for the German word "verwässert" which was first used by the German court in the *Odol* case. See- Schechter (n15) 346.

[17] Akazaki argues that utilitarian theorists use Schechter's rational regarding the quality function of trademarks; they provide that since trademarks reduce consumer search costs then this will encourage then to produce high quality products. See- L Akazaki 'Source Theory and Guarantee Theory in Anglo-American Trade Mark Policy: A Critical Legal Study' (1990) 72 J of the Patent & Trademark Office Society 259.

[18] S Wilf 'Who Authors Trademarks?' (1999) 17 Cardozo Arts & Entertainment L J 14. See also, W Ullah and TR Martino 'The Quality Guarantee Function of Trade Marks: An Economic Viewpoint' (1989) 11(8) EIPR 268-269, Ullah and Martino argue that the quality argument forms the basis for the utilitarian and economic justification of trademarks, they argue that 'trade marks lower consumer search costs[, and t]hey also act as an incentive to firms to develop and maintain consistent quality.'

current trademark legislations. His ideas led to a wide range of monopolistic rights which are currently enjoyed by the owners.

Schechter refuted the argument of the US Supreme Court in *Hanover Star Milling Co v Metcalf*[19] that trademarks are source and origin identifiers. He argues that trademarks today do not function as such, and considers this to be '[t]he orthodox definition'[20] of the function of trademarks. His argument is based on the proposition that with advances in the movement of trade, it is no longer either practical, or important for consumers to know the source and origin of the goods and/or services.[21] This is because goods are usually manufactured far away from where they are consumed. They often reach consumers after being circulated amongst manufacturers and traders. Thus, the idea that trademarks denote source and origin should be discarded, from Schechter's point of view, because 'the source or origin of the goods bearing a well-known trademark is seldom known to consumers.'[22]

He further contends that the source and origin *per se* is not of a particular importance. What is in fact important is the consumers' ability to know that the product reaches him/her

> 'through the same channels as certain other goods that have already given the consumer satisfaction, and that bore the same trademark[,] ... [thus t]he true functions of the trademark are... to identify a product as satisfactory and thereby to stimulate further purchases by the consuming public.'[23]

---

[19] The Supreme Court argued that '[t]he primary and proper function of a trademark is to identify the origin or ownership of the article to which it is affixed[, and w]here a party has been in the habit of labeling his goods with a distinctive mark, so that purchasers recognize goods thus marked as being of his production, others are debarred from applying the same mark to goods of the same description, because to do so ... may induce purchasers to believe that the goods which he is selling are the manufacture of another person'. See- *Hanover Star Milling Co v Metcalf* 240 US 403 (1916) 412-413.

[20] Schechter (n15) 334.

[21] '[T]he growth of national and international markets destroyed th[e] intimacy between producer and consumer', as such trademarks became quality identifiers 'because they denote consistent quality', rather than being origin and source identifiers. See- DM Higgins and TJ James 'The Economic Importance of Trade Marks in the UK (1973-1992) A Preliminary Investigation' (1996) The Intellectual Property Institute 5.

[22] Schechter (n15) 335.

[23] ibid 336, 337.

The quality function of trademarks is based on the premise that if the public recognize the trademark as an origin indicator, and not as a quality identifier, then there will be no rationale for choosing a certain brand. In particular when consumers are interested in the utility of certain products, then 'the trade mark serves to remind the consumer that those articles have in the past satisfactorily carried out their intended or expected purposes'.[24]

A major inadequacy, Schechter argues, results from considering trademarks as source and origin identifiers. That is, the protection of trademarks shall not find a proper justification if the mark is to be used by others over non-competing goods and/or services, even when consumer confusion is not likely to exist. This kind of protection, over non-competing products, is vital to trademark owners who provide goods of consistent quality for a long time. This is because such owners might decide to expand the scope of their businesses to include different classes of goods and/or services. They shall, therefore, be unfairly deprived of using their marks which they have invested in. Schechter supports his argument by emphasising that the origin and source function 'ignores the fact that the creation and retention of custom … is the primary purpose of trademark[s] today'.[25] The focus should be directed towards the role of trademarks protection in the 'preservation of the uniqueness [of marks]',[26] because using a trademark on non-competing goods and/or services shall lessen the distinctiveness of the mark. The real injury –which is now widely considered the definition of dilution– in such a case

> 'is the gradual whittling away or dispersion of the identity and hold upon the public mind of the mark or name by its use upon non-competing goods. The more distinctive or unique the mark, the deeper is its impress upon the public consciousness, and the greater its need for protection against vitiation or dissociation from the particular product in connection with which it has been used.'[27]

Despite the monopolistic rights defended by Schechter, many scholarly arguments have expanded the scope of his notion of quality. Such arguments aim to include "related" goods and/or services within the ambit of Schechter's quality argument, in addition to "non-competing" goods and/or services. This approach is preferred by many countries aiming to provide protection to its multinational corporations, such as the US.

---

[24] Akazaki (n17) 258.
[25] Schechter (n15) 339.
[26] ibid 339.
[27] ibid 342.

Further Expansion of Owners' Rights

Schechter's argument, albeit not convincing, is straightforward. It aims to provide a wide scope of protection to distinctive marks over *non-competing* goods and/or services, on the basis that such marks are quality identifiers. However, as Schechter's concept does not define its scope, as some have argued,[28] this matter is subject to discussions amongst scholars and courts. Some have argued that

> '[i]t is not entirely clear whether Schechter intended dilution theory to apply to noncompetitive situations *only* or to the use of certain marks on related *and* unrelated goods.'[29]

Such arguments have led to expanding the scope of the dilution concept beyond that of Schechter's intentions. They argue that the scope of dilution should not only cover the use of famous marks over *dissimilar* goods and/or services. Rather, it should cover the use of marks over *similar* goods and/or services as well.[30]

It is a matter of debate as to why dilution should protect famous marks when used over similar goods, because it is already protected under the "traditional" origin/confusion rationale. The answer is that the proponents of such expansive interpretations aim to simplify owners' burden of proof, and exempt them from proving likelihood of confusion.[31]

This approach is manifested in the European Court of Justice (ECJ) decision in *Davidoff v Gofkid Ltd*.[32] In this case, the defendant registered the trademark "Durffee" which is similar to the plaintiff's "Davidoff" well-known trademark, and is written in a very similar way. It was registered for the same class of goods for which the plaintiff was using his mark. Davidoff filed a request to the German Patent and Trade Mark Office objecting to this registration, but did not succeed, and it did not succeed either in the courts of first instance and on appeal.[33] Thus, the

---

[28] *Trademark Dilution* (n15) 17, arguing that Schechter fails to answer some 'fundamental questions concerning the scope and the application of [his] doctrine'.

[29] ibid 26-27.

[30] For example, section 10(3) of the UK Trade Marks Act of 1994 deleted the requirement that the dilutive use should be on dissimilar goods and/or services, thus, the current section 10(3) applies to similar and dissimilar goods and/or services equally. See- The United Kingdom Statutory Instrument 2004/946 Reg 7. See also, ch 5 pp 176-178.

[31] As in the case of the US. See ch 4 pp 132-134.

[32] (Case C-292/00) [2003] ETMR 42.

[33] ibid 535.

plaintiff filed the case to the Bundesgerichtshof court, and the court stayed the proceeding and requested a ruling from the ECJ as to whether Member States according to Council Directive 89/104/EEC[34] are entitled

> 'to provide more extensive protection for well-known marks in cases where the later mark is used or to be used for goods or services identical with or similar to those in respect of which the earlier mark was registered'.[35]

The hurdle which the court was dealing with was whether article 5(2) of the Directive –which protects well-known marks when used by others on *dissimilar* goods and/or services– should be interpreted widely, to cover the use of the mark on *similar* goods and/or services. The protection of this latter case was the subject of article 5(1)(b) of the Directive, which protects similar or identical marks from being used by others over similar or identical goods and/or services, but requires the existence of likelihood of confusion.

The ECJ refused observations submitted to it by the Portuguese and UK Governments, defending a narrow interpretation to article 5(2). They argued that the *Davidoff* case is already covered by article 5(1)(b) which requires the existence of the likelihood of confusion, especially insofar as 'a likelihood of confusion is found more readily in the case of well-known marks.'[36] However, the court finally ordered in favour of a wide interpretation of article 5(2) to include the case of using well-known mark even over *similar* goods and/or services regardless of the existence of likelihood of confusion. It ruled that this article is

> 'to be interpreted as entitling the Member State to provide specific protection for well-known registered trade marks in cases where a later mark or sign, which is identical with or similar to the registered mark, is intended to be used or is used for goods or services identical with or similar to those covered by the registered mark.'[37]

Such interpretation –which adheres to the utilitarian and economic theory– is wrongly based on the view of its proponents that '[d]ilution is not simply a broadening of the protection originally given to trade marks.

---

[34] First Council Directive 89/104/EEC of 21 December 1988 to approximate thc laws of the Member States relating to trademarks, OJ 1989 L40/1, Corrigendum OJ 1989 L159/60.

[35] *Davidoff* (n32) 536.

[36] ibid 541.

[37] ibid 543.

It is an entirely separate concept, with its own conditions and restrictions.'[38]

Contrary to this approach, Schechter's merits are that his concept was clear and its scope was well defined, although his argument cannot be followed. He limited the scope of marks eligible to protection under his concept, whilst arguing also that 'arbitrary, coined or fanciful marks or names should be given much broader degree of protection than symbols, words or phrases in common use',[39] and he restricted his argument on the use over non-competing goods and/or services.[40] The next section questions the credibility of the quality argument, and whether the need to return to the basics of trademark protection exists.

Function of Trademarks: Quality or Equality?

It is imperative to analyse Schechter's quality argument in order to comprehend what is the real and proper rationale of trademark protection. Thus, one should question the validity of this argument, and assess whether the origin/source argument still maintains its merits or is truly an outdated traditional argument, as Schechter denotes.

The basis of the quality argument –that the distinctiveness and the association of the trademark with the product to which it is affixed on account of the owners' efforts– is not accurate. On the contrary, the Economic-Social Planning theory argues that the essential role in establishing this association between the mark and the article derives from the consuming public. The owner might try to build the association and invest in doing so, but he/she might fail, because the association is concluded and achieved through the recognition of consumers. As such,

[38] Casparie-Kerdel (n15) 194. See also, S Chong 'Protection of Famous Trademarks Against Use for Unrelated Goods and Services: A Comparative Analysis of the Law in the United States, the United Kingdom and Canada and Recommendations for the Canadian Law Reform' (2005) 95 Trademark Reporter 643.

[39] Schechter (n15) 343. An arbitrary mark 'refers to a word in common use that has no meaning related to the product that it is used to name,' such as APPLE for computers, whereas a fanciful mark is 'the made-up name that resembles no other word, such as EXXON or KODAK.' See- WM Landes and RA Posner 'The Economics of Trademark Law' (1988) 78 Trademark Reporter 288. See also, Brown (n7) 1027.

[40] Schechter (n15) 341-345. See also, PL Roncaglia 'Should We Use Guns and Missiles to Protect Famous Trademarks in Europe?' (1998) 88 Trademark Reporter 559.

the party which deserves protection and reward for this association is the public at large.[41] This is because the consuming public are the party who attribute the association of the mark with the article, thus it remains their right to maintain this association, withdraw it or lessen its amount. Owners are by no means entitled to seize this right for themselves.

In certain instances, one may find a wide agreement and consensus among the public that a certain product bears a high quality. However, the essence of quality assessment is a relative matter, which differs from one case to the other. It is, thus, a subjective rather than objective issue.[42] What someone considers to be of high quality may be found to be different by others. This differs according to needs and expectations which are assessed on individual basis. Thus, '[t]he assumption that a trade marked product must be of high quality because it bears a trade mark, is unfounded'.[43] It is correctly argued that the quality notion 'is in principle a neutral term which can mean good or bad quality associated with a certain source of the product.'[44] When 'a consumer learns that he does not want particular goods, the mark ... becomes a significant warning signal.'[45] This argument suggests that the source and origin function is the primary function of trademarks, and that the matter of quality, whether positive or negative, is something appurtenant to this function. Indeed,

> '[t]rade mark law makes nowhere a value judgment: trade marks and their protection are available to high and low quality products alike. The

---

[41] Wilf argues that Schechter credits trademarks owners for their rationality and presumes that consumers are irrational. Wilf stresses the opposite, and argues that '[p]urchasers carefully choose material goods to construct an outward expression of identity', and this is exactly what Schechter's argument fails to acknowledge. See- Wilf (n18) 15.

[42] See ch 2 pp 25-27.

[43] A Rahmatian 'Trade Mark Infringement as a Criminal Offence' (2004) 67(4) MLR 680. See also, (Case C-10/89) *S.A. Cnl-Sucal NV v Hag GF AG* [1990] 3 CMLR 571, 583, providing that '[t]he guarantee of quality offered by a trade mark is not of course absolute, for the manufacturer is at liberty to vary the quality'.

[44] Rahmatian (n43) 680.

[45] W Cornish and D Llewelyn *Intellectual Property: Patents, Copyright, Trade Marks and Allied Rights* (6th edn Sweet & Maxwell London 2007) 621 (para 16-23). See also, the ruling of the Second Circuit Court of Appeals in the USA, arguing that the trader's 'mark is his authentic seal; by it he vouches for the goods which bear it; it carries his name for good or ill.' See- *Yale Electric Corp v Robertson Comr of Patents* 26 F.2d 972 (2d Cir. 1928) 974. See also, CDG Pickering *Trade Marks in Theory and Practice* (1st edn Hart Publishing Oxford 1998) 99.

> indicative function of the trade mark can therefore work either way –it can identify products as being goods of high quality, but it can also warn customers to avoid certain product in the future.'[46]

Moreover, the quality function argument wrongly relies upon the idea that the quality function is the only function of trademarks.[47] Schechter does not give any regard to the source and origin function, even as a primary function. Rather, he considers the quality function as the true function, implying that any other function –source and origin– is untrue. He considers that 'the preservation of the uniqueness of a trademark should constitute the *only* rational basis for its protection' (emphasis added).[48] This "only rational basis" leads to strange and unnatural conclusions. According to these, trademarks bearing products of negative or bad quality should not be protected. Moreover, trademarks with neutral quality do not merit any protection, because they do not resemble quality in the sense Schechter is arguing. In contrast to this approach, it is a matter of consensus that protection is not based upon the quality of products; i.e. trademarks are protected regardless of the merits of the goods and/or services to which they are affixed.

Schechter's argument seeks to provide as much protection as possible for the owners without regard to the rights of the public and other traders. The discussion of this quality argument shows that it cannot be reconciled with the premises of the Economic-Social Planning theory. Schechter's quality argument, and its expansion, does not help in achieving the vital goal of ensuring justice amongst the involved parties in the trademark formula.[49] As such, this assessment demonstrates the important link between theory and practice. In the remainder of this chapter, the source and origin function is introduced as a modern concept, in compliance with the suggested Economic-Social Planning approach.

The Making of a Modern Source/Origin Function

After having discussed the quality function of trademarks, and concluded that it fails to establish a rational basis for trademark protection, this section discusses the source and origin function of trademarks. In

---

[46] Rahmatian (n43) 680.

[47] Ullah and Martino (n18) 267, arguing that advocates of the quality function 'have made an exaggerated attempt to escape the strict doctrinal requirement of a known source.'

[48] Schechter (n15) 345.

[49] See ch 1 p 11.

applying the premises of the Economic-Social Planning justification, it shall be argued that the source function is the *only primary function* of trademarks. This theoretical approach provides a workable solution in its acceptance of the existence of a number of *secondary* functions, from amongst which is the quality function. To this end, the start will be to consider the roots and development of the source/origin argument and its connection with other trademarks functions. Then, a proposition –which benefits from the shortcomings of the quality argument– shall be formulated as the basis for modern trademark legislation, on the grounds of Economic-Social Planning.

Development of the Source/Origin Function

It is important to understand the concept of the source/origin argument, in order to be able to comprehend its ability to fulfil the needs of different parties in the context of trademarks. Thus, it is essential to find its roots and to assess whether its evolution could help to justify current emerging cases in trademarks, such as the issue of well-known trademarks. In this regard, it shall be argued that the notion of the source/origin argument has developed, and is, and will be able to modify in accordance with the advent of trademarks. However, first of all, a brief historical overview of the source and origin function will be given, which is necessary to assert the argument that this function establishes a real rational basis. The historical roots and development shall lead to the argument that this notion is able to evolve and transform in a manner that can follow and justify any development of trademarks. Then, the connection of the source argument with the other functions of trademarks shall be discussed, in the light of the Economic-Social Planning approach.

- Historical development

The use of trademarks finds its roots in past historical ages; perhaps it 'is one of the oldest of established human practices.'[50] In its early stages, the use of marks involved the branding of cattle and animals;[51] the

---

[50] Fletcher (n12) 301. See also, DD Domenico 'Mark Madness: How Brent Musburger and the Miracle Bra May Have Led to a More Equitable and Efficient Understanding of the Reverse Confusion Doctrine in Trademark Law' (2000) 86 Virginia L Rev 600.

[51] SA Diamond 'The Historical Development of Trademarks' (1983) 73 Trademark Reporter 223. See also, JT McCarthy *Trademarks and Unfair Competition* (2nd edn The Lawyers Co-operative Publishing Co. New York 1984) 131-132 (section 5:1).

intention of this was to distinguish the ownership of one individual's cattle from the cattle of the others, by branding the cattle with certain colours or signs or by cutting the ears thereof in certain shapes. 'This practice is portrayed in early Stone Age cave drawings and in wall paintings',[52] scholars called such marks proprietary or possessory marks.[53]

Afterwards, in mediaeval times, the use of marks to identify the source and origin took a different form, which arose because of the advent of trade and the introduction of guild marks.[54] Each guild group was obliged by statutory regulations to affix a certain mark to all examples of a certain product.[55] The aim of this practice was to identify the source and origin of the goods 'in order to permit detection and punishment of the individual responsible for a defect,'[56] 'or in order that in case of shipwreck or piracy the goods might be identified and reclaimed by the owner.'[57]

The industrial revolution witnessed the emergence of the modern use of trademarks as source and origin identifiers, because of '[t]he loss of the personal connection between producer and consumer'.[58] The 'natural result was the concentration of production capacity in larger units and this in turn required the development of methods of distribution to get the goods to the consumer.'[59] Thus emerged the use of trademarks to enable consumers to know the manufacturer and/or provider of the goods, i.e. 'to

---

[52] AH Khoury 'Ancient and Islamic Sources of Intellectual Property Protection in the Middle East: A Focus on Trademarks' (2003) 43 The J of L and Technology 156. See also, Diamond (n51) 224, arguing that wall paintings and pottery jars used in Greece, Egypt, China and Rome showed the early uses of trademarks.

[53] L Bently and B Sherman *Intellectual Property Law* (2nd edn Oxford University Press Oxford 2004) 693.

[54] Diamond (n51) 230.

[55] AS Greenberg 'The Ancient Lineage of Trade-Marks' (1951) 33 J of the Patent Office Society 882.

[56] Fletcher (n12) 301. See also, Schechter (n15) 335, Schechter provides that guild marks were 'compulsorily affixed to goods by statute, administrative order or municipal or gild regulation, so that defective work might be traced to the guilty craftsman and heavily punished, … [t]his mark was a true mark of origin'.

[57] Schechter (n15) 335. See also, SM Maniatis *The Communicative Aspects of Trade Marks: A Legal, Functional and Economic Analysis* (PhD Thesis University of London 1998) 28-29.

[58] M Blakeney 'Trade Marks and the Promotion of Trade' (1999) 5(6) Intl Trade L & Regulation 140.

[59] Diamond (n51) 237.

represent to the consumer *only* the physical source or origin of the product or service in connection with which the mark was used.'[60]

Furthermore, in modern times, with the growth of international trade and goods and/or services being distributed throughout the whole world, the source and origin function of trademarks have continued to be capable of developing, and trademarks have functioned so as to distinguish the goods and/or services of one undertaking from those of others. The significance of this development is that the exact identity of the manufacturer itself is a matter of no importance; trademarks do not tell consumers where the goods and/or services come from. Rather, consumers are now interested in knowing that certain goods and/or services emerge from a certain source and origin which could be *anonymous*, and this makes them differentiate between these goods and/or services from the goods and/or services of others of the same class.[61] As Denicola argues: 'Trademarks could be understood as indications, not necessarily of physical origin, but of a more general connection between the trademark owner and the trademarked goods.'[62]

- Primary and secondary functions

The application of the Economic-Social Planning of trademarks presumes that the source and origin function of trademarks is the primary function of trademarks. Any trademark should be able to function in this manner; otherwise it could not qualify as a trademark. Therefore, this book considers the source and origin function as the only primary function for trademarks, because protection should be based upon this function; this is achievable through the confusion test. By contrast, other functions of trademarks should be considered secondary, because protection should not be based upon them.

---

[60] *Trademarks and Unfair Competition* (n51) 110 (section 3:3). The term "physical source or origin" means concrete origin, i.e. 'that the trade mark refers to the actual producer or trader of the product ... or to a number of affiliated producers'. See- *The Communicative Aspects of Trade Marks: A Legal, Functional and Economic Analysis* (n57) 123.

[61] SA Diamond 'The Public Interest and the Trademark System' (1980) 62 J of the Patent Office Society 537, arguing that '[t]rademarks are the symbols that bridge the gap that now has grown so wide between the producer and the consumer.'

[62] RC Denicola 'Some Thoughts on the Dynamics of Federal Trademark Legislation and the Trademark Dilution Act of 1995' (1996) 59 L & Contemporary Problems 77.

Trademarks could have –and in most cases do have– other secondary functions: quality, advertising and informative functions. The quality function, as a secondary function, differs from the source and origin function. The latter should exist in all trademarks, whereas the existence of the former is not a necessity, and when it exists 'it retains a neutral character'.[63] It could inform the consumer that he/she finds a particular article with a high quality, but it could remind other consumers of bad quality.

Trademarks perform a further, secondary function besides that of quality, namely an advertising and marketing function. In today's markets, where a huge number of goods and services are available, producers are able to use their trademarks to advertise their products.[64] This allows purchasers to identify the source and origin of products, and '[t]he way in which trade marks facilitate this process is by their ability to distinguish and identify goods and services.'[65] Indeed, '[t]he mark actually *sells* the goods' (emphasis added),[66] meaning that it facilitates consumers' identification of the source and origin of the goods and/or services. In turn, this benefits the owner in selling his/her goods and/or services, because the advertising function assists in preventing of the diversion of his/her sales to other undertakings.

The advertising function is related to the Economic-Social Planning theory, according to which the creation of trademarks happens in two stages; in the first the trademark owner associates the mark with the article and in the second stage the public grant the required recognition to this association.[67] One of the ways of achieving this recognition and association by the public is through extensive advertising. It educates consumers and creates a desire for goods and/or services.[68] It also creates brand awareness in the minds of consumers, 'especially in markets

---

[63] *Intellectual Property: Patents, Copyright, Trade Marks and Allied Rights* (n45) 621 (para 16-23).

[64] JA Horwitz 'Conflicting Marks: Embracing the Consequences of the European Community and its Unitary Trademark Regime' (2001) 18 Arizona J Intl & Comparative L 248-249, arguing that 'a trademark operates like an advertisement by convincing a consumer to purchase the trademarked product.'

[65] Blakeney (n58) 141.

[66] Schechter (n15) 338. See also, *The Communicative Aspects of Trade Marks: A Legal, Functional and Economic Analysis* (n57) 155, arguing that the aim of advertising is 'to sell goods by influencing buyers.'

[67] Wilf (n18) 8.

[68] *The Communicative Aspects of Trade Marks: A Legal, Functional and Economic Analysis* (n57) 122-123.

characterised by over-capacity and increased competition'[69] which makes the public's recognition more significant.

The last secondary function of trademarks is that of being informative.[70] This function means that trademarks play an important role in providing consumers with the necessary amount of information which needs to be communicated.[71] Providing them with information about products is also related to personal experiences with certain products, which differs from one consumer to the other. This is also related to the Economic-Social Planning theory, which considers that trademarks reduce consumers' search costs.[72] This entails providing consumers with the necessary information regarding the products they wish to consume.

The informative function provides consumers with information regarding the sponsorship of the goods and/or services. This is vital in order to know the source and origin of the products, which results in lowering the search costs for consumers. In particular when the producer enters into a licence agreement with another party authorizing him/her to manufacture the products under the licensors' trademark which includes a relationship of sponsorship and affiliation that indicates a connection between the licensor (the trademark owner) and the licensee. As Ladas argues,

> '[i]t is necessary to remind ourselves of the true concept of trademarks as being essentially symbols or badges indicating source of origin of the goods bearing such. The word "origin" denotes at least that the goods are

---

[69] ibid 154.

[70] This function is also called the communicative function, because of its ability to convey information to consumers.

[71] Blakeney (n58) 141.

[72] A Griffiths 'The Impact of the Global Appreciation Approach on the Boundaries of Trade Mark Protection' (2001) 4 Intellectual Property Q 327, Griffiths argues that trademarks 'provide an economic benefit to consumers by providing them with useful information, which reduces the cost of searching for products with particular qualities.' See also, *The Communicative Aspects of Trade Marks: A Legal, Functional and Economic Analysis* (n57) 120, 121, Maniatis argues that 'humans learned through social interaction to utilise together with verbal symbols, other signs as mechanisms for communication' in order to preserve 'the spent effort with the number of purchases we make in a lifetime'. See also, Domenico (n50) 601, arguing that '[t]rademarks reduce the amount of time and money a consumer must spend to obtain a product by allowing for easier differentiation among products and producers.'

> issued as vendible goods under the aegis of the proprietor of the trademark who thus assumes responsibility for them.'[73]

For example, it is obvious that all the Coca-Cola sold in the world does not originate from Atlanta in the US.[74] Rather, the Coca-Cola Company enters into licence agreements with others to produce under its trademark. Hence, the informative function provides consumers with information that the production of Coca-Cola in a certain country is under the sponsorship and affiliation of a certain origin and source.

In conclusion, trademarks function in a number of manners. The primary function is the source and origin function, which all trademarks should perform, whereas the quality, advertising and the informative functions are secondary functions and are attached to the source and origin function.[75] It has been argued that this primary function has developed since it was first used in old historical ages until our recent years. It has proved to be a flexible notion which could be transformed to fulfil the needs of modern trade. Being able to identify that a product originates from a certain source and origin, albeit anonymous, and distinguish those products from other products by others especially when products are homogenous, alongside with being able to embrace the other secondary functions, the source and origin function is, indeed, the only rational basis for trademark protection. This is because it regards the consumer confusion criterion as the main standard, according to which consumers are protected from being confused as to the source and origin of the products, which in turn benefits trademark owners. On the basis of this conclusion, a proposition for trademark systems based on the source and origin function will now be offered.

Proposition Based on Source/Origin

The shortcomings in Schechter's argument do not mean that trademark owners should not enjoy protection. Nor do they mean that owners of well-known trademarks should not enjoy more protection than those of

---

[73] SP Ladas 'Trademark Licensing and the Antitrust Law' (1973) 63 Trademark Reporter 248.

[74] Blakeney (n58) 141.

[75] D Shanahan 'The Trademark Right: Consumer Protection or Monopoly?' (1982) 72 Trademark Reporter 238-241, arguing that the origin function is the primary function of trademarks because it plays an important role in consumer protection, whereas the other functions are secondary functions, which not every trademark should have.

ordinary marks. Rather, any trademark system should aim to provide protection for trademark owners, and at the same time protect the rights of the consuming public and other traders.[76] This could be achieved through the adherence to the source and origin function of trademarks as being the *only primary function* thereof, because there are secondary functions, which might (but not necessarily) include the quality, advertising and information functions.

Owners of ordinary marks shall enjoy their rights over their trademarks according to the origin and source function, according to which they shall use their marks and prevent others from using an identical mark over the same class of goods and/or services to which the original mark is affixed. This is because consumer confusion (as to the source or origin) is the main criterion, according to the origin and source function, and in using identical marks over the same class of goods and/or services the confusion amongst consumers is assumed,[77] and the owner shall not be obliged to prove it. In this case, the owner shall enjoy the right to ensure that his/her mark is not used by others who could unfairly take advantage by using an identical mark over the same class of goods and/or services, and the consuming public are protected from being confused. Conversely, if someone uses an identical or similar mark over an identical or similar class of goods and/or services, then the owner of the mark shall have the right to prevent such use if he/she could prove that the public will be confused by this use, or at least that the public will likely be confused by such use.[78]

Owners of well-known trademarks shall enjoy more protection than owners of ordinary trademarks. Some marks prove to have more distinctiveness, repute or fame than ordinary marks. This is achieved through the owners' investment and, more importantly, the high degree of recognition and association which the consuming public attribute to the mark, with the class of goods and/or services which they are used to. Such marks deserve more protection than ordinary marks; however, the questions are: what kind of protection should be accorded to such marks? How could this protection be formulated in a manner which preserves the owners' rights, other traders' rights and public's interests?

Schechter deals with these questions from one perspective, that of the trademark owners' rights. Due to his adherence to the quality function, he wrongly concludes that protection should be fully granted to trademarks

---

[76] Denicola (n62) 80.

[77] For example, see the Trade Marks Act 1994 (UK) c 26 s 10(1), where the existence of likelihood of confusion is not required.

[78] ibid s 10(2).

when used by others on non-related goods.[79] Schechter's policy focuses on 'offer[ing] enhanced protection to originators of unique marks.'[80] However, the proper and real injury is to provide protection to the trademark owner, thereby depriving other traders and the public from their rights. Thus, well-known marks shall enjoy protection as long as their use by others shall result in confusion or likelihood of confusion as to the source or origin. One scholar has argued, in defence of such an approach, that expanding the protection of trademarks to cover dissimilar goods and/or services should 'cover cases in which the strength of the earlier mark's reputation was such that confusion would occur despite the lack of similarity of the parties' goods, as long as confusion' exists.[81] In this way, owners of well-known trademarks shall enjoy more protection than owners of ordinary marks because of their investment in the mark, and other traders shall have the right to use the mark on other classes of goods and/or services, as long as there is no confusion or likelihood of confusion. More importantly, the public will be entitled to use the mark which they have participated in its formulation, and they will enjoy the right to enjoy cultural and expressive rights in the mark. This cultural use of trademarks is, indeed, vital to us as the public, because 'our culture is enriched by these trade marks. They tell us a story, they entertain us. They help us to express ourselves in relation to our world.'[82]

This rationale seeks equity and equality amongst the parties involved in trademarks, rather than adopting a quality argument which creates illegitimate barriers of competition and affects the social and cultural development of the society. One central aspect of the argument is therefore that the public's confusion as to the source and origin of the goods and/or services should formulate the rational basis for trademark protection. Confusion should be the basis for assessing trademark infringement, even in the case of well-known trademarks.

Once again, the importance of revisiting the philosophical foundation of trademarks comes to the surface, in order to be able to legitimize and justify the protection based on the confusion-origin/source rationale.

---

[79] Schechter (n15) 339, 345.

[80] *Trademark Dilution* (n15) 23.

[81] Michaels (n6) 339.

[82] M Richardson 'Copyright in Trade Marks? On Understanding Trade Mark Dilution' (2000) 1 Intellectual Property Q 79.

Conclusion

This chapter has emphasized that the quality function is not the appropriate rational basis for trademark protection. Therefore, the dilution test, which is based on the quality function, should not be deployed. The avoidance of the dilution arguments shall assist in preventing monopolies in trademarks. It has been clarified that the source and origin function is the only primary function on which trademark systems should be based. The test for trademark protection is, thus, the consumer confusion rationale. The approach concluded by this chapter allows other secondary functions to exist.

In this chapter, the argument was developed on the basis of the Economic-Social Planning theory. This argument adopts the confusion rationale as the proper test for infringement. Accordingly, the consuming public should enjoy two main rights,[83] amongst others. Firstly, the public should be ensured the right of having their state of mind (confusion) as the only standard of trademark infringement. Secondly, the public should be able to use trademarks for cultural and expressive uses.[84] The next two chapters deal with the first of these rights. The aim is to proving the premises of this book, namely that the philosophical foundation of current systems should be revisited. As such, it will be argued that current trademark systems in the US and the UK deploy a utilitarian approach, manifested in their adoption of the dilution rationale. They also apply the confusion rationale in a wide manner. Such a widening is responsible for turning the confusion argument into a semi-dilution concept. Chapter six deals with the second right of the public which relates to the use of trademarks in cultural and expressive purposes. It takes the case of parody as an example of the relevance of the Economic-Social Planning theory.

[83] See ch 2 pp 57-59.

[84] See ch 1 p 11.

CHAPTER FOUR

THE CURRENT PROTECTION OF TRADEMARKS IN THE USA

Introduction

In the second and third chapters, it has been argued that trademarks are founded through a two-step process. First, the owner chooses a mark and affixes it to his/her product, and in the second, the public retain the most crucial aspect in attributing an association between the mark and the product. Thus, it has been concluded that trademarks should be formulated in a manner which ensures the advent of a just and attractive culture. This necessitates the adoption of the source and origin function of trademarks as the primary function thereof, and ultimately, the appropriate test is achieved through the confusion concept.

In today's world, various systems are adopted to protect trademarks. Such systems vary according to the aims and purposes to which protection is directed. However, the value of theory is to rationalize and legitimize the adoption of a certain system. The failure of certain systems to justify the protection they provide makes it essential to discuss such systems: that is, to highlight their shortcomings in order to prove the reliability of the defended theoretical framework. The protection of trademarks in the US seems attractive to any discussion on trademark theory, because it represents an extreme point of view in favour of trademark owners, without any proper reliance on solid theoretical grounds. Additionally, the US case study is important, because its vision of trademarks' protection shall be imposed by the US over other countries through its negotiating power in international agreements,[1] or through the bilateral free trade agreements into which it enters with other countries.

---

[1] Senate Rep No 100-515 (1988 U.S.C.C.A.N. 5577) 5583-5584, although the TRIPs agreement follows the European approach, the US was trying to impose higher standards of protection for trademarks. The Senate Report accompanying the 1988 Trademark Law Revision Act (TLRA) provided that the introduction of dilution in the US would 'would also greatly assist U.S. negotiators in the Uruguay

The purpose of this chapter is to assess the US experience in the field of trademarks, to discuss the foundations of the Trademarks Act of 1946 (known as the Lanham Act)[2] and its current type of protection. The main aim of this chapter is to prove the expansion of trademark owners' rights, through the adoption of a wide notion of confusion, in addition to the dilution concept. This shall prove that the current philosophical foundation of trademarks should be revisited, and that the adoption of the Economic-Social Planning theory forms an appropriate solution to the expansion of trademark owners' rights in trademark systems such as the Lanham Act.

The first section introduces the US Trademark Act. This leads to a greater understanding of its initial foundations, and the manner by which protection was directed. This also assists in assessing whether the changes and amendments in the Act were consistent with the original aims and purposes of the Act. Next, the confusion doctrine will be considered, citing the pitfalls and inadequacies in this, and assessing the consistency of the Act with the premises of the Economic-Social Planning theory. The remaining part of this chapter sheds light on the dilution doctrine and its expansionist nature. Throughout this chapter, emphasis is directed towards assessing these doctrines according to the premises of the Economic-Social Planning justification.

Introduction to the Lanham Act

As already outlined,[3] the Supreme Court in *Trade-mark cases*[4] considered the US Trademark Act of 1870 as unconstitutional. '[T]rademark protection did not come within the scope of the Constitutional Patent or

---

Round of the General Agreement on Tariffs and Trade (GATT), who are urging other countries to provide adequate protection for trademarks and other intellectual property. At the present time, other countries can resist agreeing to higher international standards for intellectual property by pointing to the fact that the United States itself provides little protection against dilution in many States. The dilution provision would show that [the United States is not] asking other countries to give better protection than [it is] willing to give, which will be increasingly important as negotiations proceed under the new GATT trade round.'

[2] The Act was named after its sponsor Congressman Fritz Garland Lanham. See- JT McCarthy *Trademarks and Unfair Competition* (2nd edn The Lawyers Co-operative Publishing Co. New York 1984) 139 (section 5:4).

[3] See ch 2 pp 17-23.

[4] *Trade-mark cases* 100 US 82 (1879).

Copyright clause'.[5] Thus, 'Congress has exceeded its power',[6] because 'there is no specific Constitutional language giving Congress power to regulate trademarks.'[7] Afterwards, consecutive trademark statutes were 'attempt[ing] to establish a balance on the question of constitutionality.'[8] This section argues that the Lanham Act, initially, was not established on utilitarian grounds. It was formulated on the basis of the source and origin function, and considered other traders and the public as rightholders in trademarks before it shifted towards the current expansionist rights to trademark owners.

Understanding how the Lanham Act was formulated requires an investigation of its aims and purposes. Reference to such aims shall lead to the Act's recognition to other parties in the trademark formula.[9] This will support the argument that trademarks were *then* regarded as 'psychological sensations and social reactions to symbols.'[10] This, however, was before 'the emphasis of U.S. trademark law has shifted from protecting consumers to protecting trademark owners.'[11] Then, some points which accord with these aims and purposes will be discussed, such as the existence of the source function and the recognition of other parties' rights.

The Aims and Purposes of the Lanham Act

The central argument before and during the enactment of the Lanham Act was concentrated on the fears that trademark rights would turn into ferocious exclusive rights. US courts and scholars 'were troubled by the monopoly implications of recognizing exclusive rights in words of common speech.'[12] This 'anti-trademark sentiment was shared in the

---

[5] K Aoki 'Authors, Inventors, and Trademark Owners: Private Intellectual Property and the Public Domain Part 2' (1993-1994) 18 Columbia-VLA J of L & the Arts 235.

[6] *Trade-Mark cases* (n4) 89.

[7] *Trademarks and Unfair Competition* (n2) 136 (section 5:3). See also, Aoki (n5) 234-235.

[8] SM Maniatis *The Communicative Aspects of Trade Marks: A Legal, Functional and Economic Analysis* (PhD Thesis University of London 1998) 35. See also, F Beier 'Basic Features of Anglo-American, French and German Trademark Law' (1975) 3 Intl Rev of Industrial Property and Competition L 291.

[9] See ch 1 p 11.

[10] *Trademarks and Unfair Competition* (n2) 140 (section 5:4).

[11] Aoki (n5) 236.

[12] MW Handler 'Are the State Antidilution Laws Compatible with the National Protection of Trademarks?' (1998) 88 Trademark Reporter 422.

academic community that viewed trademarks as a means for creating monopoly power in favor of the trademark owner.'[13]

Courts were 'sometimes sensing intuitively that the exclusionary nature of trademarks may be in some way "monopolistic",'[14] and were reluctant to rule in favour of trademark owners because they felt that this was against the interests of the public.[15] It was argued, at that time, that 'the public interest will suffer unless the courts are very cautious either in recognizing … exclusive rights or in enlarging their scope.'[16] In addition, the US Department of Justice 'asserted that trade-marks are monopolistic and any statutory protection of them plays into the hands of big business and should be discouraged.'[17]

However, discouraging the statutory protection of trademarks provides no solution. It is true that trademark policy-makers and legislators should focus on avoiding monopolizing the rights of the owners. Nevertheless, this should not turn into a "monopoly phobia".[18] Rather, trademark systems should provide a protection to trademark owners, based on confusion, as the Economic-Social Planning theory suggests. This allows greater public access to trademarks in expressive uses, and takes into consideration other traders' rights in allowing them to invest and operate in an atmosphere of fair and just competition.[19]

Pattishall has cited this exaggeration of "trademark phobia". He argues that 'there is no public interest served in granting a monopoly for the creation [of] … [an] attractive trade-mark'.[20] However, he contends that

---

[13] M Leaffer 'Sixty Years of the Lanham Act: The Decline and Demise of Monopoly Phobia' in H Hansen (ed) *U.S. Intellectual Property Law and Policy* (1st edn Edward Elgar Cheltenham 2006) 85. See also, M Leaffer 'Fifty Years of the Lanham Act: The Decline and Demise of Monopoly Phobia' in HC Hansen (ed) *International Intellectual Property Law & Policy* (Volume 7 Juris Publishing Inc Huntington NY 2001) 38-1.

[14] DM McClure 'Trademarks and Unfair Competition: A Critical History of Legal Thought' (1979) 69 Trademark Reporter 308.

[15] BW Pattishall 'Trade-Marks and the Monopoly Phobia' (1951-1952) 50 Michigan L Rev 969.

[16] SC Oppenheim 'The Public Interest in Legal Protection of Industrial and Intellectual Property' (1950) 32 J of the Patent Office Society 906.

[17] ES Rogers 'Excerpts from the Lanham Act and the Social Function of Trade-Marks' (1972) 62 Trademark Reporter 259.

[18] Pattishall (n15) 968-970.

[19] Oppenheim (n16) 917.

[20] Pattishall (n15) 971.

> '[courts] need have no fear that in protecting a trade-mark a monopoly may be granted in anything that is public property so long as [they] adhere[…] to the likelihood of confusion test.'[21]

Congressional discussions acknowledged the fears of monopolistic trademarks rights. The Senate Report, discussing the Lanham Act, stresses that the aim and purpose of this Act is twofold:

> 'One is to protect the public so it may be confident that, in purchasing a product bearing a particular trade-mark which it favorably knows, it will get the product which it asks for and wants to get. Secondly, where the owner of a trade-mark has spent energy, time, and money in presenting to the public the product, he is protected in his investment from its misappropriation by pirates and cheats. This is the well-established rule of law protecting both the public and the trademark owner.'[22]

In order to assure that the first purpose of the Lanham Act is fulfilled, 'confusion to the public [should form] the essence of … trademark infringement'.[23] Such protection against consumer confusion shall also serve the second purpose, namely protecting the trademark owner as well.

A number of following court decisions have asserted the dual purpose of the Lanham Act. For example, in *Two Pesos Inc v Taco Cabana Inc*[24] the Supreme Court asserted that 'the Lanham Act's purposes [are to secure] to a mark's owner the goodwill of his business and protecting consumers' ability to distinguish among competing producers.'[25] The US Court of Appeals in *Avery Dennison Corp v Jerry Sumpton*[26] provided that

---

[21] ibid 978.

[22] Senate Rep No 79-1333 (1946), available at <http://ipmall.info/hosted_resources/lipa/trademarks/PreLanhamAct_026_HR_1333.htm> (26 August 2009).
See also, JA Cody 'Initial Interest Confusion: What Ever Happened to Traditional Likelihood of Confusion Analysis?' (2002-2003) 12 The Federal Circuit Bar J 648-650. See also, MJ Allen 'The Scope of Confusion Actionable under Federal Trademark Law: Who Must be Confused and When?' (1991) 26 Wake Forest L Rev 324.

[23] *Dart Drug Corp v Schering Corp* 320 F.2d 745, 116 U.S.App.D.C. 23 (1963) 750.

[24] 505 U.S. 763, 112 S.Ct. 2753 (1992).

[25] ibid 763. See also, *Hyde Park Clothes Inc v Hyde Park Fashions Inc* 204 F.2d 223 (1953). See also, J Lobur 'Trademarks – Likelihood of Confusion and the Public Interest' (1973-1974) 20 Wayne L Rev 1206.

[26] 189 F.3d 868 (1999).

> '[t]wo goals of trademark law are reflected in the federal scheme. On the one hand, the law seeks to protect consumers who have formed particular associations with a mark. On the other hand, trademark law seeks to protect the investment in a mark made by the owner.'[27]

This decision by the Court of Appeals is significant. It considers that the rights of the public derive from the "*particular associations they form with the mark*". This shows a high degree of consistency with the premises of the Economic-Social Planning theory for the justification of trademarks. It also presumes that this association is part of the process of authoring trademarks. This requires the implementation of the confusion test, because it is the most appropriate rationale to assess the extent of impairing public's association.

Still, there is a third purpose, which should have been embodied explicitly in the Senate Report, which is the right of other traders. The report did not give any regard to the rights of other traders and rivals to use similar marks in a manner which shall *not* cause confusion to the public. However, the protection of other traders could be inferred from the first aim of protecting the public. It could be construed that the owners' protection within the boundaries of the confusion rationale allows others to use similar, or identical marks if this use will not cause confusion to the public. One scholar, correctly, argues that

> 'to the extent that [the mark's] corresponding use by others is likely to result in confusion of source with the prior user, that much the prior user's individual trade identity should be protected and use denied to another – no more no less.'[28]

All in all, the Lanham Act initially aimed to protect the public against any confusion as to source and origin, as the official congressional documents indicate. Thus, the scope of the actionable confusion should be assessed in accordance with the aims and purposes stipulated by Congress.[29] If the aims and purposes on which the Act was based were followed today, protection would be consistent with the premises of the Economic-Social Planning theory. According to this theory, consumer confusion would be the only test, and dilution would not be available at all. Next, the aspects reflecting the Act's purposes will be explored, which

---

[27] ibid 873.
[28] Pattishall (n15) 979.
[29] Allen (n22) 324.

were undermined by the adoption of a wide notion of confusion, as well as the adoption of dilution.

Aspects Reflecting Lanham's Aims and Purposes

This section argues that in certain respects, the Lanham Act initially embodied aspects which accorded with its aims, as outlined above. Currently, the expansionist trend favouring monopolistic rights to trademark owners has diminished the effects of such aspects. The source function and the rights of other parties under the Act will now be discussed.

- Source/origin function under the Lanham Act

The Lanham Act, in defining trademarks, provides that they must '*identify* and *distinguish* [the owner's] goods, ... from those manufactured or sold by others and to indicate the *source* of the goods, even if that source is unknown' (emphasis added).[30] Analysing this section, two conclusions could be inferred.

First, a sign in order to qualify for registration as a "trademark" under the Lanham Act should be able to identify and *distinguish* the source of goods and/or services. Thus, '[a] trademark, to function as such, must point to the origin or ownership of the article to which it is applied.'[31] Second, the trademark system should focus on giving owners the right to use their marks in a manner which ensures product differentiation. The core of protection lies in protecting consumers from *confusion* and requiring actual confusion, or at least, the likelihood of consumer confusion as the proper test for infringment.

This interpretation shows that the main goal of the Lanham Act, when it was first enacted, was to ensure that consumers were protected from any use of trademarks which was likely to cause confusion.[32] Moreover, anyone who uses a trademark in a manner which 'is likely to cause confusion, or to cause mistake, or to deceive, shall be liable…'.[33]

Courts in the US were at first acknowledging that the proper function of trademarks is the source and origin function. A number of cases, before the introduction of the Lanham Act reflected the policy in trademark

---

[30] Trademarks Act 1946- Lanham Act (USA) 15 U.S.C. § 1127 (Section 45).

[31] SJ Liddy 'The Lanham Act- An Analysis' (1996) 86 Trademark Reporter 421.

[32] MJ Kaplan 'Antidilution Statutes and the First Amendment' (1992) 21 Southwestern U L Rev 1141.

[33] Trademarks Act 1946- Lanham Act (USA) 15 U.S.C. § 1114 (Section 32).

systems as based on the source and origin function. For instance, in the *Hanover Star Milling Co v Metcalf*,[34] the Supreme Court provided that '[t]he primary and proper function of a trademark is to identify the origin or ownership of the article to which it is affixed.'[35] Other decisions stressed that 'the trade-mark must, either by itself, or by association, point distinctively to the origin or ownership of the article to which it is applied.'[36] In *Manufacturing Co v Trainer*[37] the court argued that

> '[t]he symbol or device thus becomes a sign to the public of the origin of the goods to which it is attached, and an assurance that they are the genuine article of the original producer. In this way it often proves to be of great value to the manufacturer in preventing the substitution and sale of an inferior and different article for his products.'[38]

Afterwards, courts mixed the source and origin function with the quality function, arguing that trademarks function both to indicate source and quality of products.[39]

In conclusion, the Lanham Act admits that trademarks function as identifiers of sources and origins. Today, this is not the only function of trademarks. The quality function is present through the adoption of the dilution concept. The next section discusses instances whereby the rights of the public and other traders have been recognized under the Lanham Act.

- The rights of the public under the Lanham Act

The recognition of the rights of the public in the course of trademarks is one of the most crucial aspects of the Lanham Act. The public are not passive in trademarks. Rather, they are important players, and have the ability to make some marks, which are not eligible for registration, capable of being registered through the public's association of that mark with the product. The public also can seize hold of certain marks which they

---

[34] 240 US 403 (1916).

[35] ibid 412.

[36] *Lawrence Manuf'g Co v Tennessee Manuf'g Co* 138 U.S. 537, 11 S.Ct. 396 (1891) 546. See also, *Canal Co v Clark* 80 U.S. 311 (1871) 323. See also, *McLean v Fleming* 96 U.S. 245, 6 Otto 245 (1877) 254.

[37] 101 U.S. 51 (1879).

[38] ibid 53.

[39] See for example, *Avrick et al. v Rockmont Envelope Co* 155 F.2d 568, 69 U.S.P.Q. 431 (1946) 571-572.

believe no longer represent or denote the source of the goods and/or services to which they are affixed, rendering such marks generic.[40]

Such aspects of the entitlements of the public are justified only if the process of creating trademarks is understood. The consuming public's association of the mark with the goods and/or services is the corner-stone to the creation of trademarks. The public shall therefore enjoy the right to halt this association and render the mark generic. They might also attribute secondary meaning to certain signs which lack distinctiveness, thereby making them registrable.

Secondary meaning[41]

Trademarks should be inherently distinctive, in order to qualify for registration.[42] The Lanham Act excludes from registration 'a mark which when used on or in connection with the goods of the applicant is merely descriptive …'.[43] Since descriptive marks indicate the characteristics of products,[44] other traders 'must be left free to use, the same language of description in placing their goods before the public.'[45] This is because 'one person may not lawfully monopolize the use of words in general use … to describe [his/her goods and/or services]'[46].

According to the Economic-Social Planning theory, the consuming public are "co-authors" of trademarks; consequently, they can convert a descriptive sign into a trademark. This happens due to the public's association of the descriptive sign with the products of a particular trader. Thus, 'a firm cannot register a descriptive mark until it is able to show that consumers actually recognize the mark as distinguishing the firm's

---

[40] See *infra* pp 92-94.

[41] Also known as the "acquired distinctiveness doctrine". See- J Jacoby 'The Psychological Foundations of Trademark Law: Secondary Meaning, Genericism, Fame, Confusion and Dilution' (2001) 91 Trademark Reporter 1029. See also, A Carboni 'Distinctive Character Acquired Through Use: Establishing the Facts' in J Phillips and I Simon (eds) *Trade Mark Use* (1st edn Oxford University Press Oxford 2005) 71-72.

[42] *Trademarks and Unfair Competition* (n2) 435 (section 11:2).

[43] Trademarks Act 1946- Lanham Act (USA) 15 U.S.C. § 1052 (Section 2(e)).

[44] *Estate of P. D. Beckwith Inc v Comr of Patents* 252 U.S. 538, 40 S.Ct. 414 (1920) 543.

[45] ibid 544.

[46] ibid 540. See also, VN Palladino 'Assessing Trademark Significance: Genericness, Secondary Meaning and Surveys' (2002) 92 Trademark Reporter 858-859.

goods'.[47] This mark should 'acquire[...] the distinctiveness that characterizes a trademark, namely, the ability to indicate the goods of one producer and distinguishing them from the goods of others'.[48]

The US Court of Appeals in *J.M. Huber Corp v Lowery Wellheads*[49] provided:

> 'To acquire secondary meaning, a descriptive mark must have "been used so long and so exclusively by one producer with reference to his goods or articles that, in that trade and to that branch of the purchasing public, [the mark has] come to mean that the article is his product".'[50]

The Lanham Act acknowledges the ability of the consuming public to make descriptive marks eligible for registration. It states that 'nothing ... shall prevent the registration of a mark ... which has become distinctive of the applicant's goods in commerce'.[51] The secondary meaning doctrine, however, is not the only means of recognizing the rights of the public under the Lanham Act; it also embodies the doctrine of genericness.

Genericness

The doctrine of genericness reflects the power of the public to associate the mark with the whole class of products, rather than the products of the trader. Thus, they can end the life of the trademark. The mark then ceases to denote the source and origin of the goods and/or services.[52] As one scholar argues:

> 'Such generic designations tell the buyer what the product is, not where it came from[, and] ... [t]o grant an exclusive right to one firm of use of the generic name of a product would be equivalent to creating a monopoly in

[47] SL Carter 'The Trouble with Trademark' (1989-1990) 99 Yale L J 776.
[48] Palladino (n46) 859.
[49] 778 F.2d 146 (1985).
[50] ibid 1470.
[51] Trademarks Act 1946- Lanham Act (USA) 15 U.S.C. § 1052 (Section 2(f)).
[52] See- *Feathercombs Inc v Solo Products Co* 306 F.2d 251 (1962) 256. See also, SR Weber 'Trademarks and Genericness: Loss of a Mark to the Public Domain Through its Transformation into a Generic Term' (1989-1990) 17 Western State U L Rev 419.

> that particular product, something that the trademark laws were never intended to accomplish.'[53]

Thus, the Lanham Act gives any interested party the right to file a petition to cancel the registration of the trademark if it 'becomes the generic name for the goods or services'.[54]

One of the most famous cases regarding the doctrine of genericness[55] is that of *Bayer Co Inc v United Drug Co*.[56] In this case, the court ruled that the word "Aspirin" no longer referred to its manufacturer or to the origin and source of the goods; it was rather used 'to denote a kind of product.'[57] Judge Learned Hand asserted that:

> 'If the defendant is allowed to continue the use of the word …, there is a chance that it may get customers away from the plaintiff by deception. On the other hand, if the plaintiff is allowed a monopoly of the word as against consumers, it will deprive the defendant, and the trade in general, of the right effectually to dispose of the drug by the only description which will be understood. It appears to me that the relief granted cannot in justice to either party disregard this division; each party has won, and each has lost.'[58]

This judgment is important in a number of ways. First, the court considered the vital question in this case to be: 'What do the buyers understand by the word for whose use the parties are contending?'[59] The significance of this question is that it focuses on the role of the public and the association they grant to the mark. This is consistent with the presumptions of the Economic-Social Planning theory, which considers the public's association of the mark with the goods and/or services as the corner-stone in the creation and protection of trademarks.[60] Second, the court considered that the trademark formula included the owner, other

---

[53] *Trademarks and Unfair Competition* (n2) 520 (section 12:1), 521 (section 12:1). See also, RH Folsom and LL Teply 'Trademarked Generic Words' (1979-1980) 89 Yale L J 1324.
[54] Trademarks Act 1946- Lanham Act (USA) 15 U.S.C. § 1064 (Section 14(3)).
[55] "Thermos" is another famous example of generic marks. See- *King-Seeley Thermos Co v Aladdin Industries Inc* 321 F.2d 577 (1963) 580, 581.
[56] 272 F. 505 (1921).
[57] ibid 512.
[58] ibid 513-514.
[59] ibid 509.
[60] See ch 2 pp 57-59.

traders and the consuming public. In so doing, the court's emphasis was not so much on the need to turn the mark into a monopoly to the owner, but rather to consider the rights of other rivals and to strike a balance between those interests in the light of the meaning that the consuming public attributed to the mark. This accords with the premises of the Economic-Social Planning theory, because it considers all the parties in the trademark formula.[61]

- Other traders' rights under the Lanham Act

A further aspect which proves that the Lanham Act was not intended to provide a monopolistic tool to trademark owners is recognising the rights of other traders. This is apparent through a number of examples, one of which concerned honest concurrent use.

The 'first in time ... first in right'[62] rule is the general rule for trademark registration in the US. This rule is subject to the exception of honest concurrent use of trademarks. This exception aims to acknowledge the rights of two undertakings to register the same mark, provided that both uses do not overlap geographically. It is also essential that this concurrent use will not result in causing consumer confusion.[63]

The honest concurrent use exception is recognized by the Lanham Act.[64] It acknowledged that preventing the second user from registering the mark would result in monopolizing the mark to owner (first user). It also causes unjust prejudice to the second user who innocently used the mark and invested in creating the association in the minds of consumers through advertising. The prevention of this registration has no real justification because of the lack of interaction between the uses of both parties.[65]

---

[61] See ch 1 p 11.

[62] MJ Alexander and JH Coil 'Geographic Rights in Trademarks and Service Marks' (1978) 68 Trademark Reporter 101.

[63] S Lefkowitz 'A Concurrent Use Registration as a Reflection of Established Territorial Rights; Fact or Fiction?' (1975) 65 Trademark Reporter 71, 73. See also, DA Kaul 'Concurrent Use and Registration of Trademarks' (1972) 62 Trademark Reporter 581-582. See also, DS Barrett 'The Future of the Concurrent Use of Trademarks Doctrine in the Information Age' (2000-2001) 23 Hastings Comm/Ent L J 689.

[64] Trademarks Act 1946- Lanham Act (USA) 15 U.S.C. § 1052 (Section 2(d)).

[65] See- *Hanover Star Milling Co* (n34) 405-406, 416. See also, Barrett (n63) 690-691. See also, Kaul (n63) 581, 582 and 583. See also, Lefkowitz (n63) 73. See also, WS Creasman 'Establishing Geographic Rights in Trademarks Based on Internet Use' (2005) 95 Trademark Reporter 1020.

Analysing this section of the Lanham Act leads to a number of significant outcomes, which support the argument that the Act was designed on non-utilitarian grounds. First, it stresses that granting two traders the right to use similar, or identical marks is based on the condition that such use will not cause consumer confusion. Second, the importance of this section derives from the fact that it is not merely designed to protect other traders and give them the right of concurrent use, but also recognizes the right of the public, because they have decided to give recognition to both marks as distinct marks for different traders. This is an important point, because it falls within the premises of the Economic-Social Planning theory, which considers that the public contribute to the creation of trademarks, and are as such, the "co-authors" of trademarks, along with the owners.[66]

Honest concurrent use was not the only way by which monopolies over trademarks could be hindered. The Lanham Act requires the applicant to have 'a bona fide intention… to use a trademark in commerce'.[67] It also embodies the cancellation for non-use doctrine if the mark was not used for three consecutive years.[68] According to this rule, the owner of the mark is not allowed to keep and maintain the registration of his/her mark if he/she is not intending to use it.[69] This is because not using a mark will prevent new entrants from registering the same mark which shall constitute a monopoly promoting unfair competition, and '[i]f the mark is no longer associated with the business, in the public mind, then the mark should be regarded as abandoned'.[70]

Summarizing Remarks

In conclusion, the Lanham Act was intended to protect the different parties in the trademark formula.[71] Its aims and purposes accord with the premises of the Economic-Social Planning theory. However, it seems vital to assess whether the Act, where it stands today, still adheres to its initial goals. It shall be argued, in the coming sections, that the confusion section

---

66 See ch 2 pp 57-59.

67 Trademarks Act 1946- Lanham Act (USA) 15 U.S.C. § 1051 (Section 1(b)).

68 ibid § 1127 (Section 45).

69 B Pretnar 'Use and Non-Use in Trade Mark Law' in J Phillips and I Simon (eds) *Trade Mark Use* (1st edn Oxford University Press Oxford 2005) 15.

70 *Trademarks and Unfair Competition* (n2) 773 (section 17:3). See also, *Major League Baseball Properties Inc v Sed Non Olet Denarius Ltd* 817 F.Supp. 1103 (1993) 1130.

71 See ch 1 p 11.

is considerably widened in favour of owners. Similarly, the source function is no longer the basis of protection. This has been substituted with the introduction of the dilution concept, which is based on Schechter's quality function.

Consumer Confusion under the Lanham Act

This section aims to assess whether the Lanham Act complies with the aims and purposes for which it was enacted. More specifically, it aims to explore whether the confusion doctrine under the Act considers trademark owners and the consuming public equally. The premises of the Economic-Social Planning justification are a central argument in this assessment. The aim is to prove that the current confusion concept is widened in favour of trademark owners, and fails to consider the public and other traders as equal parties to trademark owners according to the trademark formula.[72]

In doing so, the first section discusses the notion of the confusion test, as envisioned by the Economic-Social Planning theory. Next, the texts regarding confusion in the Lanham Act in its original format will be analyzed, and the amendment introduced into this confusion sections in 1962 will be tackled. This attempts to prove that the these sections fall short of protecting trademarks on the basis of the confusion test, because they fail to determine the proper limits for confusion. This shall prove the shift towards greater rights of trademark owners, and towards less adherence to the public as the corner-stone of consumer confusion.

Economic-Social Planning and Lanham Act

The Economic-Social Planning theory considers that the existence of trademark systems is an extreme necessity in modern society. This theory calls for such systems to be formulated in a manner which fosters a just, attractive culture. This could be achieved by de-monopolizing trademark rights. This theory is translated into a practical system, which is based on the source and origin function. Accordingly, the test for trademark infringement is the consumer confusion system. The question remains, however, as to which test of confusion is required. Is it any type of confusion? Or should it have clear boundaries which define the scope of the rights of all involved parties?

Answering such questions should involve the foundations of the Economic-Social Planning justification. Trademarks are "co-authored" by

[72] ibid.

owners and the public. Therefore, the confusion test should take into account the rights of trademark owners and the consuming public. The Economic-Social Planning theory does not aim to deprive owners of their entitlement over trademarks. Rather, what is a required is a system which acknowledges both parties' rights. In addition, the confusion test should also consider the rights of other traders as a component of the trademark formula.[73] This shall encourage free and fair competition in the marketplace, without anyone of the parties dominating at the expense of others.

Consequently, an equitable confusion test is required. Such a test should focus on preventing any confusion as to the source and origin of goods and/or services. This would ensure to trademark owners that diversion of trade shall not exist. It shall also protect the consuming public in not being led to products which they do not require. At the same time, other traders will be able to use the mark when confusion is not likely to exist. If this could be achieved, it shall accord with the premises of the Economic-Social Planning theory, as well as the aims and purposes of the Lanham Act.

The coming section explores the Lanham Act's treatment of confusion. This will be assessed in accordance with the claims of the Economic-Social Planning theory, and the Lanham Act's aims and purposes. It shall be argued that the steady shift in the Lanham Act towards the extreme widening of owners rights started with the widening of the scope of the confusion test.

Likelihood of Consumer Confusion under the Lanham Act

Confusion was the basic and standard concept assessing trademark infringement before the introduction of the dilution doctrine into the Lanham Act in 1995. It was, indeed, 'the hallmark of any trademark infringement claim.'[74] This concept proved to be capable of developing and 'has manifested a remarkable flexibility in its adaptation to … new realities.'[75] It will be shown how the confusion concept is capable of developing to suit current legal needs, and can form the sole basis for trademark infringement.[76]

This doctrine functions as a warning signal to prevent any application for trademark registration, which is likely to confuse the public with the

---

[73] ibid.

[74] *Polymer Technology Corp v Emile Mimran* 37 F.3d 74 (1994) 80.

[75] Leaffer 2006 (n13) 112. See also, Leaffer 2001 (n13) 38-21.

[76] See for example, *infra* pp 99-101. See also generally ch 3.

earlier mark. Such marks which are likely to cause confusion are, therefore, not registrable. The Lanham Act provides that:

> 'No trademark by which the goods of the applicant may be distinguished from the goods of others shall be refused registration on the principal register on account of its nature unless it … [c]onsists of or comprises a mark which so resembles a mark registered in the Patent and Trademark Office, or a mark or trade name previously used in the United States by another and not abandoned, as to be *likely*, when used on or in connection with the goods of the applicant, *to cause confusion*, or to cause mistake, or to deceive' (emphasis added).[77]

Thus, the trademark owner has the right to file an opposition to any application to register a mark which is similar to his/her mark if it is likely to cause consumer confusion.[78] However, if the owner does not oppose the application and if upon examination of the application the Patent and Trademark Office finds 'that likelihood of confusion with prior marks or names exists, the application is rejected *ex officio* even if the owner of the prior mark does not oppose the registration.'[79]

The Lanham Act prohibits any use which shall result in confusing the consuming public, and creates liability in a civil action against

> '[a]ny person who shall, without the consent of the registrant use in commerce any reproduction, counterfeit, copy, or colorable imitation of a registered mark in connection with the sale, offering for sale, distribution, or advertising of any goods or services on or in connection with which such use is *likely to cause confusion*, or to cause mistake, or to deceive' (emphasis added).[80]

In addition, section 43(a) of the Lanham Act contains its main definition of confusion. It reads as follows:

> 'Any person who, on or in connection with any goods or services, or any container for goods, uses in commerce any word, term, name, symbol, or device, or any combination thereof, or any false designation of origin, false or misleading description of fact, or false or misleading representation of fact, which is *likely to cause confusion*, or to cause mistake, or to deceive

---

[77] Trademarks Act 1946- Lanham Act (USA) 15 U.S.C. § 1052 (Section 2(d)).

[78] ibid § 1071 (Section 21). For example, see- *Giant Food Inc v Nation's Foodservice Inc* 710 F.2d 1565 (1983).

[79] Beier (n8) 293.

[80] Trademarks Act 1946- Lanham Act (USA) 15 U.S.C. § 1114 (Section 32(a)).

> as to the affiliation, connection, or association of such person with another person, or as to the origin, sponsorship, or approval of his or her goods, services, or commercial activities by another person … shall be liable in a civil action by any person who believes that he or she is or is likely to be damaged by such act' (emphasis added).[81]

These confusion sections were the touchstone in relation to trademark infringement cases. Courts considered that 'under the Lanham Act the ultimate test is whether the public is likely to be deceived or confused by the similarity of the marks.'[82] Unfortunately, what was considered once "the ultimate test" for trademark infringement is considered today a traditional test of trademark infringement. It is undermined by the adoption of other doctrines, which provide monopolistic rights to trademark owners. Proponents of exclusive and monopolistic trademark rights consider that the confusion concept does constitute a rational basis for protection.

The Lanham Act should be credited for adopting the confusion test for trademark infringement. Nevertheless, while there are some positive points, others have been omitted in the course of amending the Act, and still the confusion sections are not detailed enough to specify and cover all aspects of the confusion rationale. This resulted in the courts being confused when dealing with trademark infringement cases. The confusion sections under the Lanham Act raise a number of questions, such as whether actual or likely confusion is required, and what types of confusion are actionable.

- Actual confusion or likelihood of confusion?

In the case of trademark infringement under the Lanham Act, '[i]t is not essential to show actual confusion or deception in order to establish trademark infringement.'[83] Rather, the trademark owner is only required to prove that the use of his/her mark by others is *likely* to cause consumer confusion between his/her goods and/or services and the goods and/or services of others. Thus,

> '[a] likelihood of confusion exists "when consumers viewing the mark would probably assume that the product or service it represents is

---

[81] ibid § 1125 (Section 43(a)).
[82] *The New West Corp v NYM Co of California Inc* 595 F.2d 1194 (1979) 1201.
[83] *Miller Brewing Co v Carling O'Keefe Breweries of Canada Ltd* 452 F.Supp. 429 (1978) 444.

associated with the source of a different product or service identified by a similar mark." '[84]

The flexibility of this requirement is that it does not require actual confusion. This means that the mere probability of confusion is enough to prevent the use of the mark by others. However, the likelihood of confusion test suggests that confusion should be more probable to occur than not.[85] '[C]ourts are unanimous in declaring that probability of confusion means more than a mere possibility of confusion',[86] this in turn complies with the Economic-Social Planning theory premises. It prevents any probable act which might affect or alter the association which the public attribute between the mark and the products. This should be an exclusive right accorded to the public.

The likelihood of confusion test allows the trademark owner or any interested party to file a civil action to prevent any use which might constitute confusion in future. This is one of the aspects of flexibility of the confusion test which was adopted in the Lanham Act. The reason for requiring a likelihood of confusion rather than actual confusion is to ensure that the confusion test turns into a precautionary measure to prevent actual confusion before it occurs, which would in turn pre-empt the damage before it occurs. However, although 'ordinarily evidence of actual confusion is difficult to secure,'[87] if the plaintiff –whether the trademark owner or any interested party– is capable of proving that actual confusion occurred, this would be a stronger proof.[88]

---

[84] *Citizen Financial Group Inc v The Citizens National Bank of Evans City and Citizens Inc* WL 32808575 (W.D.Pa.) (2002) 3. (Citing *Scott Paper Co v Scott's Liquid Gold Inc* 589 F.2d 1225 (1978)).

[85] JS Thomas 'Likelihood of Confusion Under the Lanham Act: A Question of Fact, a Question of Law, or Both?' (1984-1985) 73 Kentucky L J 236. (Citing *Javar Coffee Co Inc v Jos Martinson & Co Inc* 142 F.Supp. 423 (1956)). See also, *Trademarks and Unfair Competition* (n2) 45-46 (section 23:1). See also, *Board of Supervisors of the Louisiana State University and Agricultural and Mechanical College v Smack Apparel Co* 438 F.Supp.2d 653 (2006) 659.

[86] Leaffer 2006 (n13) 124-125. See also, Leaffer 2001 (n13) 38-29.

[87] *Chester Barrie Ltd v The Chester Laurie Ltd* 189 F.Supp. 98 (1960) 102. See also, *Miles Shoes Inc v R. H. Macy & Co Inc* 199 F.2d 602 (1952) 603. See also, *The Earth Technology Corp v Environmental Research & Technology Inc* WL 877 (C.D.Cal.) (1983) 4.

[88] A Bartow 'Likelihood of Confusion' (2004) 41 San Diego L Rev 763. See also, Leaffer 2006 (n13) 125. See also, Leaffer 2001 (n13) 38-29, 38-30. See also, *Gilbert/Robinson Inc v Carrie Beverage-Missouri Inc* 758 F.Supp. 512 (1991) 524.

Some scholars object to the likelihood of confusion test, claiming that it is not based on real foundations, and argue that 'actual confusion is the best evidence of likelihood of confusion.'[89] They also contend that survey evidence shows the existence of actual confusion in a number of cases.[90] As such, they consider that actual confusion should be the test for confusion cases.

However, the likelihood of confusion test is a means of preventing the occurrence of irreparable harm. We need not wait until irreparable damage happens to give the owner, or the interested party, the right to file a case of trademark infringement. Thus 'harm can be stopped before it starts and before significant costs have been incurred'.[91] Moreover, actual confusion is, indeed, the best evidence of trademark infringement. However, this should not be a substitute for the likelihood of confusion test, because it has been incorrectly stated that the 'lack of actual confusion is proof that no likelihood of confusion exists.'[92] Thus, '[i]t is well settled … that the plaintiff is not required to prove any instances of actual confusion in order to be entitled to a finding of a likelihood of confusion.'[93]

Thus, it should be stressed that the likelihood of confusion is the "minimum standard test" of trademark infringement. It gives the plaintiff the option of proving actual confusion, which might strengthen his/her allegation of the existence of infringement.

- Types of confusion or expansion of confusion?

Trademarks are source and origin identifiers; as such, the only *primary* type of confusion is related to source and origin. Source and origin confusion occurs when the second user's adoption of an identical or similar mark confuses customers as to the source and origin of the products in question. However,

> 'it is important to note that the public need not know the identity of the senior source in order for actionable confusion to exist; it is sufficient that

---

See also, *24 Hour Fitness USA Inc v 24/7 Tribeca Fitness LLC* 447 F.Supp.2d 266 (2006) 277.

[89] ES Clark 'Finding Likelihood of Confusion with Actual Confusion: A Critical Analysis of the Federal Courts' Approach' (1992) 22 Golden Gate U L Rev 398-399.

[90] ibid 397-398.

[91] *Barbecue Marx Inc v 551 Ogden Inc* 110 F.Supp.2d 689 (2000) 693.

[92] Clark (n89) 409.

[93] *Elvis Presley Enterprises Inc v Barry Capece* 950 F.Supp. 783 (1996) 796.

> the public simply believes the products bearing the marks emanate from a single, though anonymous, source.'[94]

Trademarks might have other secondary functions, and they could also fall under the ambit of the confusion doctrine if the nature of such functions is compatible with the confusion doctrine principles. As such, the confusion rationale accepts the advertising and informative functions (regarding sponsorship and affiliation) within its ambit. Accordingly, any confusion in this regard is also actionable. This is correct, because any confusion regarding advertising, sponsorship or affiliation leads to indirect confusion as to the source and origin. On the contrary, the quality function by its very nature, especially because quality is subjective and differs from one consumer to the other,[95] could not be assessed according to the confusion test.

Therefore, advocates of a broad trademark protection in favour of the owners[96] "invented" a number of types of consumer confusion other than the source and origin confusion. The aim of this was to make an implicit introduction of the quality argument within the ambit of the confusion doctrine. Such attempts have widened the scope of confusion applicability, and made it 'danc[e] with dilution'.[97] As a result, a semi-dilution concept was introduced within the confusion concept. Such new types will now be discussed, as will their effects on expanding the confusion concept, through various means.

Confusion of sponsorship and subliminal confusion

The newly invented types of confusion include the confusion of sponsorship.[98] This type of confusion suggests that confusion might occur if the consuming public is not confused as to the source; rather they are confused because they will think that the infringing user is using the mark under the sponsorship or affiliation of the trademark owner.[99] Another type of confusion is the subliminal confusion, which

---

[94] Allen (n22) 325.

[95] See ch 3 pp 70-72.

[96] Such as those named by the Senate Report of the 1962 as "Interested Private Organizations". See- Senate Rep No 87-2107 (1962 U.S.C.C.A.N. 2844) 2845.

[97] Leaffer 2006 (n13) 111. See also, Leaffer 2001 (n13) 38-20.

[98] Also known as confusion of affiliation or connection. See- *Worthington Foods Inc v Kellogg Co* 732 F.Supp. 1417 (1990) 1430. See also, Trademarks Act 1946-Lanham Act (USA) 15 U.S.C. § 1125 (Section 43(a)).

[99] Leaffer 2006 (n13) 114-115. See also, Leaffer 2001 (n13) 38-22.

> 'occurs on a subliminal or subconscious level, [when it causes] the consumer to identify the properties and reputation of one product with those of another, *although he can identify the particular manufacturer of each*' (emphasis added).[100]

This expansionist trend in favour of trademark owners was unable to divert the Lanham Act to comply with its premises rapidly. It was a process of steady change throughout more than sixty years of the applicability of the Act, giving rise to a drift towards more absolute rights in trademarks. Still, this is an ongoing process which shall not end until it gives the owner full exclusive rights. Thus, as part of this process, the expansionist's aim was to diminish the confusion concept as an introduction to the dilution concept, without any objections as to the constitutionality of the rights conferred by such concept, as has happened with the 1870 Act.[101]

Accordingly, the original sections of the Lanham Act regulating confusion were amended in order to broaden the confusion rationale to include certain types such as subliminal confusion. For example, the original wording of section 32(a) of the Act required that confusion should be 'as to the source of origin of … goods or services',[102] whereas the current proviso after the amendment of 1962 does not require the likelihood of confusion to be as to source and origin. The Senate Report accompanying this amendment did not give any purpose for this unjustifiable excision other than 'rearranging the language.'[103] Courts contended that 'the purpose of the amendment was to broaden the scope of

---

[100] *Ortho Pharmaceutical Corp v American Cyanamid Co* 361 F.Supp. 1032 (1973) 1044. See also, *Farberware Inc v Mr. Coffee Inc* 740 F.Supp. 291 (1990) 302. See also, Jacoby (n41) 1045-1046.

[101] See *supra* pp 84-85.

[102] The original wording of section 32(a) of the Lanham Act provides that: 'Any person who shall, in commerce, use, without the consent of the registrant, any reproduction, counterfeit, copy, or colorable imitation of any registered mark in connection with the sale, offering for sale, or advertising of any goods or services on or in connection with which such use is *likely to cause confusion* or mistake or to deceive purchasers *as to the source of origin of such goods or services*' (emphasis added). This should be compared with the wording of the current section. See *supra* pp 97-99.

[103] Senate Rep No 87-2107 (1962 U.S.C.C.A.N. 2844) 2850. See also, Allen (n22) 331, arguing that '[b]eyond this "clarification," the amendment and its legislative history provide no further guidance.'

the situations in which confusion would result in infringement',[104] and by eliminating the source and origin phrase, Congress

> 'evinc[ed] a clear purpose to outlaw the use of trademarks which are likely to cause confusion, mistake, or deception of any kind, not merely of purchasers nor simply as to source of origin.'[105]

Contrary to the courts' approach, the purpose of this amendment was not to introduce new situations and types of confusion. Rather, the aim was to introduce the quality function, which is based on the utilitarian and economic justification.

If the aim was really to introduce new types of confusion, then there was no need to delete the source and origin phrase in the 1962 amendment. The drafters could simply have maintained this phrase and provided new examples of confusion. There is no point in removing one type of confusion (source and origin confusion) and keeping the (sponsorship or affiliation confusion). Moreover, the sponsorship or affiliation confusion is a sub-category of source and origin confusion, because when the consuming public are confused as to sponsorship or affiliation, then they are *ex officio* confused about the source and origin of the goods and/or services. One scholar argues that '[a] corollary to source confusion is confusion as to affiliation, sponsorship, connection, relationship, or approval.'[106] The real problem is that the omission of the source and origin confusion shall result in including semi-dilution concepts, such as subliminal confusion.[107] However, this was not the only attempt to "erode" the confusion test; other attempts aimed to include the notion of post-sale confusion.

Pre-sale confusion and post-sale confusion

In addition to the traditional pre-sale confusion, a new type of confusion could be applied to trademark infringement cases; that is, post-sale confusion. Scholars argue that the introduction of the post-sale

---

[104] *Ortho Pharmaceutical Corp* (n100) 1043.

[105] *Syntex Laboratories Inc v The Norwich Pharmacal Co* 437 F.2d 566 (1971) 568. The court in the *Syntex Laboratories* case had 'adopted the expansive view that the Lanham Act protects confusion of any kind on the part of anyone, without any … limitations, [relying] upon the 1962 Amendment.' See- Allen (n22) 349.

[106] Allen (n22) 325.

[107] Leaffer 2006 (n13) 131. See also, Leaffer 2001 (n13) 38-34.

confusion was not available before the amendment of 1962,[108] because of the Lanham Act's reference to the source and origin confusion. 'Therefore the possibility of post-sales confusion of a group beyond immediate purchasers was precluded.'[109] The concept of post-sale confusion suggests that consumers are not confused whilst purchasing; rather, 'the use by … purchasers of [the] goods is likely to cause others to be confused with respect to the marks.'[110] In *Lois Sportswear U.S.A. Inc v Levi Strauss & Co*,[111] the court held that according to its interpretation, the Lanham Act was meant to prevent the likelihood of confusion when the products in question 'are observed in the post-sale context.'[112] This means that the confused parties are 'persons who have not yet bought the goods at issue. [Hence, post-sale] confusion arises on the part of observers of the goods that are already purchased and in use.'[113]

However, dividing the confusion concept into pre-sale and post-sale confusion is not based on real grounds. If the confusion test as to source and origin is fully and strictly applied, there will be no need to introduce a new category of post-sale confusion. If one were to suppose, for the sake of argument, that the trademark "Rolex" was used by another infringer, then the concept of post-sale confusion suggests that consumers buying the replica of the original Rolex watches would not be confused as to the source and origin of the goods which they are buying, especially that the low price of the watches will inform them that they are not buying original Rolex watches. The post-sale concept is not directed towards those consumers; rather it is directed towards those who will observe the replicas and will be confused about such items.

If the confusion doctrine is applied appropriately to this hypothetical example, then using a mark which is identical to the original mark, and on the same class of goods and/or services, is prohibited, because the confusion doctrine provides that in such cases, consumer confusion as to the source and origin of the goods and/or services is presumed. Thus, the confusion doctrine will suffice to prevent such use, and the owner of the mark "Rolex" will be able to file a case of trademark infringement where

---

[108] *Trademarks and Unfair Competition* (n2) 47 (section 23:1).
[109] DM Tichane 'The Maturing Trademark Doctrine of Post-Sales Confusion' (1995) 85 Trademark Reporter 401.
[110] Allen (n22) 345.
[111] 799 F.2d 867 (1986).
[112] ibid 871. See also, *Jordache Enterprises Inc v Levi Strauss & Co* 841 F.Supp. 506 (1993) 515. See also, *Dorr-Oliver Inc v Fluid-Quip Inc* 94 F.3d 376 (1996) 381.
[113] Leaffer 2006 (n13) 128. See also, Leaffer 2001 (n13) 38-32.

there is no burden of proving confusion, as is presumed in such cases. This is before the infringing replicas are used by purchasers, and before their use is likely to confuse observers of the item.

In conclusion, new invented types of confusion do not aim to prevent consumer confusion. The goal of such attempts is to expand the confusion types and to widen the scope of confusion, in order to give trademark owners more monopolistic rights in their marks. It shall be argued below that the failure of the Lanham Act to define the scope of the confusion concept was the reason for such unnatural expansion in the confusion rationale.

- Scope of confusion under the Lanham Act

In the light of the broad language of the confusion provisions, the Lanham Act suffers from a problem as regards the scope of confusion. This problem is apparent in two respects. First, there is a lack of specification as to the similarity between the marks and the goods and/or services in question. Secondly, the Act does not refer to the characteristics of the confused public.

Specifications of marks and products

One major insufficiency of the confusion doctrine under the Lanham Act is that it does not differ between the different situations and expected scenarios of confusion. That is, it does not refer to the different instances to which confusion could be applied in respect of the degree of similarity between the marks and products in each particular case.

Three main scenarios of confusion could be introduced, on the basis of the degree of similarity or dissimilarity between the marks and the goods and/or services in question. The first is the use of an identical trademark on identical products, and in this situation, confusion is presumed. The second category is the use of similar or identical marks over similar or identical products. In this case, the likelihood of confusion should exist to establish a case of trademark infringement. Finally, the third category is the case of "well-known marks". In this case, protection is extended to dissimilar goods and/or services if such use fulfils a number of conditions. Such categories shall define the exact boundaries of trademark protection.

In many instances, courts were unable to determine the scope of confusion under the Lanham Act. For example, in one aspect courts provided that

> 'the protection which the law gives the owner of a trademark is not confined to the goods upon which it is used by the owner, but extends to articles which would reasonably be thought to come from the same source if bought under the same name.'[114]

This statement by courts shows a degree of adherence to the source function of trademarks. It also stresses confusion, but continues to show and assert that the scope of confusion is indefinite, and that the protection of trademarks might extend to dissimilar products.

Therefore, courts started to apply the confusion test over ordinary marks, even on non-competing goods and/or services, and were confused as to the proper scope of the confusion concept. For example, in *Dallas Cowboys Cheerleaders Inc v Pussycat Cinema Ltd*,[115] the plaintiff owned the Dallas Cowboys Cheerleaders team. The defendants used an outfit almost identical to the uniform of the plaintiff's team in a sexual film. The plaintiff raised a case of trademark infringement, claiming that the defendant's use of its trademark caused consumer confusion. The defendants argued 'that the Lanham Act requires confusion as to the origin of the film … [and] that no reasonable person would believe that the film originated with plaintiff.'[116] However, the court eventually ruled in favour of the plaintiff on the basis that 'it is hard to believe that anyone who had seen defendants' sexually depraved film could ever thereafter disassociate it from plaintiff's cheerleaders.'[117]

The unsavoury use of the mark by the defendants in this case could be described as "depraved use". However, the court should have objectively dealt with the business of the defendants as a certain class of goods and/or services. This is because the registrability of trademarks is a matter of public policy, and as long as the Lanham Act does not consider "pornography" contrary to public order and morality, then the court should not take the nature of the business into consideration in the assessment of infringement on the basis of confusion. The second step in analysing the court's decision in the light of confusion is that the use of the defendants of the mark was for dissimilar goods and/or services. The defendants' use is thus permissible, because such protection over dissimilar goods and/or services is restricted to well-known marks. Nothing in the facts of the case indicates that the plaintiff's mark is well-known or famous. Finally, if the

---

[114] JR Lunsford 'Trademark Infringement and Confusion of Source: Need for Supreme Court Action' (1949) 35 Virginia L Rev 218-219.

[115] 604 F.2d 200 (1979).

[116] ibid 204.

[117] ibid 204-205.

plaintiff is insulted by the use of its mark in this context or if such use would injure its business reputation then trademark infringement cases are not the proper means for such claims.[118] Rather, defamation cases could be the proper solution. Thus, this case 'd[oes] not meet the traditional standard of likelihood of confusion',[119] therefore, 'the continued validity of the Dallas Cowboy holding is questionable.'[120]

The court in *Dallas Cowboys Cheerleaders* case, probably impelled by its intuitive intentions against "immoral and depraved films", benefited from the broad language of the confusion sections under the Lanham Act and 'suggest[ed] that Lanham Act § 43(a) supports the claim of trademark dilution.'[121] This expansionist trend is supported by the fact that there is little or no guidance under the Lanham Act confusion sections as to the scope of the confusion doctrine. If there were any adherence to the premises of the Economic-Social Planning theory, the courts' decision would focus on different aspects, such as the degree of similarity between the goods and/or services to which both marks were used and if such use would result in confusing the public. Therefore, the decisive question which the court should have addressed is whether the plaintiff mark's ability to indicate the source and origin of his/her products was lessened or at least weakened.

It should be borne in mind that the *Dallas Cowboys Cheerleaders* case holds very specific facts. However, it is indicative in terms of the results of expanding the scope of the confusion doctrine, namely enabling trademark owners to contest different uses of trademarks where confusion is not likely. This is not the only insufficiency regarding the scope of confusion; the lack of reference to the requirements of the confused party is another aspect of the scope of confusion under the Lanham Act.

Who should be confused?

The ideal assessment of the amount of confused consumers should be decided upon the basis of the Economic-Social Planning theory, according to which the focus on the role of the public in the creation of trademarks

---

[118] DK Park 'Trademark Infringement – Lanham Act § 43(a) – Source Confusion' (1980-1981) 48 Tennessee L Rev 192, Park argues that 'the court should not have used trademark law to reach its result.'

[119] ibid 185.

[120] *WHS Entertainment Ventures v United Paperworkers International Union* 997 F.Supp. 946 (1998) 953.

[121] T Farmany 'Dallas Cowboys Cheerleaders v. Pussycat Cinema' (2001-2002) 12 J of Contemporary Legal Issues 275.

plays an important role.[122] Thus, due to the fact that a wide cross-section of the consuming public attribute their association to the mark, confusion should exist or be likely to exist amongst the majority of the public who granted their association to the mark. This is required because the right of the public and their association is crucial, and confusion amongst a minority will not suffice. However, this does not mean that confusion or likelihood of confusion should exist for the public at large; rather, confusion should be assessed amongst the majority of prospective and expected consumers.

The Lanham Act fails to refer to the number of consumers who have to be confused in order for infringement to occur. This has led courts and scholars to introduce a criterion for the amount of confused consumers. For example, in *McGregor-Doniger Inc v Drizzle Inc*,[123] the court provided that 'the crucial issue is confusion on the part of an "appreciable number" of consumers.'[124] Other courts provided that

> '[t]he touchstone of trademark infringement under the Lanham Act … is "likelihood of confusion": whether a *substantial number of ordinarily prudent purchasers* are likely to be misled or confused as to the source of the different products' (emphasis added).[125]

Scholars supported the courts' tendency to consider that a relatively high number of consumers are required to be confused in order to establish trademark infringement. For example, McCarthy argues that '[i]f an appreciable number of reasonable buyers are likely to be confused by the similar marks, then there is liability for trademark infringement'.[126]

Although it could be argued that courts' and scholars' approach as regards the standard of the confused public is generally acceptable,

---

[122] This results from the adoption of the source and origin function as the primary function of trademarks. See generally ch 3.

[123] 599 F.2d 1126 (1979).

[124] ibid 1138. See also, *Montblanc-Simplo GmbH v Aurora Due S.R.L.* 363 F.Supp.2d 467 (2005) 477.

[125] *Mushroom Maker Inc v R. G. Barry Corp* 441 F.Supp. 1220 (1977) 1225. See also, *McDonald'S Corp v McBagel's Inc* 649 F.Supp. 1268 (1986) 1273. See also, *Western Publishing Co Inc v Rose Art Industries Inc* 910 F.2d 57 (1990) 59. See also, *W.W.W. Pharmaceutical Co Inc v The Gillette Co* 984 F.2d 567 (1993) 571. See also, *Design Solange Ltd Inc v Lane Bryant Inc* WL 599552 (S.D.N.Y.) (1997) 4.

[126] *Trademarks and Unfair Competition* (n2) 44 (section 23:1). See also, PW Smith 'Trademarks, Parody, and Consumer Confusion: A Workable Lanham Act Infringement Standard' (1990-1991) 12 Cardozo L Rev 1541.

possible shortcomings might derive from the fact that their approach is not constructed on a theoretical basis, and is subject to change and modification. Hence, the Lanham Act should have referred to this subject and addressed this problem.

- Test of confusion

To comply with the Economic-Social Planning theory in achieving a just and attractive culture, trademark legislations should adopt a test which provides courts with a clear, unified criterion for confusion. It shall also assist new entrants when they attempt to choose their marks. A clear and well-established test will indicate to competitors that if the factors of the test are likely to occur, then such use might confuse consumers. Thus, it would give them more predictability in the course of choosing their mark, which would save them money and time in choosing a different mark, rather than entering into a long and complicated process of litigation. This, in turn, would result in the protection of the public in preventing the adoption of any mark which shall confuse them. It shall also alter the association they make between the senior mark and the products to which it is affixed.

The Lanham Act does not embody any test for confusion; nor does it provide any guidance as to the manner of assessing confusion. Courts noticed this insufficiency in the Act,[127] and were keen to invent a test for confusion. There was, however, no consensus amongst courts as to the factors required for the confusion test; each of the eleven Circuit Courts adopted its own test for confusion.[128]

---

[127] *Freedom Savings and Loan Association v Vernon Waw Jr. d/b/a Freedom Realty* 757 F.2d 1176 (1985) 1182.

[128] First Circuit Court test, see- *Boston Athletic Association v Mark Sullivan* 867 F.2d 22 (1989) 29. Second Circuit Court test, see- *Polaroid Corp v Polarad Electronics Corp* 287 F.2d 492 (1961) 495. Third Circuit Court test, see- *Fisons Horticulture Inc v Vigoro Industries Inc* 30 F.3d 466 (1994) 473. Fourth Circuit Court test, see- *Lone Star Steakhouse & Saloon Inc v Alpha of Virginia Inc* 43 F.3d 922 (1995) 933. Fifth Circuit Court test, see- *Westchester Media v PRL USA Holdings Inc* 214 F.3d 658 (2000) 664. Sixth Circuit Court test, see- *U.S. Structures Inc v J.P. Structures Inc* 130 F.3d 1185 (1997) 1189-1190. Seventh Circuit Court test, see- *Barbecue Marx Inc v 551 Ogden Inc* 235 F.3d 1041 (2000) 1043-1044. Eighth Circuit Court test, see- *Duluth News-Tribune v Mesabi Publishing Co* 84 F.3d 1093 (1996) 1096. Ninth Circuit Court test, see- *Surfvivor Media Inc v Survivor Productions* 406 F.3d 625 (2005) 631. Tenth Circuit Court test, see- *Sally Beauty Co Inc v Beautyco Inc* 304 F.3d 964 (2002) 972. Eleventh

Despite the importance of the intervention of the courts, especially in the case where the legislation does not cover a certain area, US Circuit Courts were not successful in this particular situation. Firstly, the tests developed by courts are very similar in practice.[129] However, the regulation of trademarks at a federal level aims to provide a unified system for protection; therefore, the Lanham Act should have embodied the factors for this test. This would overcome the possibility of future split between Circuit Courts in respect of this test; and ensures the harmonization which the federal legislation aims to achieve. Secondly, and most importantly, the test developed by Circuit Courts is designed to be applied in cases where the question of confusion concerns dissimilar goods and/or services.[130] It is argued that this kind of protection should only be applied to well-known marks, not to ordinary marks.

In this context, it would be beneficial to discuss the distinction between "dissimilar" products and "non-competing" products. This distinction is not usually addressed by scholarship; however, it would be helpful in terms of identifying the scope of trademark protection. It is suggested that the term "dissimilar" is more strict than the term "non-competing". Dissimilarity requires that the products should be totally non-related products, while non-competing products infers that the goods might be possibly related.[131] A proper example of non-competing products is that of *Aunt Jemima Mills Co v Rigney & Co.*[132] In this case the mark was used for pancake flour and syrup.[133] These two uses of the mark could be classified as non-competing, but related, uses. Nevertheless, such uses could not be classified as dissimilar uses. Thus, it could be concluded that using the term dissimilarity is more approapriate because it limits the range of marks eligible for protection, as it requires the use to be totally different and unrelated.

Circuit Court test, see- *Planetary Motion Inc v Techsplosion Inc* 261 F.3d 1188 (2001) 1201.

[129] MH Blerman and JD Wexler 'Toward a Reformulation of the Test for Determining Trademark Infringement' (1990) 80 Trademark Reporter 4.

[130] Some courts started an argument that '[t]he multi-factor test used to determine likelihood of confusion between noncompeting goods should also be applied in cases involving directly competing goods.' See- *Checkpoint Systems Inc v Check Point Software Technologies Inc* 269 F.3d 270 (2001) 280.

[131] *AMF Inc v Sleekcraft Boats* 599 F.2d 341 (1979) 348, referring to the possibility of non-competitive but similar uses of trademarks.

[132] 247 F. 407 (1917).

[133] See *infra* p 116.

However, courts should not be blamed for this situation. This was a result of the indeterminate scope of the confusion section under the Lanham Act. The Act does not provide whether the scope of the confusion sections covers similar or dissimilar goods and/or services, or whether protection over dissimilar goods is confined to well-known marks. This insufficiency regarding the scope of confusion has led courts to develop their own criteria, which resulted in confusing the courts as to the proper scope of the confusion doctrine.

Summarizing Remarks

It has been argued that the Economic-Social Planning requires the existence of an equitable test of confusion. Such a test should be able to recognize the rights of all the parties in the trademark formula.[134] It should clearly define the scope of confusion in order to achieve the goals of the Economic-Social Planning theory in a just culture and a free and fair competition.

Throughout this section, it has been clearly proved that the current confusion concept, under the Lanham Act, does not provide the desired notion of confusion. While confusion was initially the corner-stone of trademark protection under the Act, it seems today to be a wide notion, which is out of context. It has been argued that many attempts have widened confusion in a manner which benefited only trademark owners. This has been proved through a number of instances. The explicit reference of confusion as to source and origin has been removed, as this was claimed to open the way for new types of confusion. The result was the introduction of subliminal confusion, which was described by one scholar as 'an anti-dilution notion smuggled into federal trademark law.'[135] In addition, post-sale confusion is now actionable. It aims to substitute the confusion test with the mere association which does not lead to confusion. It is also argued that the Lanham Act does not define a scope for confusion. It does not provide for when confusion is presumed or when it is required. It also fails to denote whether well-known trademarks are actionable under the confusion protection. Similarly, the Act does not provide a test for confusion, and therefore there is no link with the public's association between the mark and the products.

All in all, the confusion concept under the Lanham Act is too wide. It does not accord with the premises of the Economic-Social Planning

[134] See ch 1 p 11.

[135] Leaffer 2006 (n13) 131. See also, Leaffer 2001 (n13) 38-34.

theory; nor does it comply with the aims and purposes on which the Act was based. Presently, courts should be aware that in protecting a trademark on the basis of confusion, they might be granting to the mark owner something that is public property. There is thus a need to rethink the foundations of current trademark systems.

Dilution under the Lanham Act

After having discussed the confusion concept under the Lanham Act, and proved its current expansion in favour of trademark owners, this section discusses the dilution concept. Dilution is the effective tool for trademark owners to monopolize rights in trademarks. This section aims to explore the introduction of dilution under the Lanham Act, exploring its aims and purposes. This will assist in proving the utilitarian grounds of dilution, which are responsible for the current expansion of trademark owners' rights under the Lanham Act. As a result, revisiting the foundations of trademark systems will become evident.

This section starts with the Economic-Social Planning theory's vision of creation and entitlement in the case of well-known trademarks. This is important because many calls defending the introduction of the notion of dilution argue that the confusion concept fails to provide proper protection to owners. Then, the substance of the dilution theory in the US will be presented. To do this, it is necessary to tackle the history, definition, types and requirements of the dilution action under the Lanham Act. The evaluation of the current state of protection under dilution is essential for the conclusion of a normative approach which aims to provide a substitute for the dilution concept in relation to the protection of well-known marks, in order to conclude an improvement to this area of trademark protection. In doing so, the conclusion will apply the dilution theory within the scope of the Economic-Social Planning theory. The aim is to challenge the concept of dilution and to devise the argument in favour of more public access to well-known marks trademarks, and in the need to balance the rights in trademarks rather than giving more exclusivity in well-known marks.

Economic-Social Planning of Well-Known Marks

Arguments defending the dilution theory consider that trademarks are the sole creation of their owners.[136] Accordingly, they consider the rights of trademark owners, which should be remunerated for the creation of trademarks. They should also be assured the proper incentives. This scenario for the creation of trademarks is unrealistic. Rather,

> 'trademark[s are] not ... word[s] or symbol[s] but an association of an object with a sign. [They are] not authored by the production/marketing of an object in its package but by a joint interpretive enterprise between author and public.'[137]

The Economic-Social Planning theory, as developed by this book, provides a clear vision to well-known trademarks. This vision is based on the flexible premises of this theory, as opposed to the rigid approach of other theoretical approaches which are individualistic in nature, and consider only the owners' interests.

This theory provides a new process for the creation and authoring of *well-known* trademarks, as well as a new concept as to the type of protection of such marks. It is important to note first of all that a well-known mark, before it became well-known, was an ordinary mark, and the original scenario as to the "co-authorship" of ordinary marks is still applicable. The difference in well-known marks is that there are two other steps for an ordinary mark to become well-known. The first step is that the owner of the mark starts to provide a more extensive effort in advertising his/her mark, and in enhancing the association of the mark with his/her mark. The second and most crucial step is that the public will attribute a higher degree of association between the mark and the products of the owner than the association attributed in the case of ordinary marks. It is this second step which is decisive in the process of authoring a well-known mark. In other cases, the mark will remain an ordinary mark and will never turn into a well-known mark.

The type of protection accorded to well-known marks should be assessed upon the foundations of the Economic-Social Planning theory, according to which the focus should be directed towards 'the public authorial role in associating a symbol with an object ... [which] creates

---

[136] R Callmann 'Unfair Competition without Competition?' (1946-1947) 95 U of Pennsylvania L Rev 464.

[137] S Wilf 'Who Authors Trademarks?' (1999) 17 Cardozo Arts & Entertainment L J 45-46.

competing interests of the public as creator.'[138] Therefore, one concludes from this analysis that the consuming public should have more access to use the well-known mark, namely in cultural and expressive manners, and this shall be their reward for their role in authoring such marks. In the meantime, owners of well-known marks shall enjoy extra protection than owners of ordinary marks; this is their reward for the effort they exerted in their marks.

Accordingly, the protection of well-known marks should result in achieving a just and attractive culture.[139] Hence, trademarks should function as source and origin identifiers. It follows that any confusion as to this source and origin should be prevented. Consequently, owners of well-known trademarks shall enjoy the extra protection *only* within the boundaries of the confusion rationale. This could be achieved by giving the owners of well-known marks the right to prevent the use by others of any identical or similar marks on *dissimilar* goods and/or services *provided* that the owners of such marks can prove the existence of likelihood of confusion. This proposition shall provide owners with extra protection in cases of well-known trademarks, but it also considers the confusion of the public as the parameter for trademark infringement. The rights of other traders are recognized, in allowing them to use well-know marks, *if* confusion is not likely. If protection of well-known marks is based as such, then a just culture would be achieved, and competition would be fair and free.

Tackling the dilution concept under the Lanham Act, shall prove its monopolistic nature. It shall therefore assist in showing how distinct it is from the suggested Economic-Social Planning theory, and consequently shall prove that the philosophical foundations of current trademark systems should be revisited.

The Dilution Concept under the Lanham Act

This section discusses the dilution doctrine under the Lanham Act. This requires discussing the origins of dilution; this shall set out the aims and purposes of the doctrine, which proves the individualistic nature of rights. Thereafter, the introduction of dilution under the umbrella of the Lanham Act, which was originally based on the dual purpose of protecting the interests of the public and the owners' interests, will be tackled.

---

[138] ibid 3-4.

[139] W Fisher 'Theories of Intellectual Property' in S Munzer (ed) *New Essays in the Legal and Political Theory of Property* (1st edn Cambridge University Press Cambridge 2001) 172.

- Origins of dilution

Arguably, the first traceable indication of the dilution doctrine is the US Court of Appeals decision of 1917 in the *Aunt Jemima Mills* case.[140] In this case, the court dealt with the critical question of whether the protection of the complainant's mark should be extended when the use by the defendants was for non-competing goods. The court then concluded that the products of both parties, although not directly competing, are interrelated, with similar marks falling within the same class of products.[141] Therefore, this case does not seem to be the root of the dilution doctrine, because the court expressly found that the products on which the mark was used were similar goods. The court applied the case of confusion resulting from the use of an identical mark over similar goods, and concluded that confusion is likely to result, and prevented the defendants' use. Despite this conclusion, proponents of the dilution doctrine use the term "Aunt Jemima doctrine" to refer to the use of a trademark on non-competing goods and/or services.[142]

The roots of the dilution concept could be traced back to the year 1924 in the German *Odol* case.[143] In this case, the German word "verwässert" which means "diluted" in English, was first used by the court.[144] It was held that owners of the well-known trademark "Odol" should enjoy protection over non-competing goods. The court reasoned that the use for a dissimilar product 'shall lead[…] the public to assume that it is of good *quality*' (emphasis added),[145] and the '[c]omplainant's ability to compete with other manufacturers of mouth wash will be impaired [because] the significance of its mark is lessened.'[146]

Tackling the history of dilution and the *Odol* case decision is of crucial importance in understanding this concept in current legal systems. The court's emphasis in the *Odol* case was directed towards the idea that protection should be accorded to well-known trademarks, even over non-competing products, because the public would link the superior quality of

---

140 *Aunt Jemima Mills Co* (n132).
141 ibid 409-410.
142 Leaffer 2006 (n13) 116. See also, Leaffer 2001 (n13) 38-23.
143 T Martino *Trademark Dilution* (1st edn Clarendon Press Oxford 1996) 4. (Citing *Odol* case (1925) 25 *Juristiche Wochenschrift* 502; XXV *Markenschutz und Wettbewerb* 264).
144 See ch 3 pp 64-67.
145 FI Schechter 'The Rational Basis of Trademark Protection' (Reprint in 1970 of the 1927 text) 60 Trademark Reporter 346.
146 ibid.

the well-known mark with the inferior quality of the junior mark. This shall affect the mark's 'selling power if others were allowed to use it … even for totally different products.'[147] It follows that such use shall incline the incentive of well-known trademark owners to produce superior quality products. This argument is in harmony with the utilitarian and economic justification, which mainly argues that owners of well-known trademarks shall enjoy full protection against any use by others whatsoever.[148]

Nevertheless, the American Scholar Schechter 'rais[ed] the idea of dilution within the United States'[149] in 1927. Influenced by Schechter's exposition, that trademarks shall face "real injury"[150] if others are permitted to use trademarks over non-competing goods, many states enacted their own state anti-dilution statutes. Massachusetts was the first state having such an Act on 1947, only one year after the enactment of the Lanham Act.[151] The first, but unsuccessful, attempt to introduce the dilution concept at a federal level was the "Vestal Bill" of 1932, in support of which Schechter provided a testimony before the House of Representatives,[152] and 'argued that federal protection against dilution ought to be available for certain trademarks.'[153] The second attempt to introduce dilution federally was in the same year, but the "Perkins Bill" had the same destiny of the "Vestal Bill".[154]

Afterwards, the first modern attempt to introduce dilution was in 1988, but this was not successful. However, in 1995 the Federal Trademark Dilution Act (FTDA 1995) was passed by Congress. Later, in 2006, proponents of dilution were successful in enhancing the protection of trademark owners through the enactment of the Trademark Dilution Revision Act (TDRA 2005). Before discussing these legislations, it is essential to start with the purposes of the dilution concept, to assess whether this concept is compatible with the aims and purposes of the Lanham Act.

---

[147] WJ Derenberg 'The Problem of Trademark Dilution and the Antidilution Statutes' (1956) 44 California L Rev 449.

[148] For example, see- Carter (n47) 763. See also generally ch 2 pp 17-23.

[149] K Port 'The "Unnatural" Expansion of Trademark Rights: Is a Federal Dilution Statute Necessary?' (1995) 85 Trademark Reporter 529.

[150] Schechter (n145) 342.

[151] J Gilson 'A Federal Dilution Statute: Is it Time?' (1993) 83 Trademark Reporter 109. See also, Port (n149) 530. See also, *Trademark Dilution* (n143) 29.

[152] Derenberg (n147) 449-450.

[153] DS Welkowitz *Trademark Dilution Federal, State, and International Law* (1st edn The Bureau of National Affairs Washington 2002) 154.

[154] ibid 154-155.

- Aims and purposes of the dilution concept

> *'If KODAK may be used for bath tubs and cakes, MAZDA for cameras and shoes, or RITZ-CARLTON for coffee, these marks must inevitably be lost in the commonplace words of the language ...'*[155]

With these words, Schechter expressed the aims of dilution. He directed dilution towards the protection of well-known marks, and 'limited it to the protection of unique marks against use on different products'.[156] To safeguard such "unique" marks, Schechter's proposal aims to maximize the protection thereof, even when used over non-competing products. This is achieved, from Schechter's perspective, through the protection of the distinctiveness of the mark. Therefore, the dilution concept aims to protect the quality of the mark, in order to provide the incentive to owners of "unique" marks to produce or provide high quality products. The dilution concept does not accept the consumer confusion concept. As dilution proponents argue, in the case of dilution, the 'injury is materially different from that arising out of mere confusion.'[157] Therefore, the focus is not directed towards the confused public. It is, rather, directed to the injury to the owner's interests to whom rights should be enhanced and entitlement should be maximized, on the wrong premise 'that the real wrong arises out of dilution.'[158]

Proponents of dilution admit that Schechter's rationale 'was not overly concerned with public deception.'[159] Such a claim aims to "dilute" the dark sides of dilution. This concept is designed only to suit trademark owners and to allow them to monopolize the use of "unique" marks, through the protection of the mark, even when used on non-competing products.[160]

This emphasis on owners' rights embraces two issues. First, it denies the role of the public as "co-authors" of trademarks with the owners, and thus does not accord with the aims and purposes of the Lanham Act. Second, it allows trademark owners to monopolize words in the English language in return for a really low price,[161] and deprives the public of

---

[155] Schechter (n145) 344.
[156] Handler (n12) 425.
[157] Callmann (n136) 448.
[158] ibid 449.
[159] Gilson (n151) 109.
[160] See *supra* pp 110-112.
[161] J Davis 'European Trade Mark Law and the Enclosure of the Commons' (2002) 4 Intellectual Property Q 342.

having their state of mind as the test for infringement, in addition of not being able to use the mark in cultural and expressive uses. As such, dilution is the 'basis of trademark exclusivity that has nothing to do with protecting consumers from being confused or deceived',[162] and 'severs the link between trademark protection and consumer protection'.[163]

In *L.L. Bean Inc v Drake Publishers Inc*,[164] the court asserted that '[t]he law of trademark dilution aims to protect the distinctive quality of a trademark from deterioration caused by its use on dissimilar products.'[165] The court further reasoned that

> '[t]he overriding purpose of anti-dilution statutes is to prohibit a merchant of noncompetitive goods from selling its products by trading on the … reputation of another's mark.'[166]

The court's interpretation is not correct; the court incorrectly concluded that the rights of the owners emerge from any probable diversion of trade. It seems that the court ignored the fact that it is not possible for any diversion of trade to occur unless the consuming public is *confused*. Moreover, in the case of well-known trademarks it is more probable that consumers would be able to recognize the senior mark, to which they have attributed a high degree of association, and thus are less likely to be confused.

In conclusion, the aims and purposes of the dilution concept contradict the aims and purposes of the Lanham Act. It has already been argued that the original aims and purposes of the Lanham Act are consistent with the premises of the Economic-Social Planning theory.[167] Thus, it is no surprise that the dilution concept does not refer to balancing the rights in trademarks throughout the relevant parties. Rather, the owner of a well-known trademark is the only player in the dilution field. Therefore, the initial aims and purposes of the Lanham Act are disrupted, and every time a court rules in favour of owners on the basis of dilution, there is something given to the owner which is the public interest, and the original idea of the Lanham Act is "betrayed".

---

[162] JT McCarthy 'Proving a Trademark has been Diluted: Theories or Facts?' (2004-2005) 41 Houston L Rev 727.
[163] *Trademark Dilution Federal, State, and International Law* (n153) 5.
[164] 811 F.2d 26 (1987).
[165] ibid 30.
[166] ibid.
[167] See *supra* pp 95-96.

- 1988: Congressional failure to adopt dilution

In 1988, a draft of the Trademark Law Revision Act (TLRA) was introduced. From amongst the various amendments to the Lanham Act was an addition of paragraph (c) to section 43 of the Act, which deals with trademark infringement. This suggested subsection aims to introduce the dilution concept into the Lanham Act. Fortunately, this attempt ended in failure because of 'its potential[] anti-competitive aspects and freedom of speech consideration.'[168] However, examination of this unsuccessful attempt is helpful in the process of judging the following amendments, which established the current dilution section under the Act.

The Senate Report accompanying the Bill provides that '[d]ilution occurs when a person adopts the mark of another for use on noncompeting goods or services.'[169] To contest this deficiency the 'traditional trademark infringement questions such as likelihood of confusion and competition between the parties are not at issue.'[170] The report also indicates that marks eligible for protection should not be only inherently distinctive, but should also be famous. It also provides a number of factors which should be weighed *cumulatively* in order for the mark to be eligible for protection, as 'no one of them is determinative.'[171]

This Bill is credited, over later propositions, for its stress on proving that the mark should be famous, and that all the factors should be taken *cumulatively* in assessing the mark's distinctiveness and fame. Such requirements are not applicable to the currently applied notion for dilution.

When the TLRA was introduced in the House of Representatives it was not passed because of the opposition held by Representative Robert Kastenmeier and his concerns about the clash of dilution with the First Amendment.[172] Therefore, the attempt to monopolize the rights and entitlements in trademarks for the owners' benefit and to ensure the domination of US trademarks worldwide failed. Unfortunately however, the year 1995 was different, and witnessed the first federal introduction of dilution.

---

[168] S Maniatis *Trade Marks in Europe: A Practical Jurisprudence* (1st edn Sweet & Maxwell London 2006) 710 (para 10-068).

[169] Senate Rep No 100-515 (1988 U.S.C.C.A.N. 5577) 5604.

[170] ibid.

[171] ibid 5604-5605.

[172] Gilson (n151) 114.

- 1995: Dilution into effect

The Federal Trademark Dilution Act of 1995 (FTDA) was the first successful introduction of dilution at a Federal level. The elements of the FTDA shall be discussed in order to prove its monopolistic nature. This requires exploring the definition, types, test and requirements of dilution under the FTDA. It shall be clarified that this Act forms an important step in the ongoing expansion of owners' rights.

Definition of dilution

The FTDA defines dilution as:

> '[T]he lessening of the capacity of a famous mark to identify and distinguish goods or services, regardless of the presence or absence of
> (1) competition between the owner of the famous mark and other parties, or
> (2) likelihood of confusion, mistake, or deception.'[173]

This definition has a number of defects. First, as the dilution concept lacks justification, the drafters of the FTDA have attempted to override the principles of the confusion rationale in order to legitimize this concept. Considering that dilution is a lessening of the capacity of the mark to distinguish the products to which they are affixed, they have used the source and origin function to overcome any objections to the quality argument upon which dilution is based. However, if one were to use the source and origin function, then logically confusion should be the test for any use which would lessen the ability of the mark to distinguish the source and origin of the products. Therefore, the reliance on this notion is not in conformity with the results of applying dilution.

The court in *Ringling Bros.-Barnum v Utah Division of Travel Development*[174] 'interpret[ed the definition of dilution under] the Act … as requiring for proof of … an actual lessening of the senior mark's selling power, expressed as "its capacity to identify and distinguish goods or services." '[175] The court attempted to draw a link between the distinguishing function of the mark with the "selling power" of marks, which Schechter argued 'the value of the modern trademark lies in'.[176]

---

[173] Trademarks Act 1946- Lanham Act (USA) 15 U.S.C. § 1127 (Section 45).
[174] 170 F.3d 449 (1999).
[175] ibid 458.
[176] Schechter (n145) 345.

However, such an approach contradicts Schechter's starting point of refusing the source and origin function of trademarks. Therefore, the combination of the source function with the dilution doctrine is strange.

Second, the definition provides that competition and likelihood of confusion between the marks should not be regarded in assessing dilution. As regards the competition part, it is not clear what input this addition has; it has been already argued that the likelihood of confusion test can adopt the protection of well-known marks when used on dissimilar products, provided that confusion exists. This shall provide more equity in balancing the rights of the public and other traders with the rights of the owner, because any use for dissimilar products which might confuse the public is harmful to both the public and the owner and prohibited as such, whereas if such use does not cause confusion then there is no harm neither to the owner nor to the public, it rather considers the discretion of the public in the meaning-making of signs and marks.

In contrast to the approach of confusion, the FTDA aims to provide protection to the owners of well-known trademarks against any use which might lessen their ability to distinguish the source and origin, and does not require the owners of such mark to prove the existence of confusion which is the tool to assess and measure any lessening in the marks' ability to distinguish the source and origin. It follows that the monopolizing nature of the dilution concept is clear from its definition, by protecting the owner without any burden of proving confusion. This is also apparent in the disregarding of the role of the public in creating trademarks, and not protecting them in this process.

For example, the legislative history of the FTDA clearly indicates that 'the use of DUPONT shoes, BUICK aspirin, and KODAK pianos would be actionable under this legislation.'[177] It seems elementary even to inexperienced purchasers that BUICK aspirin does not originate from the same source as BUICK automobiles; it would seem rather that such use might strengthen the public's association with the first user.[178] Thus, the source and origin function is maintained. Moreover, the public is the party who made BUICK for automobiles, a well-known sign, and they should retain the right to alter or withdraw the amount of association they attribute. By prohibiting further use of this mark for dissimilar goods when confusion does not exist, we prevent the possibility of the benefits of this new use, and infringing the rights and entitlements of the public and other traders.

---

[177] House Rep No 104-374 (1996 U.S.C.C.A.N. 1029) 1030.

[178] McCarthy provides a similar argument. See- McCarthy (n162) 746.

Types of dilution

The dilution concept embraces two types of dilution: dilution by blurring and dilution by tarnishment.

(i) Blurring

This type of dilution presumes that the use by a third party of a famous mark shall blur the distinctiveness of the mark 'if such use begins after the mark has become famous and causes dilution of the distinctive quality of the mark,'[179] regardless of the existence of likelihood of confusion.[180] Thus, '[t]he wrong that the Dilution Act prohibits is the reduction of the distinctiveness of the plaintiff's famous mark',[181] which is manifest through the erosion of 'the strength of the mark as a unique identifier of the senior holder's goods'.[182]

The reliance of this type of dilution upon the mark's "distinctive quality" seems to be totally inaccurate. Distinctiveness is the ability of the mark to denote the source and origin of products and to distinguish the goods of one undertaking from those of others. Therefore, distinctiveness is a prerequisite for any sign to become a mark. As one scholar argues, 'all trademarks must be distinctive either inherently or through acquired meaning',[183] and appropriately asks, '[i]f all marks are distinctive, … what marks would be outside the protection of the FTDA?'[184] This sheds the light on the crucial role of the public in trademarks and well-known marks in particular, in which the matter of distinctiveness lies in the hands of the consuming public. This role, however, is totally ignored under dilution by blurring.

---

179 Trademarks Act 1946- Lanham Act (USA) 15 U.S.C. § 1125 (Section 43(c)(1)).

180 ibid § 1127 (Section 45).

181 C Hein 'Confused About the Federal Trademark Dilution?' (1997) 87 Trademark Reporter 384.

182 KB McCabe 'Dilution-by-Blurring: A Theory Caught in the Shadow of Trademark Infringement' (2000) 68 Fordham L Rev 1842.

183 L Krafte-Jacobs 'Judicial Interpretation of the Federal Trademark Dilution Act of 1995' (1998) 66 U of Cincinnati L Rev 690.

184 ibid.

(ii) Tarnishment

Tarnishment refers to a situation where the second user's use of the mark affects the positive connotations which the well-known mark enjoys. This occurs when the subsequent use of the mark is used over an inferior class of goods and/or services, the link with which shall affect the image of the mark in the eyes of consumers. As courts have provided, tarnishment

> 'arises when the plaintiff's trademark is linked to products of shoddy quality, or is portrayed in an unwholesome or unsavory context likely to evoke unflattering thoughts about the owner's product.'[185]

It is questionable whether the FTDA includes this type of dilution.[186] Through its section 43(c), the FTDA only refers to the distinctive quality of the mark, which is the subject-matter of blurring. Denicola argues that the drafters of the FTDA intentionally omitted the reference to tarnishment from the Act, and that the '[s]eparation of the tarnishment and dilution of distinctiveness theories was not an accident[, … and t]he drafters should be held to their statutory language.'[187] He argues that broadening the dilution concept in this way, so as to include tarnishment, shall lead to rulings of dilution in cases where dilution does not exist.[188]

However, the House Report clearly provides that the purpose of this Act 'is to protect famous trademarks from subsequent uses that blur the distinctiveness of the mark or *tarnish* or disparage it' (emphasis added).[189] In the light of this contradiction between the wording of the Act and its legislative history, one court decided that it 'need not … delve into the difficult question of how conceptually to fit tarnishment within a theory of dilution.'[190] However, a substantial number of court decisions consider

---

185 *Deere & Co v MTD Products Inc* 41 F.3d 39 (1994) 43. See also, *Perkins School for the Blind v Maxi-Aids Inc* 274 F.Supp.2d 319 (2003) 326-327.

186 JT McCarthy 'The 1996 Federal Anti-Dilution Statute' (1998) 16 Cardozo Arts & Entertainment L J 593.

187 RC Denicola 'Some Thoughts on the Dynamics of Federal Trademark Legislation and the Trademark Dilution Act of 1995' (1996) 59 L and Contemporary Problems 89-90.

188 ibid 89.

189 House Rep No 104-374 (1996 U.S.C.C.A.N. 1029) 1029.

190 *Ringling Bros.-Barnum* (n174) 452.

that the FTDA encompasses dilution through blurring and tarnishment as being the two types of dilution.[191]

Nonetheless, this is not the only hurdle under the FTDA; the clash between tarnishment and the definition of dilution seems more problematic. If the FTDA considers dilution to be defined as the lessening of the famous mark's ability to distinguish the source and origin of the products, then there seems to be the problem of classifying tarnishment under this definition. It is, by any means, unclear how the use of the mark on inferior goods and/or services would result in reducing the ability of the famous mark to denote the source of the products. Consequently, tarnishment could not fall under the definition of dilution under the FTDA. Welkowitz raises similar concerns, and argues that

> '[n]othing in th[e] definition [of dilution] directly refers to business reputation, trademark tarnishment, or trademark disparagement[,] … [and t]arnishment does not attack the distinctiveness of the mark. … [Thus,] the unsavory association does not mean that the consumer sees the mark as designating more than one *source*.'[192]

This means that tarnishment does not fit under the FTDA's definition of dilution.

Scope of dilution under the FTDA

Not only does the dilution doctrine widen the scope of protection in favour of trademarks owners, but its proponents have succeeded in widening the scope of its applicability so that it becomes an effective monopolistic tool for the owners of trademarks. It is suggested that dilution under the FTDA is extended to include different types of trademarks.

(i) Fame and its test

When Schechter envisioned his concept of dilution, he focused on extending protection to the limited class of marks even in relation to noncompeting goods. This could be easily inferred from Schechter's

[191] See for example, *American Family Life Insurance Co v Timothy Hagan* 266 F.Supp.2d 682 (2002) 692. See also, *Jews For Jesus v Steven C. Brodsky* 993 F.Supp. 282 (1998) 306.

[192] *Trademark Dilution Federal, State, and International Law* (n153) 259.

eagerness to maintain the "uniqueness"[193] of marks; he stressed that only "coined marks"[194] are the types of marks subject to this expansive protection as opposed to "commonplace marks".[195] He restricted his argument to the rejection of any use responsible for "impairing the individuality"[196] and "singularity"[197] of such marks. The emphasis was on the fact that a dilution type of protection should only be limited to a truly exclusive set of marks, retaining a high degree of fame.

A number of scholars have argued that the dilution concept was formulated and founded to cover a limited class of marks. For example, McCarthy argues that the dilution concept should 'be reserved for a small, select group of truly eminent and widely recognized marks'.[198] Thus the FTDA, Jacobs argues, 'is meant to protect only famous marks'.[199] However, the vagueness and general language of the FTDA open the way for a wide interpretation, leading to an expansion of the scope of dilution beyond its limits.[200]

The FTDA provides that the entitlement for legal action under section 43(c) be restricted to '[t]he owner of a *famous* mark' (emphasis added),[201] it provided a list of factors which might be taken into consideration '[i]n determining whether a mark is *distinctive* and *famous*' (emphasis added).[202] The legislative history of the FTDA shows that this list provides '*nonexclusive* factors that a court *may* consider in determining whether a mark qualifies for protection' (emphasis added).[203] Therefore, this list is not compulsory for courts to follow, and it is not exclusive; this is the first indication of the widening the scope of dilution, by not requiring a compulsory set of factors that a mark should fulfil in order to qualify for dilution protection. This could be distinguished from the 1988 Bill, which required such factors to be taken cumulatively when assessing a mark's

---

193 Schechter (n145) 340, 342 and 345.
194 ibid.
195 ibid.
196 ibid 344.
197 ibid 345.
198 McCarthy (n162) 733.
199 Krafte-Jacobs (n183) 690.
200 JF Hacking 'Trademark Dilution: Setting the Dilution Standard under the Federal Trademark Dilution Act' (2003) 5 Tulane J of Technology & Intellectual Property 123.
201 Trademarks Act 1946- Lanham Act (USA) 15 U.S.C. § 1125 (Section 43(c) (1)).
202 ibid.
203 House Rep No 104-374 (1996 U.S.C.C.A.N. 1029) 1034.

fame.[204] Consequently, the standard of fame differed from one court to the other. Some courts considered the plaintiff's mark to be "strong", and directly concluded that the mark is famous by virtue of its mere distinctiveness;[205] meanwhile, other courts did not even bother to discuss the famousness of the mark.[206]

In conclusion, such decisions show the widening of the fame requirement. They also de-emphasize the public's association between the mark and the products, which should be the real injury in the field of trademarks.

(ii) Non-registered marks

The FTDA considers that if the mark is registered, then this is a factor which promotes its fame and distinctiveness, and renders the mark eligible for protection.[207] This indicates that registration is not a requirement for dilution protection, but only a factor in deciding its famousness. And if the user of a non-registered mark could prove that it is a famous mark, then protection is provided 'to [such] famous marks, whether or not the mark is the subject of federal trademark registration.'[208]

However, The Lanham Act was founded by the motive to provide protection for registered marks at a federal level. It was also intended to promote the registrability of trademarks at a federal level. Hence, it was not meant to cover non-registered trademarks by any means.

The FTDA's inclusion of non-registered trademarks under its scope of subject-matter contradicts the intentions of the Lanham Act. This widens the scope of its applicability, granting monopolistic rights to negligent large businesses who do not take the initiative of registering their signs. It also broadens the scope of dilution protection, to include an area which falls under the ambit of common law. This raises the fears of some

---

[204] Senate Rep No 100-515 (1988 U.S.C.C.A.N. 5577) 5604. See also, *supra* pp 120-122.

[205] *Clinique Laboratories Inc v Dep Corp* 945 F.Supp. 547 (1996) 551.

[206] JR Hughes 'The Federal Trademark Dilution Act of 1995 and the Evolution of the Dilution Doctrine – Is it Truly a Rational Basis for the Protection of Trademarks?' (1998) Vol 1998 Issue 3 Detroit College L Rev 799.

[207] Trademarks Act 1946- Lanham Act (USA) 15 U.S.C. § 1125 (Section 43(c) (1) (H)).

[208] House Rep No 104-374 (1996 U.S.C.C.A.N. 1029) 1034.

scholars[209] of turning the American legal system into a civil law system, because the inclusion of non-registered marks in the FTDA provides protection which already exists in common law.

This inclusion of non-registered marks under the ambit of the FTDA is significant. Non-registered marks are protected by English courts under the doctrine of passing off,[210] and in the US under the doctrine of unfair competition.[211] It is agreed that where there is no competition, there can be no unfair competition.[212] Therefore, in principle, it could be argued that non-registered marks are protected under the unfair competition doctrine only in the case of competition between the two uses of the mark.

Rendering non-registered marks actionable under the dilution doctrine means that protection of such marks is extended, because the dilution protection is available 'regardless of the presence or absence of competition between the owner of the famous mark and other parties'.[213] As such, protecting non-registered marks under the FTDA forms a real expansion of trademark protection.

Burden of proof: Likelihood or actual dilution?

The burden of proof is a crucial issue in the field of dilution. That is, there should be a need to ensure that the requirement to prove dilution is difficult, and only extremely well-known marks which have suffered actual harm can succeed in such cases. Nevertheless, the FTDA is silent as regards the requirement of proving the existence of actual dilution, or the mere likelihood of dilution. The legislative history provides no indication either.[214]

One would expect the courts to provide a clear answer concerning this requirement. However, there was a split amongst courts;[215] some have

---

[209] See for example, KL Port 'The Congressional Expansion of American Trademark Law: A Civil Law System in the Making' (2000) 35 Wake Forest L Rev 827-914.

[210] See ch 5 pp 148-151.

[211] Schechter (n145) 338.

[212] *Bond Stores v Bone Stores* 104 F.2d 124 (1939) 125. See also, Callmann (n136) 443.

[213] Trademarks Act 1946- Lanham Act (USA) 15 U.S.C. § 1127 (Section 45). See also, *supra* pp 121-122.

[214] K Ruwe 'The Federal Trademark Dilution Act: "Actual Harm" or "Likelihood of Dilution"?' (2001-2002) 70 U of Cincinnati L Rev 1175.

[215] *Cable News Network L.P. v CNNews.com* 177 F.Supp.2d 506 (2001) 521, providing that 'there is a circuit split regarding whether a plaintiff seeking to prove

argued that the FTDA necessitates actual dilution,[216] whereas others have stressed that it only requires that dilution is likely to occur.[217] For example, the US fourth Circuit Court in the *Ringling Bros.-Barnum* case[218] argued that dilution consists of a number of factors, amongst which is the requirement that the junior use of the famous mark causes '*actual harm* to the senior marks' economic value as a product-identifying and advertising agent' (emphasis added).[219] The court reasoned by arguing that if no actual economic harm is required, 'property rights in gross' would be created in famous marks, making them comparable to patents and copyrights.[220] The court correctly concluded that this interpretation of requiring actual harm 'confines the federal dilution claim to a … narrow scope'.[221]

In contrast, other courts have argued in favour of requiring the mere likelihood of dilution. The second Circuit Court in *Nabisco Inc v PF Brands Inc*[222] criticized the *Ringling Bros.-Barnum* case decision. It considered that

> 'requir[ing] proof of actual loss of revenue seems inappropriate[,] … [as] it would be extraordinarily speculative and difficult to prove that the loss was due to the dilution of the mark.'[223]

The court also stressed that the *Ringling Bros.-Barnum* case requirement of actual harm opens the door for a type of 'injury [that] would never be compensated.'[224] Therefore, the court concluded that the Act 'permit[s] adjudication granting or denying an injunction, … before the dilution has actually occurred.'[225]

---

dilution must show actual economic harm to its famous mark or merely a threatened injury.'

[216] For example, see- *Westchester Media* (n128) 670. See also, *International Bancorp L.L.C. v Societe Des Bains De Mer Et Du Cercle Des Etrangers A Monaco* 192 F.Supp.2d 467 (2002) 484.

[217] For example, see- *Eli Lilly & Co v Natural Answers Inc* 233 F.3d 456 (2000) 468. See also, *Trans Union LLC v Credit Research Inc* 142 F.Supp.2d 1029 (2001) 1045.

[218] *Ringling Bros.-Barnum* (n174).

[219] ibid 453.

[220] ibid 456.

[221] ibid 458.

[222] 191 F.3d 208 (1999).

[223] ibid 223-224.

[224] ibid 224.

[225] ibid 224-225.

In the light of this split amongst Circuit Courts, there was a need for the intervention of the Supreme Court to settle this controversy. The Supreme Court's decisive answer was in *Moseley v V Secret Catalogue Inc.*[226]

Moseley v V Secret Catalogue Inc

The *Moseley* case is of crucial importance. The core of the Supreme Court's decision was whether the FTDA required actual dilution or likelihood of dilution. In this case, the mark "Victor's Secret" was used by the petitioners on their retail store for adult videos, novelties and lingerie. The respondents argued that the mark was similar to, and diluted their famous mark "Victoria Secret" which is used on lingerie. The respondents sent a letter to the petitioners requesting that they stop using their mark, as it caused confusion and dilution to the "Victoria Secret" famous mark. Hence, the petitioners changed their trademark to "Victor's Little Secret", but this was of no conciliation to the respondents.[227] Thus, the owners of the "Victoria Secret" mark filed a suit and succeeded in the District Court,[228] and on appeal to the Circuit Court.[229] Therefore, the Moseleys petitioned to the Supreme Court.

The court shed light on the language of the FTDA itself, in particular on the phrase: 'if such use … *causes dilution* of the distinctive quality of the mark' (emphasis added).[230] The court provided that '[t]his text unambiguously requires a showing of actual dilution, rather than a likelihood of dilution.'[231] The court also linked this interpretation to the FTDA's definition of the term dilution itself,[232] and ruled that

> '[t]he contrast between the initial reference to an actual "lessening of the capacity" of the mark, and the later reference to a "likelihood of confusion, mistake, or deception" in the second caveat confirms the conclusion that actual dilution must be established.'[233]

---

[226] 537 U.S. 418, 123 S.Ct. 1115 (2003).
[227] ibid 422-424.
[228] See- *V Secret Catalogue Inc v Victor Moseley* 2000 WL 370525 (W.D.Ky.) (2000).
[229] See- *V Secret Catalogue Inc v Victor Moseley* 259 F.3d 464 (2001).
[230] Trademarks Act 1946- Lanham Act (USA) 15 U.S.C. § 1125 (Section 43(c) (1)).
[231] *Moseley v* (n226) 433.
[232] See *supra* pp 121-122.
[233] *Moseley v* (n226) 433.

The Supreme Court has set out a more flexible notion for actual harm, which falls between the *Ringling Bros.-Barnum* case requirement of *actual economic harm*, and the *Nabisco Inc* case requiring the mere *likelihood of dilution*. Conversely, the Supreme Court argued that there is no need to prove 'actual loss of sales or profits'.[234] However, the court argued that 'the mere fact that consumers mentally associate the junior user's mark with a famous mark is not sufficient to establish actionable dilution.'[235] This is correct, because the public's association is a rational decision on their part, and could not be manipulated by the junior use of the mark. Yet, the mental association does not of necessity mean that the mark's capacity to distinguish the source of products is lessened. Consequently, mental association is only relevant when the public are confused as regards the source and origin of the products, and this is an area which falls out of the dilution zone.

Not only does the significance of this decision derive from the fact that it resulted in settling the dispute amongst Circuit Courts, but more importantly, it narrows the scope and restricts the applicability of the dilution concept. Although not totally satisfactory, this decision was the only procedure that courts could undertake to limit the owners' broad rights under the FTDA. In part, this is consistent with the Economic-Social Planning theory in restraining owners' rights. However, the part relating to harm to the public is missing, especially insofar as the court's decision 'still acknowledged some property rights in trademark[s]'.[236]

Proponents of the dilution concept opposed the Supreme Court's decision in the *Moseley* case. Some scholars argued that this decision failed to discuss 'how to prove "actual" dilution'.[237] Others argued that during the hearings of the FTDA, 'Congress was concerned with the severe implications that might result if dilution occurred and was allowed to continue', which contradicts the rigid rule of the court.[238] Consequently,

---

[234] ibid.

[235] ibid.

[236] A Walker 'The Burden of Actual Dilution: In the Wake of *Moseley v. Victoria Secret Catalogue*' (2003) Volume 8 Number 2 Intellectual Property L Bulletin 25.

[237] DM Cendali CM Matorin and J Maltby 'Moseley v. V Secret Catalogue, Inc.: One Answer, Many Questions' (2003) 93 Trademark Reporter 836. See also, AE Pulliam 'Raising the Bar Too High: *Moseley V. V Secret Catalogue, Inc.* and Relief under the Federal Trademark Dilution Act' (2004) 53 Catholic U L Rev 902. See also, JR Higgins and SA Duvall 'The FTDA after Moseley v. V Secret' (2003) 93 Trademark Reporter 818. See also, T Rangel 'What's the Secret? – Proving Actual Harm in Trademark Dilution' (2005-2006) 47 South Texas L Rev 145.

[238] Pulliam (n237) 904.

'[i]n the wake of *Moseley*, Congress has begun to consider amending the FTDA,'[239] which opened the way for the introduction of the Trademark Dilution Revision Act of 2005.

- 2006: Introduction of "Trademark Dilution Revision Act"

The Trademark Dilution Revision Act of 2005 (TDRA) became effective on 2006. Dilution proponents argue that the TDRA provides clarity to the FTDA, and is 'a sensible and progressive reform of American federal antidilution protection',[240] forming 'an appropriate solution to the interpretive difficulties plaguing the courts.'[241] The effects of the TDRA are manifold. On the one hand, the TDRA expanded the scope of dilution, while on the other, it required a high standard for marks eligible for dilution protection. This strict standard of fame could form an effective tool to limit the scope of dilution actions.

Dilution extended

The TRDA has expanded the rights of trademark owners to limits that were never previously available. It may be argued that the current exposition of the TRDA provides large businesses with extremely wide rights. Indeed, the TDRA 'greatly favors big businesses',[242] to the detriment of small businesses and the consuming public.[243] As Bone argues, the expansion of dilution by the TDRA 'risks creating high social costs without corresponding benefits.'[244]

Unlike the Supreme Court's decision to interpret the FTDA as requiring the plaintiff to prove actual harm,[245] the TDRA reversed the

---

239 Walker (n236) 26.

240 B Beebe 'A Defence of the New Federal Trademark Antidilution Law' (2006) 16 Fordham Intellectual Property Media & Entertainment L J 1144.

241 K Goodberlet 'The Trademark Dilution Revision Act of 2006: Prospective Changes to Dilution Definition, Claim Analyses, and Standard of Harm' (2006) 6 J of High Tech L 279.

242 CR Kinkade 'Is Trademark Dilution Law Diluting Rights? A Survey of the Trademark Dilution Revision Act of 2006' (2007) 31 Seton Hall Legislative J 437.

243 ibid 457.

244 RG Bone 'A Skeptical view of the Trademark Dilution Revision Act' (2007) 11 Intellectual Property L Bulletin 198.

245 See *supra* pp 130-132.

decision in the *Moseley* case, requiring merely the likelihood of harm to prevail in a dilution claim.[246] It provides that:

> '... the owner of a famous mark ... shall be entitled to an injunction against another person who ... commences use of a mark or trade name in commerce that is *likely* to cause dilution by blurring or dilution by tarnishment of the famous mark ...' (emphasis added).[247]

The House Report, accompanying the TDRA, provides that '[t]he Mosely standard creates an undue burden for trademark holders who contest diluting uses',[248] hence 'in response to the Mosely decision, actual harm is not a prerequisite to injunctive relief.'[249]

The importance of this lower standard is that it simplifies the burden of proof for trademark owners, 'particularly with dilution by blurring, [because] proving actual dilution is far more difficult than establishing that it is likely.'[250] It is, therefore, easier for owners of famous mark to protect the exclusivity of their marks under the new TDRA standards. However, this is not the only tool of expansion of dilution, the TDRA

> 'explicitly provides that both "dilution by blurring" and "dilution by tarnishment" are forms of dilution actionable under Section 43(c) and formulates definitions of "dilution by blurring" and "dilution by tarnishment."'[251]

The TDRA defines tarnishment as the 'association arising from the similarity between a mark or trade name and a famous mark that harms the reputation of the famous mark.'[252] In regards to its recent decision, the Supreme Court relied on such grounds (tarnishment) in favour of the plaintiff in the *Moseley* case,[253] although the court was previously

---

[246] SA Duvall 'The Trademark Dilution Revision Act of 2006: Balanced Protection for Famous Brands' (2007) 97 Trademark Reporter 1258.

[247] Trademark Dilution Revision Act 2005 (USA) § 2 – Trademarks Act 1946-Lanham Act (USA) 15 U.S.C. § 1125 (Section 43(c) (1)).

[248] House Rep No 109-23 (2005 U.S.C.C.A.N. 1091) 5.

[249] ibid 8.

[250] JF Beerline 'Anti-Dilution Law, New and Improved: The Trademark Dilution Revision Act of 2006' (2008) 23 Berkeley Technology L J 521.

[251] Beebe (n240) 1156.

[252] Trademark Dilution Revision Act 2005 (USA) § 2 – Trademarks Act 1946-Lanham Act (USA) 15 U.S.C. § 1125 (Section 43(c) (2) (c)).

[253] The *Moseley* case returned to the Supreme Court after the enactment of the TDRA. See- *V Secret Catalogues Inc v Victor Moseley* 558 F.Supp.2d 734 (2008).

speculative as to whether tarnishment was embodied within the FTDA.[254] Clearly, this also contributes to the expansion of rights in favour of trademark owners,[255] although proponents of dilution argue that 'many past cases involving tarnishment claims would not be actionable under the TDRA'.[256] However, the *Moseley* case leads to the contrary.

Standard of fame

It is claimed that the expansion of trademark owners' rights deriving from the inclusion of tarnishment, and the associated lower burden of proof, is balanced by the introduction of a new standard of fame. Prior to the TDRA, fame in niche[257] markets was sufficient to satisfy the requirement of fame under the FTDA, i.e. fame amongst prospective consumers in the relevant trade. This has been shown in *Times Mirror Magazines Inc v Las Vegas Sports News LLC*[258] for example, where the court held that the appellant's mark "The Sporting News" 'was famous in its *niche* and therefore entitled to protection under the FTDA' (emphasis added).[259] However, the TDRA 'denies protection for marks that are

---

[254] *Moseley v* (n226) 432, providing that '[w]hether [tarnishment] is actually embraced by the statutory text, however, is another matter. Indeed, the contrast between the state statutes, which expressly refer to both "injury to business reputation" and to "dilution of the distinctive quality of a trade name or trademark," and the federal statute which refers only to the latter, arguably supports a *narrower* reading of the FTDA.' (emphasis added).

[255] PA Levy 'The Trademark Dilution Revision Act – A Consumer Perspective' (2006) 16 Fordham Intellectual Property, Media & Entertainment L J 1197, arguing that 'tarnishment cases tend to involve commentary on the trademark holder- sometimes nasty commentary, but commentary nonetheless.'

[256] SL Burstein 'Dilution by Tarnishment: The New Cause of Action' (2008) 98 Trademark Reporter 1224.

[257] The term "niche fame" is used 'to describe marks that enjoy a high level of recognition that is confined to a certain segment of the public, a smaller geographic area, a particular industry or a limited group of specialized purchasers or users.' See- MHH Luepke 'Taking Unfair Advantage or Diluting a Famous Mark – A 20/20 Perspective on the Blurred Differences Between U.S. and E.U. Dilution Law' (2008) 98 Trademark Reporter 797.

[258] 212 F.3d 157 (2000).

[259] ibid 165.

famous only in "niche" markets',[260] which was the standard under the FTDA.

The TDRA considers that 'a mark is famous if it is widely recognized by the *general consuming public of the United States* as a designation of source of the goods or services of the mark's owner' (emphasis added).[261] However, the Act 'does not make it clear precisely who is included in the general consuming public of the United States.'[262] It states that courts may consider all relevant factors in determining whether the mark is famous or not, and for this purpose, the TDRA provides a number of non-exhaustive factors which the court *may* take into consideration in this process.[263] Today,

> 'the mark must be famous across the entire public (precluding niche product-market fame) and across the entire United States (precluding fame in a particular geographical locality).'[264]

As such, the TDRA 'require[s] nationwide fame, not simply regional recognition.'[265] This is not an easy requirement, especially given the wide geographical area, and the level of population in the US. On its face, it could be argued that this change in the standard of fame is extremely important, in terms of its ability to limit the scope of marks capable of fulfilling the requirement of fame. However, it will now be discussed

---

[260] House Rep No 109-23 (2005 U.S.C.C.A.N. 1091) 8. See also, ML Delflache S Silbert and C Hillson 'Life After Moseley: The Trademark Dilution Revision Act' (2007) 16 Texas Intellectual Property L J 142-143.

[261] Trademark Dilution Revision Act 2005 (USA) § 2 – Trademarks Act 1946-Lanham Act (USA) 15 U.S.C. § 1125 (Section 43(c) (2) (a)).

[262] SS Diamond 'Trademark Dilution: of Fame, Blurring, and Sealing Wax, with a Touch of Judicial Wisdom' (2007-2008) 24 Santa Clara Computer & High Technology L J 528, arguing that 'all people living in the United States are presumably included in the general consuming public, with the arguable exception of those in jails, prisons, and nursing homes who, although they consume goods, are not in a position to make any of their own purchasing decisions.' See also, J Jacoby 'Considering the Who, What, When, Where and How of Measuring Dilution' (2007-2008) 24 Santa Clara Computer & High Technology L J 602-606.

[263] Trademark Dilution Revision Act 2005 (USA) § 2 – Trademarks Act 1946-Lanham Act (USA) 15 U.S.C. § 1125 (Section 43(c) (2) (a)).

[264] IS Fhima 'The Fame Standard for Trademark Dilution in the United States and European Union Compared' (2008) 17 Transnational L and Contemporary Problems 644.

[265] Beerline (n250) 525. See also, Beebe (n240) 1157, arguing that 'the use of the language "widely recognized" and "general consuming public of the United States" repudiates outright the strange doctrine of "niche fame."'

whether the new standard of fame is helpful in terms of narrowing down the boundaries of dilution.

Effects of the TDRA

Two main issues should be discussed in assessing the effect of TDRA. Firstly, it is important to consider the treatment by courts of the new standard of fame; the TDRA has been effective for more than two years now. Following this, it may be seen as beneficial to look at the role of state anti-dilution statutes in the light of the TDRA.

In terms of the courts' treatment of the new standard of famous marks, it seems that this has been treated inconsistently. Although the new fame requirement was regarded by some courts,[266] it is clear from a number of courts' decisions that this requirement was not fully considered. For example, in *Diane Von Furstenberg Studio v Catherine Snyder and Richard Snyder*,[267] the court ruled in favour of the plaintiff[268] without any assessment of the fame of its mark.[269] Another example is that of *Pet Silk Inc v Maria Jackson*.[270] In this case, the court referred to the requirement that the plaintiff's mark should be famous. The court, however, concluded that the plaintiff's mark was famous. In the absence of significant clarification, the court relied on the fact that the defendants did 'not contest[] the characterization of the Pet Silk mark as famous',[271] and that a review of the conditions of fame under the TDRA 'demonstrates that th[is] characterization is valid.'[272] Beebe considers that such decisions show that 'the TDRA's newly heightened standard for fame has failed to limit the subject matter of federal antidilution protection only to truly deserving marks.'[273] Indeed, 'in some cases it is hard to see how the court came to the conclusion that the plaintiff's mark was famous, at least under the criterion of the TDRA.'[274]

---

[266] *Nike Inc v Nikepal International Inc* 2007 WL 2688499 (E.D.Cal.). See also, *Pepsico Inc v #1 Wholesale LLC* 2007 WL 2142294 (N.D.Ga.).
[267] 2007 WL 2688184 (E.D.Va.).
[268] ibid 4.
[269] ibid 7.
[270] 481 F.Supp.2d 824 (2007).
[271] ibid 830.
[272] ibid.
[273] B Beebe 'The Continuing Debacle of U.S. Antidilution Law: Evidence from the First Year of Trademark Dilution Revision Act Case Law' (2007-2008) 24 Santa Clara Computer & High Technology L J 466.
[274] Diamond (n262) 529.

It could thus be argued that the alleged reform by the TDRA was not successful. Port argues that although 'Congress did eliminate regional fame with the Trademark Dilution Revision Act of 2006, but this tension [between regional and nationwide fame] has not gone away.'[275] This conclusion is also supported by a statement of the court in the *Pet Silk Inc* case that '[t]he Texas anti-dilution statute explicitly requires only distinctiveness, not fame.'[276] This is extremely important, in that it brings the significance of the state anti-dilution statutes to the surface again.[277] 'Thus, a questionable level of fame is one situation in which there may be an advantage to suing only under state law.'[278] As such, if one would assume, for the sake of argument, that the TDRA's requirement of fame is strictly applied, it seems that state anti-dilution statutes would provide owners of marks with "niche fame" an escape route, where the likelihood of dilution to marks with "niche fame" is sufficient.[279]

Summarizing Remarks

This section has demonstrated that the Economic-Social Planning theory is capable of providing a justification for extra protection of well-known trademarks over dissimilar products, on the grounds of confusion. However, it has been argued that the origins of the dilution concept, in addition to its aims and purposes, contradict the approach of the Economic-Social Planning theory in recognizing all the parties under the trademark formula.[280]

The FTDA was the first successful attempt to introduce dilution at a federal level. Although it provides wide protection to trademark owners, it was followed by the TDRA, which provides the utmost protection to owners. It prohibits any association between the famous mark and other similar marks, which shall blur its distinctiveness. It also prevents any use

---

[275] KL Port 'Judging Dilution in the United States and Japan' (2008) 17 Transnational Law and Contemporary Problems 676.

[276] *Pet Silk Inc* (n270) 830.

[277] Especially that approximately more than 37 States have enacted state anti-dilution statutes.

[278] C Chicoine and J Visintine 'The Role of State Trademark Dilution Statutes in the Light of the Trademark Dilution Revision Act of 2006' (2006) 96 Trademark Reporter 1169. See also, DS Welkowitz 'State of the State: Is There a Future for State Dilution Laws?' (2007-2008) 24 Santa Clara Computer & High Technology L J 697.

[279] Chicoine and Visintine (n278) 1181.

[280] See ch 1 p 11.

which might affect and tarnish the reputation of the famous mark. The current formula of dilution protection does not require a high burden of proof; the mere likelihood of harm is sufficient.[281]

The Economic-Social Planning theory advocates more public access to well-known trademarks, in return for the high degree of association they attribute to such marks. This, in turn, embraces the need to allow other rivals and traders to use similar marks on dissimilar goods and/or services to open the door for the public to decide whether they wish to alter the association of the senior mark. This allows the public to practice their right in the meaning-making of cultural signs. The TDRA introduced exceptions in this regard; this will be the matter of further discussion in chapter six.[282]

A central piece of argument lies in applying the dilution doctrine under the Lanham Act over the principles of the Economic-Social Planning theory, to conclude as to whether this concept fits under this theoretical framework. Apparently, dilution falls far away from the premises of the Economic-Social Planning theory, for a number of reasons.

First, as regards the creation of marks, the dilution concept wrongly supposes that the mark becomes famous because of the owners' efforts, while the Economic-Social Planning theory acknowledges the role of the public in "co-authoring" trademarks and in rendering them famous. Second, as to the scope of rights, the dilution concept aims to maintain the singularity of the famous mark. This requires imposing a monopoly over the use of the mark in favour of the owner. This contradicts the Economic-Social Planning theory rationale of achieving a just and attractive culture, where each is given his/her due. Rather than admitting the public, the owner, and other traders as the parties in trademark formula, dilution undermines the public and other traders' rights by focusing on the owner.

In addition, the application of the Economic-Social Planning theory requires the adoption of the source and origin function as the primary function of trademarks. And if dilution is the lessening of the mark's ability to distinguish the source of the products, then the only way to assess this lessening is to question the party to whom this lessening has occurred. In other words, the abandonment of the confusion test to assess the lessening of the mark's ability to distinguish the source makes dilution immeasurable. Thus, owners' protection should exist when the junior use causes confusion to the public as to the source and origin of the products in question. This is important because it constitutes a practical tool for measuring the infringement. Meanwhile, the requirement of likelihood of

---

[281] CH Farley 'Why we are Confused about the Trademark Dilution Law' (2006) 16 Fordham Intellectual Property Media & Entertainment L J 1184.

[282] See ch 6 pp 208-209.

harm under the dilution concept seems to be a vague speculation, leaving more questions regarding the efficiency of dilution.

All in all, situating dilution within the Economic-Social Planning theory is, indeed, impossible. There is no way of reconciling these two. As such, the dilution concept also fails to accord with the aims and purposes of the Lanham Act. Therefore, there are sound utilitarian grounds in the concept dilution under this Act. This raises the old concerns of the constitutionality of this Act, as was the case with the 1870 Act,[283] and proves the need to rethink its philosophical foundations.

Conclusion

Throughout this chapter, it has been argued that the aims and purposes of the Lanham Act, when it was first founded, were focused on the dual purpose of protecting trademark owners and the consuming public. This was reflected in the original text through the adoption of different aspects; namely was the embodiment of the confusion test as the norm for trademark infringement. However, various attempts to widen the confusion test resulted in the introduction of semi-dilution concepts. Thereafter, the adoption of the FTDA in 1995 and the TDRA amendment of 2006 opened the way to getting the Lanham Act out of its context and far away from its original purposes. As Dinwoodie argues,

> '[d]ilution protection moves trademark law away from its basic purpose of mutual consumer and producer protection, and instead focuses solely on protecting the producer.'[284]

Scholarly arguments defending the dilution concept undermine the confusion concept. This idea seems to lack accuracy for a number of reasons. First, the dilution concept is clearly directed to protecting trademark owners. This is apparently in conflict with the general aims and purposes of the Lanham Act, which give attention to protecting the consuming public side by side to the owner. Second, the monopolistic nature of dilution contradicts the general outline of any trademark system in promoting just and fair competition amongst traders, by preventing other trader's rights of using similar marks over dissimilar products when confusion is not at question. Third, dilution denies the role of the public in "co-authoring" trademarks and therefore denies their right to use

---

[283] See *supra* pp 84-85.

[284] GB Dinwoodie 'The Rational Limits of Trademark Law' in H Hansen (ed) *U.S. Intellectual Property Law and Policy* (1st edn Edward Elgar Cheltenham 2006) 76.

trademark as cultural signs and symbols. Thus, the dilution concept as perceived under the Lanham Act contradicts the Economic-Social Planning theory.

The theoretical approach envisioned and adopted by this book regards the confusion test as the sole manner of assessing the mark's ability to denote the origin and source of goods and/or services.[285] The significance of this test lies in its ability to provide extra protection to owners of well-known trademarks, in that protection extends to cover their uses over dissimilar goods and/or services *if* such uses are likely to confuse the public.

If an effective trademark system based on confusion, which is founded according to a convincing theoretical framework, acknowledging the rights of the owners, other traders and the consuming public, and which makes trademarks effective tools to promote the cultural movement of communities then why do we need the dilution notion at the first place? Indeed, as McCarthy argues:

> 'If a legal system has a test of likelihood of confusion that broadly encompasses confusion over sponsorship, affiliation, or connection, then many of the "deficiencies" cited by proponents of a broad antidilution law disappear. In such a setting, the alleged "need" for a separate system of protection though a dilution theory is much less pressing, and the burden of persuasion on proponents who advocate a broad scope to antidilution laws is much greater.'[286]

Returning to Schechter, Welkowitz argues:

> 'It is unclear ... whether today Schechter would have divined the same need for promoting a doctrine that potentially protects highly distinctive marks from virtually any unauthorized use on other goods and or services.'[287]

[285] See ch 2 pp 57-59. See also, ch 3 p 81.
[286] McCarthy (n162) 720.
[287] *Trademark Dilution Federal, State, and International Law* (n153) 9.

CHAPTER FIVE

THE CURRENT PROTECTION OF TRADEMARKS IN THE UK

Introduction

As has previously been indicated, the proper justification for trademark systems lies in the premises of the Economic-Social Planning theory. This means that trademark systems should be formulated in order to promote the existence of a just and attractive culture, which acknowledges that trademarks are the result of "co-authorship" by the owner and the consuming public. This could be achieved through a system which adopts the source and origin function as the only primary function which could be assessed through the deployment of the confusion rationale. This shall result in acknowledging all the parties in the trademark formula,[1] thereby promoting free and fair competition, and enhancing the cultural movement of societies.

This chapter evaluates the UK Trade Marks Act of 1994 (TMA). This is a particularly good example, because to a large extent, the UK TMA is a reflection, and implementation of Directive 2008/95/EC, which aims to approximate trademark legislations in the countries of the European Community. It also adheres to the minimum standards required by international treaties: in particular, the agreement on Trade-Related Aspects of Intellectual Property Rights (TRIPs). Thus, to a certain extent, this Act seems to reflect a large amount of trademark legislation, whether in Europe[2] or at an international level. This serves as an attractive example when tackling trademark policy in general.

The experience of the UK TMA is different from that of the American experience. Both types of legislation are different in a number of aspects.

---

[1] See ch 1 p 11.

[2] Excluding the trademark system adopted in the Benelux countries, which adopts an expansionist approach to trademark rights, making it similar in its general approach to the US Lanham Act.

The US and Europe in general hold different approaches regarding the policy towards intellectual property rights in general, each trying to protect its interests. For example, Europe has always been keen to expand protection to geographic indications, as it has retained the lion's share in this field, while the US's keenness to protect trademarks is now evident, as concluded from Chapter Four above, being the country to have the highest number of valuable well-known trademarks in the world. As such, studying the UK experience is indicative in order to gain a different view. After all, the US has been successful in ensuring due adherence to its policy in distributing its utilitarian dilution principles at an international level through its negotiating power of the TRIPs agreement, for example. Nevertheless, the approach of many other countries is less radical than that of the US.

The purpose of this chapter is to consider the evaluation of the UK TMA within the boundaries of the proper theoretical approach, developed and adopted by this book, as demonstrated in the Economic-Social Planning theory. It aims to assess whether a certain theoretical approach was deployed in its formulation, and to what extent it complies with the premises of the Economic-Social Planning theory. This shall be of benefit in proving the premises of this book, namely that the philosophical foundations of current trademark systems should be revisited.

In so doing, the starting point will be to introduce the UK TMA and Directive 2008/95/EC; this shall assist in gaining an insight into the theoretical approaches on which they were built. Following this, the nature of rights in trademarks will be discussed. The core of this chapter lies in the section that discusses confusion-based protection and dilution-based protection under the UK TMA and Directive 2008/95/EC, in the light of the European Court of Justice (ECJ) and English case law. It is the purpose of the final section to provide a normative approach, which applies the British experience to the premises of the Economic-Social Planning theory, in order to make appropriate conclusions regarding this piece of legislation. In the conclusion of this chapter, the aim is to prove that the UK TMA is an intuitive example, which proves the need to revisit the philosophical foundations of this Act.

Introduction to the UK TMA and Directive 2008/95/EC

At a European level, efforts to harmonize trademark legislations resulted, in 1988, in the adoption of the First Council Directive 89/104/EEC to approximate the laws of the member states relating to trademarks.[3] This Directive (89/104/EEC) has been repealed by Directive 2008/95/EC.[4] The importance of the Directive in tackling the UK TMA lies in the fact that the Act finds its roots and historical source in this Directive. Thus, an overview of the Directive's rules and the ECJ's decisions shall assist in interpreting how trademarks are protected in the UK. More widely, it will also provide an indirect indication as to the situation of trademark protection within Europe in general.

On the face of it, the Directive refers to the source and origin function in two particular instances. First, the Directive plainly requires that a sign should be able to denote the source and origin of the goods and/or services in order to qualify as a trademark.[5] Second, the eleventh recital of the Directive provides that: '… the function of [a registered trade mark] is *in particular* to guarantee the trade mark as an indication of origin …' (emphasis added).[6] Some scholars argue that the use of the words "*in particular*" denotes the Directive's intention to include cases where confusion is not in question. As Gielen writes:

> 'Note the words "in particular". The Directive had to leave other functions open since it provides for the possibility of wide protection of reputed marks even if no *confusion* arises. Such protection can only be given if one accepts that the trade mark has functions other than being an indicator of origin' (emphasis added).[7]

This conclusion by Gielen cannot in itself be supported because he has a different reference for the functions of trademarks. The reference to the source and origin function "*in particular*" does not result in protecting reputed marks where confusion does not arise. This reference is included because the source and origin function is, indeed, the primary function of

---

[3] First Council Directive 89/104/EEC of 21 December 1988 to approximate the laws of the Member States relating to trade marks, OJ 1989 L40/1, Corrigendum OJ 1989 L159/60.

[4] Directive 2008/95/EC of the European Parliament and of the Council of 22 October 2008 to approximate the laws of the Member States relating to trade marks, OJ L 299, 08/11/2008.

[5] Directive 2008/95/EC art 2, providing that: '[a] trade mark may consist of any signs capable of being represented graphically, particularly words, including personal names, designs, letters, numerals, the shape of goods or of their packaging, *provided* that such signs are capable of distinguishing the goods or services of one undertaking from those of other undertakings.' (emphasis added).

[6] Directive 2008/95/EC.

[7] C Gielen 'Harmonisation of Trade Mark Law in Europe: The First Trade Mark Harmonisation' (1992) 14(8) EIPR 264.

trademarks. The use of the words "*in particular*", however, is to open the gate for other secondary functions; namely the advertising and informative functions,[8] to which confusion is an essential element. This conclusion is supported by the decision of the ECJ in *Canon Kabushiki Kaisha v Metro-Goldwyn-Mayer Inc*,[9] where the court provided that

> 'according to the settled case-law of the court, the *essential function* of the trade mark is to guarantee the identity of the *origin* of the marked product to the consumer or end user by enabling him, without any possibility of *confusion*, to distinguish the product or service from others which have another origin' (emphasis added).[10]

However, some ECJ decisions provided an approach which is contrary to the view of the *Canon* case. For example, in *Arsenal Football Club Plc v Reed*,[11] the court provided that:

> 'The Court has consistently stated that the function of trade marks is not only to indicate the undertaking of origin of the goods or services to which they apply and that the intention is, through identification of origin, to protect the status and reputation of its proprietor and the *quality* of his creations' (emphasis added).[12]

The implications of these roots of the source and origin function of trademarks under the Directive are sound, within the UK TMA. The Act provides a modern approach to the notion of the source function, according to its modern standard, in that it does not require the mark to denote the physical source of the products. It stipulates that:

---

[8] (C-337/95) *Parfums Christian Dior v Evora* [1997] ECR I-6013, the ECJ provided protection to the advertising function of trademarks. See also, W Cornish and D Llewelyn *Intellectual Property: Patents, Copyright, Trade Marks and Allied Rights* (6th edn Sweet & Maxwell London 2007) 625 (para 16-30).

[9] (Case C-39/97) [1999] RPC 117.

[10] ibid 133. This statement is important, because it links the confusion concept with the essential function of trademarks, and deploying the confusion test for any infringement which shall affect the mark's ability to denote the source and origin of the products.

[11] (Case C-206/01) [2003] 1 CMLR 12.

[12] ibid 357.

> '[A] "trade mark" means any sign capable of being represented graphically which is capable of distinguishing goods or services of one undertaking from those of other undertakings.'[13]

Questions remain as to which theoretical basis the UK TMA was based upon. Indeed, does it provide any explicit indication as to its theoretical foundations?

The legislative history of the UK TMA provides little indication regarding the theoretical grounds on which it was formulated. However, a thorough look at the discussions of the UK TMA at the House of Lords and the House of Commons shows the desire to formulate the Act in a manner which complies with the Council Directive.[14] In introducing the Bill at the House of Lords, Lord Strathclyde[15] observed that 'the rights conferred by registration of a trade mark will be broadened.'[16] Similarly, in the House of Commons, it was provided that 'the Bill make[s] it easier for industry and commerce to register their trade marks and will provide owners of registered trade marks with wider infringement rights.'[17] Mr McLoughlin[18] remarked that: 'The Government believe that it reflects industry's needs for a law that *maximises* the protection given to owners of registered trade marks' (emphasis added).[19]

This shows the adherence to the current trend favouring trademark owners, and bases protection on their interests and needs. Nonetheless, some members of the Parliament were concerned about the consumers' interests. For instance, in the House of Commons, Mr Bruce emphasized that 'the suggestion that branding requires the additional protection of law

---

[13] Trade Marks Act 1994 (UK) c 26 s 1(1). The 1938 Act recognized the origin function, it defines a trademark as 'a mark used or proposed to be used in relation to goods for the purpose of *indicating … a connection* in the course of trade between the goods and some person having the right either as proprietor or as registered user to use the mark, *whether with or without any indication of the identity of that person …*' (emphasis added). See- Trade Marks Act 1938 (UK) 1 & 2 Geo 6 c 22 s 68(1).

[14] Lord Strathclyde –the Parliamentary Under-Secretary of State, Department of Trade and Industry– stated that: '[O]ur aim must be to use the wording of the directive whenever possible in the bill …, also to ensure that the interests of UK *owners* of trade marks are not put at risk' (emphasis added). See- *Hansard* HL Deb Vol 552 Col 731 (24 February 1994).

[15] The Parliamentary Under-Secretary of State, Department of Trade and Industry.

[16] *Hansard* HL Deb Vol 550 Col 750 (6 December 1993).

[17] *Hansard* HC Deb Vol 241 Col 658 (18 April 1994).

[18] The Parliamentary Under-Secretary of State for Technology.

[19] *Hansard* HC Deb Vol 241 Cols 658-659 (18 April 1994).

is contrary to the consumer's interest.'[20] During discussions of the Bill at the Public Bill Committee, Lord Peston expressed his concerns regarding the rights of the public in trademarks. He said: '[T]he ability to use words in the English language in contexts other than the specific trade mark context … should not be limited.'[21] The Minister, however, replied that the Lord's suggestion 'is a difficult one to accommodate.'[22]

As such, the legislative history does not provide any clear aims and purposes, as in the case of the Lanham Act.[23] It merely shows the desire to comply with the Directive, with more emphasis on owners' rights. As Pickering puts it:

> 'The problem which confronts us is that there is currently no expressly articulated policy guiding English trade mark law[,] … there seems to exist a blind acceptance of the obligations imposed by the EC Directive and of the belief that trade mark protection must somehow be necessary.'[24]

This view is supported by the preamble of the UK TMA, which provides that it is

> '[a]n Act to make new provision for registered trade marks, implementing Council Directive No. 89/104/EEC of 21st December 1988 to approximate the laws of the member states relating to trade marks …'.[25]

Some scholars even proclaim that the introduction of this Act heralds a shift towards more protection to owners, an argument which implies utilitarian and economic roots. Davis argues:

> 'Before the introduction of the 1994 Trade Marks Act, the prevailing assumption among both the judiciary and law-makers in the United Kingdom was that the protection of a public interest, as opposed to the interests of proprietors, was central to any system of trade mark registration.'[26]

---

[20] ibid Col 665 (18 April 1994). See also, the statement of Mr Griffiths, *Hansard* HC Deb Vol 241 Cols 663-665 (18 April 1994).
[21] Public Bill Committee on Trade Marks Bill HL (1994) 3 LA8/3 Job 1-5 Col 25.
[22] ibid.
[23] See ch 4 pp 85-89.
[24] CDG Pickering *Trade Marks in Theory and Practice* (1st edn Hart Publishing Oxford 1998) 96.
[25] Trade Marks Act 1994 (UK) c 26 Preamble.
[26] J Davis 'To Protect or Serve? European Trade Mark Law and the Decline of the Public Interest' (2003) 25(4) EIPR 180.

At the outset, one may argue that the Directive, as the source of the Act, is the result of negotiations, and as such, its formation was the result of compromise between conflicting views towards the appropriate theoretical approach.[27] This resulted in a mixing of the foundations of the Directive, because it was not based on a solid theoretical basis. However, we shall explore and identify the identity of the TMA and the Directive in the remainder of this chapter. Europe in general has traditionally deployed a more moderate and balanced approach towards intellectual property rights protection, but ultimately it was not beyond the expansionist implications of the Americans. After this introduction to the UK TMA, the nature of rights conferred to owners as a result of trademark registration shall be explored.

The Nature of Property Rights in Trademarks

The UK TMA looks at the nature of rights in trademarks in an excessively rigid manner. It provides that '[a] registered trade mark is a *property right* obtained by the registration of the trade mark under this Act ...' (emphasis added),[28] and that '... equities in respect of a registered trade mark may be enforced in like manner as in respect of other personal or moveable property.'[29]

The view of trademarks as the registrants' property rights is, indeed, a radical one. Even Schechter, the founder of the concept of dilution, avoided giving property rights in trademarks. Although some scholars argue that '[t]he concept of a nearly absolute property right for ... marks is

---

[27] *Hansard* HC Deb Vol 241 Col 659 (18 April 1994).

[28] Trade Marks Act 1994 (UK) c 26 s 2(1). It is noteworthy that the 1938 avoided describing trademarks as property rights, however, it considered that '... the registration ... of a person ... as proprietor of a trade mark ... in respect of any goods shall, if valid, give or be deemed to have given to that person the exclusive right to the use of the trade mark in relation to those goods ...' See- Trade Marks Act 1938 (UK) 1 & 2 Geo 6 c 22 s 4(1).

[29] Trade Marks Act 1994 (UK) c 26 s 26(2). It is noteworthy that Directive 2008/95/EC was silent as regards the nature of rights in trademarks and whether they constitute property rights. However, Council Regulation (EC) No 207/2009 regarded trademarks as 'objects of property'. See- Council Regulation (EC) No 207/2009 of 26 February 2009 on the Community trade mark, OJ L 78, 24/03/2009, Section 4, in particular art 16(1), and the eleventh recital of Council Regulation 207/2009.

generally attributed to … Schechter',[30] Schechter's own words lead to the contrary. He argued that:

> 'Nothing is to be gained, in determining the nature of a trade-mark and the basis of its protection by describing the trade-mark as "property". The real heart of the matter seems to be that a trade-mark, both as a symbol and as a creative agency of its owner's good will, depends for its value upon its hold upon the public mind'.[31]

It is significant that the reason for Schechter's avoidance in considering trademarks as property lies in the fact that trademarks are, in essence, the "hold upon the public mind". This indirectly implies an adherence to the role of the public in trademarks, but which is obviously not credited, according to Schechter's exposition.

However, if Schechter, who is, at least in the US, considered as the intellectual source of the current expansion of trademark rights, avoided the argument regarding the nature of rights in trademark, it seems essential to look at the grounds of such rights under the UK TMA. The approach of the UK TMA should be discussed in two ways. It should be assessed within the historical outline, in the light of the passing off effects at first, and then the theoretical basis of such an argument should be examined.

Passing Off Effects

Some scholars argue that:

> 'Trademark law was not intended to protect consumers, but rather to protect producers from fraudulent diversion of their customers by competitors who passed off their goods.'[32]

Passing off protection for trademarks aims to protect the owners and the public, and recognizes the function of trademarks as source and origin identifiers. However, it shall be argued that although passing off protection

---

[30] J Abdel-khalik 'To Live in in-"Fame"-Y: Reconceiving Scandalous Marks as Analogous to Famous Marks' (2007) 25 Cardozo Arts & Entertainment L J 215.

[31] FI Schechter 'Fog and Fiction in Trade-Mark protection' (1936) 36 Columbia L Rev 65. See also, T Martino *Trademark Dilution* (1st edn Clarendon Press Oxford 1996) 79, (Citing FI Schechter *The Historical Foundations of the Law Relating to Trade-Marks* (1925 Unpublished) 156). It should also be noted that the Directive 2008/95/EC is silent as to the nature of rights in trademarks.

[32] MP McKenna 'The Normative Foundations of Trademark Law' (2006-2007) 82 Notre Dame L Rev 1869.

was directed towards protecting owners and consumers, its protection began to be oriented towards expanding owners' rights. This could have an effect on the UK TMA's view of trademarks as property rights.

In *Reckitt & Colman Products Ltd v Borden Inc*,[33] the House of Lords referred to the source and origin function by stating that 'no man may pass off his goods as those of another.'[34] It has also held that to prevail in a passing off case,

> 'there [should be] a goodwill or reputation attached to the goods or services which [the owner] supplied in the *mind* of the purchasing public by *association* with their identifying get-up, [and] that there was a misrepresentation to the public likely to lead the public to believe the goods or services offered by him were the goods or services of the plaintiff' (emphasis added).[35]

This decision is clearly in keeping with the premises of the Economic-Social Planning theory in its recognition of the source and origin function.[36] It also regards the role of the public in creating of trademarks, which is derived through the association they attribute to the mark with the goods and/or services. Therefore, the traditional approach of passing off was the protection of owners' goodwill, through the prevention of diversion of trade, which should be assessed through a confusion test. However, the expansionist trend aims to undermine this confusion rationale. For example, McKenna comments that

> '[c]onsumer confusion was relevant to the traditional determination of infringement not for its own sake, but because deceiving consumers was a particularly effective way of stealing a competitor's trade.'[37]

Regardless of the merits of this argument, the ultimate conclusion is that consumer confusion as to source and origin forms an important part of passing off. It shall also be argued that, in applying the premises of the Economic-Social Planning theory, the goodwill which is at the core of the passing off protection retains a high role by the consuming public. As such, passing off should be directed towards protecting the public and

[33] [1990] RPC 341 (HL). Also known as the "Jif Lemon" case.
[34] ibid 342.
[35] ibid.
[36] ibid, providing that: 'It was irrelevant whether or not the public was aware of the plaintiff's identity as the manufacturer or supplier of the goods in question, as long as they were identified with a particular source'.
[37] McKenna (n32) 1848.

owners as the parties of the trademark formula.[38] This precludes the adoption of the dilution doctrine, based on the quality and incentive arguments upon which this doctrine is based. In support of this argument, Dawson argues that a number of

> 'aspects of the historical development of the action for passing off have mitigated against the emergence of an action for trade mark dilution as such within the confines of passing off[, mainly because of] the rejection of any notion of protectable property in a trademark itself'.[39]

However, there was a shift in the English courts towards the dilution concept within the scope of passing off, even before the enactment of the UK TMA in 1994. In *Taittinger SA v Allbev Ltd*,[40] the plaintiffs challenged the defendants' use of the word "Champagne" on their Elderflower soft drink on the basis of passing off. The Court of Appeal considered that 'it [is not] realistic to suppose that there is any likelihood of confusion as between the parties' businesses.'[41] On the contrary, the Court of Appeal expanded the scope of passing off cases by the adoption of dilution.[42] It observed that there is a further type of damage, that is,

> 'if the defendants continue to market their product then there will take place a blurring or erosion of the uniqueness that now attends the word "champagne," so that the exclusive reputation of the Champagne Houses will be debased.'[43]

This shift in passing off cases, from protecting the owners and the public from confusion to protecting owners solely on dilution-based propositions, is indicative. It shows the dominance of the dilution concept in the field of trademarks, because this concept aims to maximize the

---

[38] See ch 1 p 11.
[39] N Dawson 'Famous and Well-Known Trade Marks – "Usurping a Corner of the Giant's Robe" ' (1998) 4 Intellectual Property Q 365.
[40] [1993] FSR 641 (CA).
[41] ibid 655.
[42] H Carty 'Dilution and Passing off: Cause for Concern' (1996) 112 L Q Rev 638-639. See also, H Carty 'The Common Law and the Quest for the IP Effect' (2007) 3 Intellectual Property Q 246-247, arguing that '[d]ecisions throughout the twentieth and into the twenty-first century have reflected the protean nature of the tort with their recognition of extended passing off … [through] dilution'. See also, *Intellectual Property: Patents, Copyright, Trade Marks and Allied Rights* (n8) 656 (para 17-38).
[43] *Taittinger SA* (n40) 655.

protection in favour of trademark owners. As such, it seems that the granting of property rights *solely* to trademark owners is a rational conclusion. This is because this shift in passing off cases towards dilution presupposes a link between dilution and goodwill.

However, this approach could be overcome through the deployment of the Economic-Social Planning theory. It could be argued that the goodwill retained in the mark is "authored" in the same manner by which the mark itself is "authored". The consuming public may attribute this association between the owner and the mark through the goodwill, i.e. the goodwill is one way of manifesting the association of the public. 'Good will is [thus] an identification created by the public.'[44] As such, property rights should be conferred equally to both owner and public.

All in all, in determining the nature of rights in trademarks, one cannot rely upon an argument based on the rights in the goodwill as a basis for property rights, because this goodwill is "co-authored" between the owner and the public. Thus, if property rights are to be granted, then such rights should be the "co-property" in equal measure for both the owner and the consuming public. Hence, it seems essential to look at the theoretical justification of property in order to conclude whether this granting of property rights is legitimized or not.

Theoretical Considerations

The view that registration confers property rights to trademark owners should be assessed within theoretical boundaries. After all, granting property rights of this nature to trademark owners requires justification for their existence,[45] because 'whenever property rights are permitted at all, their accumulation in one hand is a potential result.'[46] This raises fears from turning trademarks into tools of monopoly, because 'the continual treatment of trademarks as property has led to serious concerns regarding the scope of rights granted to "owners." '[47]

---

[44] S Wilf 'Who Authors Trademarks?' (1999) 17 Cardozo Arts & Entertainment L J 12.

[45] J Waldron 'What is Private Property?' (1985) 5 Oxford J of Legal Studies 349, Waldron argues that the 'philosoph[ical] argu[ment] about the justifiability of private property … [focuses on] whether there are good reasons, on grounds of individual liberty, utility, equality, or other values for preferring [such] property systems …'.

[46] A Rahmatian 'Copyright and Commodification' (2005) 27 (10) EIPR 374.

[47] CJ Doellinger 'A New Theory of Trademarks' (2007) 111 Penn State L Rev 845.

The first consideration from which property should be tackled is the source of the entitlement of the right itself, which is the registration process. This book suggests that registration should not be sufficient to claim property rights in trademarks, because at this stage the consuming public have not yet attributed any association to the mark. The nature of trademarks rejects the sole ownership thereof by owners; they are different from the case of tangible property. For instance, if one buys a house in a street,[48] owners of other houses in the same street are not entitled to snatch away this house if the house owner does not use it for a certain period of time, five years for instance.[49] Similarly, no one is entitled to the concurrent use of a house with its owner.[50] A house is either the owner's property or it is not, unless he/she buys the property with others, and this clearly contradicts the case of trademarks. Therefore, the nature of trademarks *ab initio* rejects the sole proprietary nature, and conferring property rights to trademark registrants contradicts the inclusion of doctrines such as "cancellation for non-use" and "honest concurrent use".

Using the Lockean, Hegelian or utilitarian arguments to legitimize the granting of property rights is not of much assistance. As has been argued above, the mark itself and the goodwill pertaining in the mark are the "co-authorship" of the owner and the public. Contrary to this view, the above-mentioned theoretical approaches are individualistic in their approach.[51] Therefore, the nature of such theories, in addition to the insufficiencies already discussed,[52] fails to provide a helpful justification as to the property nature of trademarks. This individual nature of such theories should be taken in the light of the effects of the grant of property rights.

---

[48] This scenario is influenced by an example provided by Raz, who argues that buying all the houses in a certain street does not entail the owner of the houses to own the street itself. See- J Raz 'On the Nature of Rights' (1984) 93 Mind 197-198.

[49] As is the case in trademarks, see- Trade Marks Act 1994 (UK) c 26 s 6A. Implementing Directive 2008/95/EC art 10.

[50] Trade Marks Act 1994 (UK) c 26 s 7. The doctrine of "honest concurrent use" is directed to overcome any confusion which might arise from the use of the marks by two users, by restricting any preventing any overlap in the use of the mark. It also recognizes the rights of other traders, which fulfils the goal of the Economic-Social Planning theory in promoting a fair and free competition.

[51] J Waldron 'When Justice Replaces Affection: The Need for Rights' (1988) 11 Harvard J of L & Public Policy 630, Waldron argues that such 'theories of rights have been attacked for their individualism, for the way they parade the desires and interests of the human individual as the be-all and end-all of politics, at the expense of notions like … shared social good.'

[52] See generally ch 2.

Granting property rights in trademarks, in this sense, leads to an important conclusion: the owner shall enjoy the exclusive right to use, exploit and alienate the mark.[53] This shall exclude the consuming public from using the mark, especially in cultural and expressive contexts, even if this use does not cause any harm to the owner. By totally ignoring the rights of the public in the mark, this individualistic nature of property rights shall constitute a monopoly over marks. It shall also provide the minority of trademark owners with the ability to control the public at large. On these grounds, this book strongly disagrees with the view that the granting of property rights solely to trademark owners could be the best and most effective way to safeguard the integrity of the culture.[54]

Some scholars have adopted the approach that intellectual creations such as trademarks should not be regarded as property rights. For instance, Doellinger argues that '[t]rademarks are not property.'[55] Moreover, Bouchaert in his attempt to answer the title of his article "What is Property?", argues that '[t]he history of the origin of the several kinds of intellectual property' indicates that they could not be regarded as corporeal property rights.[56] Therefore,

> 'conferring property rights in words and symbols has a significant negative impact on the manner in which we are able to express ourselves; and … placing constrains on how we otherwise might communicate our ideas, thoughts, or dreams inevitably constrains our ability to evolve as individuals and as a society.'[57]

---

[53] J Hughes 'The Philosophy of Intellectual Property' (1988-1989) 77 The Georgetown L J 291, Hughes argues that '[i]n the final analysis, intellectual property shares much of the origins and orientation of all forms of property.' See also, RN Klieger 'Trademark Dilution: The Whittling Away of the Rational Basis for Trademark Protection' (1997) 58 U of Pittsburgh L Rev 839, (Citing-Statement of Nils Victor Montan -HR Rep No 104-374 1995 5), providing that '[t]he basic principle is that the trademark owner who … create[d] and maintain[ed] the property, should be the sole determinant of how that property is to be used …".'

[54] T Dougherty 'Group Rights to Cultural Survival: Intellectual Property Rights in Native American Cultural Symbols' (1998) 29 Columbia Human Rights L Rev 400.

[55] Doellinger (n47) 842.

[56] B Bouckaert 'What is Property?' (1990) 13 Harvard J of L & Public Policy 790.

[57] PC Chalk 'The True Value of Trademarks: Influencing who we are and who we Want to be' (2001-2002) 12 J of Contemporary Legal Issues 20.

Clearly, the traditional form of property rights does not fit in with the field of trademarks. In particular, '[a]ccording to article 6 of the EU Directive, the scope of the right is limited so as to preserve its essential function of a trademark, being to act as a guarantee of origin.'[58] Therefore, there exists the need to find a substitute system eligible to clarify the nature of rights in trademarks, in the light of the process of "authoring" trademarks and their main function as source identifiers.

Reference to the Economic-Social Planning theory is, thus, vital. It allocates a system which identifies the process of producing a trademark and the goodwill as the "co-authorship" of both the owner and the consuming public. As such, trademark systems should give the owner and the public the ownership of a certain bundle of rights. This legitimizes the use of the word "owner" in reference to the registrant of the mark, in the same sense that the public own certain rights as well. Therefore, the view that trademarks are the owners' sole property rights should be re-estimated. One scholar argues:

> 'As the property foundations of intellectual property have weakened and become tenuous, the claim that intellectual rights represent merely state-granted monopolies or privileges has gained prominence.'[59]

However, in revisiting the foundations of trademarks, the role of the Economic-Social Planning theory is to provide a justifiable allocation of these entitlements amongst parties in trademark context, and to diminish monopolies in the hands of one party on the expense of other parties. Thus, the solution does not lie in denying the property nature of rights in trademarks; rather the question should focus on the parties eligible for the enjoyment of such rights.

In applying of the moral claims of the Economic-Social Planning theory, the owner of a trademark and the consuming public are the major parties who retain certain rights in the mark. Accordingly, the owner has the right to use the mark, and to prevent other traders from using the mark if such use shall result in confusing the public. The consuming public enjoy the right to be protected from any confusion as to the meaning they attribute to the mark and the goodwill, and, most importantly, they shall enjoy the right to use trademarks in cultural and expressive uses. Moreover, other traders shall also have the right to use identical and/or

---

[58] GI Zekos 'Trademarks and Cyberspace' (2006) 9(5) The J of World Intellectual Property 506.

[59] A Mossoff 'What is Property? Putting the Pieces Back Together' (2003) 45 Arizona L Rev 413.

similar marks if such use shall not result in confusing the public. This is vital, because it might motivate the public to trigger a new association and meaning-making in the mark. This shall, in turn, result in promoting a free and fair environment of competition. As Levine argues:

> '[T]rademark allows the fair use of a mark to be invoked as an affirmative defense because there is a "public interest in allowing competitors to make free use of the English language to describe their goods." '[60]

This picture, as a whole, establishes the proper application of the Economic-Social Planning theory's goal in fostering the creation of a just and attractive culture as the basis for trademark systems.

In conclusion, rights in trademarks take the form of a bundle of rights enjoyed by the "owner", the consuming public, as the "co-authors" of trademarks. Rights in the form of property rights to trademark owners solely lack justifiability and do not form any rational grounds for trademarks, as is, equally, the case for other intellectual creations. It has also been seen that trademarks differ from other types of property in the manner of acquiring rights. Since trademarks are the result of the "co-authorship" of both the owner and the public, a bundle of rights should be granted to both parties. Consequently, the approach of the UK TMA is indeed a rigid one. It has been shown that the dilution concept, based on utilitarian grounds, has led to the adoption of this conception which confers property rights to trademark owners without taking into account the same nature of rights in favour of the public. Nevertheless, in order to completly assess the basis of the UK TMA, the next section discusses the details of protection accorded to trademarks, in the light of Directive 2008/95/EC.

Protection of Trademarks in the UK in the Light of Directive 2008/95/EC

In order to gain a full and clear grasp of the UK TMA, and to support the main theme in this book, which focuses on the shift from protecting both the trademark owner and the public, to the sole protection of owners, it seems vital to explore the registrability of trademarks under the UK system of trademarks. This could have important implications for the form

---

[60] JK Levine 'Contesting the Incontestable: Reforming Trademark's Descriptive Mark Protection Scheme' (2005-2006) 41 Gonzaga L Rev 44. (Citing SD Kane *Trademark Law, A Practitioner's Guide* (4th edn 2004) § 12.2.4)

of protection which this system aims to provide. Following this, the standards of trademark infringement under the UK TMA will be discussed.

Registrability of Trademarks

Tackling the registrability of trademarks under the UK TMA is beneficial; it clarifies and mitigates the rigid approach of this Act in considering trademarks as owners' sole property rights. It also clarifies that the consuming public play a decisive role in the process of registering of trademarks. The UK TMA provides two grounds for the refusal of the registration of marks: absolute grounds of refusal, and relative grounds of refusal. Relative grounds of refusal occur when the registration of the mark conflicts with earlier rights or earlier marks.

In this context, the issue of conflict with earlier rights is of little importance. However, conflict with earlier marks reflects whether the UK TMA is connected with the adoption of the source and origin function as the primary function of trademarks, and whether it considers the confusion concept as the test for assessing whether the registration of a certain mark would affect the ability of the senior mark to denote the source and origin of the products to which they are affixed. It also shows whether the new registration of the junior mark might result in a mark which fulfils the role of marks as source identifiers, in accordance with the requirement of the ability to distinguish, as the definition of trademarks requires.

The importance of article 5 of the UK TMA,[61] which regulates relative grounds of refusal, is that it deploys the confusion test. However, it also opens the gate for a "semi-dilution" concept in its section (3). Although Directive 2008/95/EC did not impose the obligation on member states to adopt this paragraph, the UK TMA did embody this controversial section.[62] This article shall not be discussed in detail, because it is almost identical to section 10 regarding infringement, which will be analysed below.[63]

- Absolute grounds for refusal and the consuming public

It is suggested that despite considering trademarks as owners' property rights, the UK TMA does recognize the rights of the consuming public,

[61] Implementing Directive 2008/95/EC art 4.
[62] See *infra* pp 174-176.
[63] See *infra* pp 176-178.

and in fact takes them into consideration in determining whether the mark is eligible for registration, and thus for protection. Clearly, this regard to the role of the public supports the argument that trademarks are not the sole property rights of trademark owners, since the granting of property rights does not depend upon the state of mind of the consuming public. This is a feature of the granting of property rights, which plainly contradicts the situation of trademarks.

As has already been argued, the UK TMA requires that a sign should be able to distinguish goods and/or services of one undertaking from those of other undertakings, in order to qualify for registration.[64] Therefore, the Act considers that 'signs which do not satisfy th[is] requirement' shall not be registered.[65] The ECJ in *Dyson Ltd v Registrar of Trade Marks*[66] considered that

> 'the conceivable shapes of a transparent bin or collection chamber forming part of the external surface of a vacuum cleaner, is not a "sign" within the meaning of [article 2 of the directive, the equivalent of section 1(1) of the UK TMA] and therefore is not capable of constituting a trade mark within the meaning thereof.'[67]

The court considered that the subject-matter of registration should be a "sign". '[T]he purpose of that requirement is in particular to prevent the abuse of trade mark law in order to obtain an unfair competitive advantage.'[68] This category 'prohibits the registration of "*signs*" which do not satisfy the requirements of [trademarks]'.[69] It embodies two kinds of signs; first, 'those signs which have never been capable of distinguishing the goods of one undertaking from those of other undertakings',[70] and second, 'those which once had the capacity to distinguish but have, through use, ceased to be capable of doing so.'[71]

---

[64] Trade Marks Act 1994 (UK) c 26 s 1(1), in addition to the condition that the sign should be 'capable of being represented graphically'.

[65] ibid s 3(1)(a). This section reflects the Directive which provides that 'signs which cannot constitute a trade mark' shall not be registered. See- Directive 2008/95/EC art 3(1)(a).

[66] (Case C-321/03) [2007] 2 CMLR 14. See also, ch 2 pp 38-40.

[67] *Dyson Ltd* (n66) 331.

[68] ibid 314.

[69] *AD2000 Trade Mark* [1997] RPC 168, 173.

[70] *Bach and Bach Flower Remedies Trade Marks* [2000] RPC 513 (CA) 533.

[71] ibid.

The Act also prohibits the registration of 'trade marks which are *devoid of any distinctive* character' (emphasis added):[72] that is, marks which are not distinctive either through inherent or acquired distinctiveness.[73] Moreover, the Act considers that marks which are *descriptive* as to the 'kind, quality, intended purpose, value, geographic origin, the time of production of goods or of rendering of services, or other characteristics of goods or services,' are not eligible for registration,[74] because such marks should remain in the public domain.[75] On this basis, the application to register the mark "Day by Day" for milk was refused, since it was descriptive of the quality and characteristics of the product, and thus, was considered devoid of distinctiveness.[76] Moreover, the Act prohibits the registration of generic marks 'which consist exclusively of signs or indications which have become customary in the current language or in the *bona fide* and established practices of the trade'.[77]

Such grounds for refusal are significant because 'behind each one of the[m] … there is an underlying public interest.'[78] This derives from their focus on the source and origin function as the primary and essential function, which all marks should satisfy in order to qualify as trademarks in the first place. More importantly, on this basis, if a mark is registrable because it is able to distinguish the products of the undertaking from those of others, then any use of the mark by others should be assessed through

---

[72] Trade Marks Act 1994 (UK) c 26 s 3(1)(b). Implementing Directive 2008/95/EC art 3(1)(b).

[73] See for example, (Case C-299/99) *Koninklijke Philips Electronics NV v Remington Consumer Products Ltd* [2002] ECR I-5475, providing that the three-headed rotary shaver is devoid of any distinctiveness.

[74] Trade Marks Act 1994 (UK) c 26 s 3(1)(c). Implementing Directive 2008/95/EC art 3(1)(c).

[75] See for example, (Case C-191/01) *OHIM v Wm Wrigley Jr Co (Doublemint)* [2003] ECR I-12447, para 31, providing that the aim of prohibiting the registration of descriptive marks is to keep such mark freely used by all, which serves a public interest.

[76] *R. v Besnier S.A.'s Trade Mark Application* [2002] RPC 6, 258. See also, *Linkin Park LLC's Application* [2006] ETMR 74, 1034, (the sign "Linkin Park" was refused by the Registrar. The Applicant appealed the Registrar's decision, however it was held that the mark's registration is precluded because it is describes some characteristics of the goods.)

[77] Trade Marks Act 1994 (UK) c 26 s 3(1)(d). Implementing Directive 2008/95/EC art 3(1)(d). See for example, (Case C-517/99) *Merz & Krell GmbH & Co* [2001] ECR I-6959.

[78] S Maniatis *Trade Marks in Europe: A Practical Jurisprudence* (1st edn Sweet & Maxwell London 2006) 85 (para 4-091).

the confusion as to source and origin, to determine whether such use is legitimate or not. Furthermore, it refers, implicitly, to the role of the public in the "life" of marks, through doctrines such as secondary meaning and genericness.

Genericness

The UK TMA does not allow the continuance of the registration of a trademark if 'it has become the common name in the trade for a product or service for which it is registered',[79] and considers this situation a valid case for the revocation of registration of such a mark.

Trademarks become generic when the consuming public start to associate the mark with the whole class of goods and/or services, rather than associating the mark with the goods and/or services of the undertaking. This could result either from the decision of the public, which is resembled in their consensus in altering the association attributed to the mark, or from some kind of negligence on the part of the owner.[80] The UK TMA only recognizes this last scenario as the only ground for rendering a mark generic, and considers this to be 'in consequence of acts or inactivity of the proprietor'.[81] However, even if the mark becomes generic through the owner's acts, the decisive factor is the decision of the public to alter the association of the mark and ascribe a new meaning to it. The recognition of the role of the public as such contradicts the owners' sole property rights in trademarks. In other forms of property rights, the public do not have the authority, nor the right, to prevent someone from ownership of their house simply because they decide to do so, whereas, in trademarks, the public retain this right because they are the "co-authors" of such rights, according to the Economic-Social Planning theory.

As such, the decisive factor in trademark genericness is that the consuming public are the party who render the mark generic, not the evaluation of traders. Traders could be considered experts in this field to support a claim of a mark being generic, but it is not their acts which transform the mark into a generic word.

---

[79] Trade Marks Act 1994 (UK) c 26 s 46(1)(c). Implementing Directive 2008/95/EC art 12(2)(a).

[80] The owner of a mark could take some actions which would prevent the mark becoming generic. See generally, D Kaufmann 'How to Prevent Your Mark Becoming Generic' (2007) 168 Managing Intellectual Property 125-127.

[81] Trade Marks Act 1994 (UK) c 26 s 46(1)(c). Implementing Directive 2008/95/EC art 12(2)(a).

Secondary meaning

The absolute grounds for refusal of the registration of trademarks, under the UK TMA, clearly focus on the distinctiveness of a mark in order to qualify for registration. This reflects the idea that certain marks, which do not retain any kind of inherent distinctiveness, but which acquire distinctiveness through the association which the public decide to attribute between the mark and the owner's products, have valid grounds for being registered. This is another important aspect which plainly clarifies the role of the public in the creation of marks. According to the Economic-Social Planning theory, the "authoring" of a trademark passes through a two step process; the use of an inherently distinctive sign by the owner, and the second crucial step, which lies in the association which the public attribute between the mark and the products.

However, the secondary meaning doctrine recognizes the ability of the public not only to draw a link between the mark and the products, but also to grant a distinctiveness to the marks which were initially devoid of distinctiveness. That is, the public grant a meaning to the mark as indicator of the source and origin of the products in question. The High Court of Justice provides that: 'A mark which is prima facie descriptive will only be protected if it can be shown to have acquired a secondary meaning: that is to say, if it has become distinctive of the [owner]'.[82]

Significantly, this association, which results in the granting of distinctiveness to descriptive marks, also supports the argument that the goodwill is "co-authored" by the public as well. The Court of Appeal in *Phones 4u Ltd v Phone4u.co.uk. Internet Ltd*[83] concluded that the trademark "Phones 4u", although descriptive, still retained goodwill which resulted from the distinctiveness it acquired.[84] This approach by the court concealed a number of issues. It could be inferred from this decision that the public granted the secondary meaning to the mark as an indicator of source and origin; this secondary meaning provided distinctiveness to the mark, and this in turn resulted in the goodwill of the mark. Thus, goodwill partly results from acts of the public, but it still involves "co-authorship" with the owner, because he/she contributes, through advertising, for instance.

A further important conclusion from this decision is the emphasis on the source and origin function. That is, when a descriptive mark starts to indicate the source of the products due to the public's association, such a

---

[82] *Knight v Beyond Properties Pty Ltd* [2007] FCR 34 (Ch) 819.
[83] [2007] RPC 5 (CA).
[84] ibid 96.

mark acquires distinctiveness, which renders it eligible for protection. This gives considerable prominence to the source and origin function as the only *primary* function of trademarks.

Trademark Infringement in the UK TMA

This section examines more extensively the criterion adopted by the UK TMA as regards the infringement of registered trademarks, and the test deployed to assess such infringement. It shall set out the current state of art under the Act in order to be able to assess whether it complies within the suggested theoretical framework. The first section discusses the scope of rights conferred to trademark owners, and then, confusion-based protection and dilution-based protection will be argued.

- General scope of applicability of section 10 of the UK TMA

Section 9 of the UK TMA sets out the rights conferred to trademark owners. It refers to '[t]he proprietor of a *registered* trade mark' (emphasis added)[85] as the party eligible to protection. Although this discredits the public as a protectable party in the trademark formula,[86] it is a better approach than in other jurisdictions, where non-registered trademarks are protected by the same statutory means of protecting registered marks.[87]

This section provides that the owner of a registered mark shall have 'the exclusive right[] in the trade mark'.[88] Legislative history shows the failure of the attempt to limit such exclusivity; indeed this particular attempt failed to insert the following sentence at the end of section 9(1):

> 'In particular, the proprietor has the exclusive right to use the mark on or in relation to the goods or services for which it is registered in the course of business so as to indicate a commercial connection with such goods or services.'[89]

---

[85] Trade Marks Act 1994 (UK) c 26 s 9(1). Implementing Directive 2008/95/EC art 5(1). The 1938 Act explicitly considers that there is no protection against infringement for unregistered marks. See- Trade Marks Act 1938 (UK) 1 & 2 Geo 6 c 22 s 2. Such protection for unregistered trademarks falls under passing off.
[86] See ch 1 p 11.
[87] Such as the situation in the US under the Lanham Act. See ch 4 pp 125-127.
[88] Trade Marks Act 1994 (UK) c 26 s 9(1). This was the same approach of the 1938 Act. See *supra* pp 147-155.
[89] *Hansard* HL Deb Vol 552 Col 732 (24 February 1994).

Thus, exclusivity of rights in trademarks again raises the fears of the monopolistic nature of marks as the owner's sole property right. This exclusivity supports the individualistic nature of the dilution principle, and precludes the rights of the public and other traders. The Economic-Social Planning theory suggests that trademarks are source and origin identifiers, and that any infringing use should be the use of the mark as source identifier by others, which should in turn result in confusing the public in order to amount to infringement.

Contrary to this approach, this section considers that exclusive rights shall be exercised against the "use" of the mark without the consent of the proprietor.[90] It does not specify what kind of "use" amounts to infringement; this could have opened the scope of infringing uses to high limits, had the subsequent section not referred to the "use in the course of trade".[91] Section 10(4) sets out a list of four non-exhaustive examples of "use";[92] however, this list is open-ended, and allows for unlimited further examples of uses, which would broaden the owners' rights to include many prohibited infringing uses one could imagine. Most importantly, this might also lead to the inclusion of cases of "use" in contexts other than trademarks. Rather, it should have focused on one particular instance: that is, any use of the mark by others as a source and origin identifier, i.e. as a trademark.[93]

- Confusion-based protection

Confusion-based protection of trademarks under the UK TMA includes two scenarios for protection. The first is identical/identical confusion, while the second deals with identical/similar confusion.

Identical/identical confusion

The first type of trademark infringement under the UK TMA is concerned with the use 'in the course of trade [of] a sign which is identical with the trade mark in relation to goods or services which are identical

[90] Trade Marks Act 1994 (UK) c 26 s 9(1).
[91] ibid ss 10(1),(2) and (3).
[92] ibid s 10(4).
[93] Under the 1938 Act, it is noteworthy that to establish infringement it was required that the mark is used as a trademark. See- Trade Marks Act 1938 (UK) 1 & 2 Geo 6 c 22 s 4(1)(a).

with those for which it is registered.'[94] The Act considers such a case to be an infringement of the registered mark in question. It does not require the trademark registrant to prove any kind of confusion.

This type of confusion-based scenario is consistent with the premises of the Economic-Social Planning theory. It presumes the existence of confusion, because the ability of the senior mark to denote the source and origin of the senior user shall be diminished. This shall protect the trademark owner in maintaining his/her mark's ability to denote the source of his/her products, and in turn protects the public from any confusion which they will suffer in this case.

The only likely problem in this case is the interpretation of the word "identical" as regards the phase of marks and the phase of goods or services, i.e. whether the junior mark should mirror the senior mark, or that the products are identical. As regards the identical nature of marks, this should not be left to the discretion of courts to decide on a case by case basis. Courts should, rather, assess whether the junior mark mirrors exactly the senior mark in order for infringement to occur. This is because this section deals with situations where the *exact* identicality between the marks would make confusion inevitable. The strict application of identicality results from the fact that the trademark owner is exempted from proving confusion, and in such a case, there is a need to make sure of the inevitability as to the raising of confusion, in order the ensure that the scope of this section is not widened.

English courts' interpretation of the matter of identicality follows a strict approach. For example, in *Origins Natural Resources Inc v Origin Clothing Ltd*,[95] it was considered that the mark "Origin" was not identical to the mark "Origins". The court provided that they 'are different in that the plaintiff's mark is in the plural whereas the defendants use the word "Origin" alone,'[96] and as such out of the scope of section 10(1) of the UK TMA. Similarly, the ECJ provided that '[t]he criterion of identity of the sign and the trade mark must be interpreted strictly.'[97] Thus, 'a sign is identical with the trade mark where it reproduces, without any

---

[94] Trade Marks Act 1994 (UK) c 26 s 10(1). Implementing Directive 2008/95/EC art 5(1)(a).

[95] [1995] FSR 280 (Ch).

[96] ibid 284. See also, *R. v IDG Communications Ltd's Trade Mark Application* [2002] RPC 10, 287, finding that the mark "Digit" is not identical to the mark "Digits".

[97] (Case C-291/00) *LTJ Diffusion SA v Sadas Vertbaudet SA* [2003] FSR 608 para 50.

modification or addition, all the elements constituting the trade mark'.[98] English courts interpreted this ECJ decision to support their strict approach of identicality.[99]

Regarding the identicality of the goods and/or services, they should also be totally identical. This should be differentiated from the use of the mark. As has already been argued,[100] the Economic-Social Planning theory argues that the only *primary* function of trademarks is the source and origin identification function, and forms the real rational basis for trademark protection. As such, trademarks could provide other *secondary* functions such as: quality, advertising and informative functions. The difference is that the latter functions could not form the basis of trademark protection, and there is no prerequisite that they be available in all trademarks, as opposed to the source and origin function. However, the quality function could not be assessed through confusion; thus, it should not be considered when looking at trademark infringement, and as such, cannot be relied upon by Art 10(1). The case of the other secondary functions is different; such uses are assessable through confusion, and if the mark and products in question are identical, then confusion is presumed even if it was related to these secondary functions. In keeping with this approach, the ECJ in its decision in *Arsenal* case[101] provides that:

> '[W]here a third party uses in the course of trade a sign which is identical to a validly registered trade mark on goods which are identical to those for which it is registered, the trade mark proprietor of the mark is entitled, … to rely on Art.5(1)(a) of th[e] Directive to prevent that use. It is immaterial that, in the context of that use, the sign is perceived as a badge of support for or loyalty or affiliation to the trade mark proprietor.'[102]

Identical/similar confusion

Confusion is the ideal test for assessing trademark infringement.[103] It protects both the public and other traders 'by helping to preserve the integrity of the free market',[104] and in allowing other traders to use the

[98] ibid para 54.
[99] *Intellectual Property: Patents, Copyright, Trade Marks and Allied Rights* (n8) 717 (para 18-53).
[100] See generally ch 3.
[101] *Arsenal Football Club Plc* (n11).
[102] ibid 380-381.
[103] Also to assess the eligibility of trademarks to be registered.
[104] *Trade Marks in Theory and Practice* (n24) 98.

mark or any similar sign where confusion is not likely to occur. This promotes an environment of free and fair competition and removes any possibility of monopolizing rights in trademarks. It must be acknowledged that this form of protection, based on the Economic-Social Planning premises, is the most equitable approach. This should form the modern a substitute for the utilitarian monopolistic approach in denying the rights of the public in trademarks.

The second level of confusion-based protection, under the UK TMA, is provided in Art 10(2). This section includes three types of infringement: identical *v* similar, similar *v* identical, and similar *v* similar. It provides that:

> 'A person infringes a registered trade mark if he uses in the course of trade a sign where because—
> (a) the sign is identical with the trade mark and is used in relation to goods or services *similar* to those for which the trade mark is registered, or
> (b) the sign is *similar* to the trade mark and is used in relation to goods or services identical with or *similar* to those for which the trade mark is registered,
> there exists a *likelihood of confusion* on the part of the public, which includes the *likelihood of association* with the trade mark' (emphasis added).[105]

This section raises questions on two counts; first, as to the test for interpreting similarity, and second, as to interpretation of the likelihood of association. Each of these concerns shall have serious effects on the scope of trademark protection.

(i) Sequential test v global appreciation test

The UK TMA and the Directive provide no guidance as to the interpretation of "similarity" for the purposes of this section. *British Sugar Plc v James Robertson & Sons Ltd*[106] was one of the early case law interpreting and applying this section. The court provided six factors to be taken into consideration when assessing the availability of similarity.[107] The court considered that the sequence of implementation of section 10(2) should start by assessing similarity, before turning to the matter of

---

[105] Trade Marks Act 1994 (UK) c 26 s 10(2). Implementing Directive 2008/95/EC art 5(1)(b).
[106] [1996] RPC 281 (Ch).
[107] ibid 296-297.

confusion. This means that the court should first assess whether the marks and products are similar in the light of its six factors test, before tackling the likelihood of confusion. Accordingly, the court developed the three step test:

> '(1) Is the mark used in the course of trade?
> (2) Are the goods for which it is used similar to those covered by the registration?
> (3) Is there a likelihood of confusion because of that similarity?'[108]

As such, the court did not find that the products were similar, and consequently –without discussing confusion– no infringement arose under this section.[109]

The *British Sugar* case provided a strict approach to the interpretation of "similarity". However, this 'sequential approach'[110] differs from the one adopted by the ECJ. In *Sabel BV v Puma AG*,[111] the ECJ held that:

> '[L]ikelihood of confusion must … be appreciated globally, taking into account all factors relevant to the circumstances of the case. [As such,] … global appreciation of the visual, aural or conceptual similarity of the marks in question, must be based on the overall impression given by the marks, bearing in mind, in particular, their distinctive and dominant components.'[112]

The ECJ's decision in the *Sabel* case contradicts the *British Sugar* case in its result that 'the more distinctive the earlier mark, the greater will be the likelihood of confusion.'[113] This outcome was precisely what the *British Sugar* case aimed to avoid; that is, by not giving extra protection to strong marks under this type of confusion-based protection. Therefore, 'there is a clear message coming through from the ECJ that the three questions set by [the *British Sugar* case] should be elided into a single test

---

[108] ibid 294, the court considered that this sequence is vital in order not to provide more extra protection for strong marks under section 10(2).
[109] ibid 297.
[110] Griffiths provides the term "sequential approach" to the test of the court in *British Sugar* case. See- A Griffiths 'The Impact of the Global Appreciation Approach on the Boundaries of Trade Mark Protection' (2001) 4 Intellectual Property Q 333.
[111] (Case C-251/95) [1998] RPC 199.
[112] ibid 224.
[113] ibid.

of "global appreciation".'[114] Griffiths defends the ECJ's approach,[115] and considers that the sequential approach of the *British Sugar* case

> 'would establish a uniform and narrow scope of protection for all registered trade marks without taking account of the particular circumstances of the first mark, which might in practice have a bearing on the likelihood of confusion.'[116]

Thus, Griffiths considers that '[m]arks are similar if in practice they resemble each other enough to be likely to confuse consumers about trade origin.'[117]

In assessing the appropriate approach in this regard, it seems essential to follow a strict approach. The global appreciation approach aims to widen the scope of this level of protection by overcoming the requirements of similarity and confusion. This test is of no relevance at this level, because at this level of protection, no distinction between ordinary marks and well-known marks is drawn. This is not to say that owners of well-known marks could not use this type of protection, but rather, they should adhere to the requirement of proving similarity and proving the existence of likelihood of confusion. Therefore, the premise of the global appreciation test that the likelihood of confusion embodies the presumption of similarity is not accurate, and if this is the case, then proving similarity would be easy. In addition, the aim of this approach is to overcome the requirement of proving similarity to widen the scope of protection; this is correctly referred to by one scholar as the "similarity-therefore-confusion" concept.[118] In the same context, the ECJ in the *Canon* case provided that:

> '[T]he distinctive character of the earlier trade mark, and in particular its *reputation*, must be taken into account when determining whether the

[114] N Briggs 'Infringement under Section 10(2) and 10(3) of the 1994 Trade Marks Act in Perspective' (2000) 22(9) EIPR 430.
[115] See also, C Howell 'A Loaded Question: On Section 5(3) of the Trade Marks Act 1994' 2002 13(3) Intl Company and Commercial L Rev 120, arguing that '[i]t is wrong to consider the question of similarity separately from confusion.'
[116] Griffiths (n110) 333.
[117] ibid.
[118] NLW Loon 'Time to Re-think the Ever Expanding Concept of Trade Marks? Re-calibrating Singapore's Trade Mark Law after the Controversial US-Singapore FTA' (2008) 30(4) EIPR 153.

similarity between the goods or services covered by the two trade marks is sufficient to give rise to the likelihood of confusion' (emphasis added).[119]

Consequently, the global appreciation approach aims to overcome cases where similarity does not amount to likelihood of confusion, namely in well-known trademarks, because they 'are so well ingrained in the memories of consumers that consumers are able to distinguish them even from very similar signs on similar products.'[120] Therefore, confusion is not likely to occur because of the high degree of recognition that the public attribute to the mark; instead, the use of similar marks would strengthen the association with the well-known marks rather than resulting in a likely confusion. Thus, the ECJ's deployment of the global appreciation approach[121] 'has confirmed that the likelihood of confusion is ... to be seen as a quite broad concept'.[122]

As such, the presumption of global appreciation, namely that all relevant factors such as aural, visual and conceptual elements should be taken into consideration could be reconciled with the strict sequential approach of the *British Sugar* case. One may argue that similarity should first be proved, and thereafter, the likelihood of confusion. Throughout this process, aural, visual and conceptual elements could be deployed to this end. This shall ensure not only the need not to expand the scope of this level of protection beyond its rationale scope and limits, but at the same time to provide a degree of flexibility, which overcomes this hurdle.

(ii) Likelihood of confusion including likelihood of association

Section 10(2) requires that in order for an infringement to occur there should exist 'a likelihood of confusion on the part of the public, which includes the likelihood of association with the trade mark.'[123] There is a wide agreement that this phrase is ambiguous and vague,[124] as the wording

---

[119] *Canon Kabushiki Kaisha* (n9) 134. See also, S Maniatis 'Dilution in Europe?' in HC Hansen (ed) *International Intellectual Property Law & Policy* (Volume 7 Juris Publishing Inc Huntington NY 2001) 43-6.

[120] PL Roncaglia 'Should We Use Guns and Missiles to Protect Famous Trademarks in Europe?' (1998) 88 Trademark Reporter 554.

[121] As in the *Sabel* case.

[122] *Trade Marks in Theory and Practice* (n24) 112.

[123] Trade Marks Act 1994 (UK) c 26 s 10(2).

[124] AK Sanders 'The Wagamama Decision: Back to the Dark Ages of Trade Mark Law' (1996) 18(1) EIPR 3. See also, Griffiths (n110) 341. See also, *Sabel BV* (n111) 221.

of this requirement seems to be confusing as to whether non-origin association could be interpreted as a substitute for confusion as to source and origin. This is a concern because if it could be construed as a substitute for confusion, then the scope of section 10(2) would simplify the owner's burden of proof to an extent which amounts to the grant of full monopolies. As a result of such an interpretation, the rights of the public would be affected because adherence to their confusion is no longer necessary and is not the criterion for trademark infringement. In addition,

> '[a]dopting association as the infringement standard for all trademarks, ... not only would have provided a rigorous criterion upon which to rely but also would make it virtually impossible to avoid trademark infringement.'[125]

This also affects the rights of other traders, because it does not allow them to use the mark if such use shall not cause any confusion, and mental association with the senior mark would constitute trademark infringement, even in the absence of confusion.

According to the premises of the Economic-Social Planning theory, confusion is the central test for trademark infringement. It has been clarified that the only *primary* function is the source and origin function, and confusion is the criteria to be used in this regard. The flexibility of this theory lies in its ability to include other *secondary* functions, one of which is the informative function. This function provides the public with information regarding the sponsorship of the products, and therefore, plays an important role in maintaining the primary function of trademarks in identifying the source and origin. Thus, by applying of the Economic-Social Planning theory any uses by others which shall lead the consuming public to associate the senior mark with a junior mark, and would lead them to believe that a relation of affiliation or sponsorship exists shall be prohibited.[126] Yet this should be assessed through the confusion test. As such, mere association could not be interpreted as a substitute for confusion.

In contrast, the drafting of this section infers that association occurs when consumers, when confronted with the junior mark, would be reminded of the senior mark without the necessity of proving confusion as to source and origin for infringement to occur at this level of protection.

---

[125] Roncaglia (n120) 561.

[126] Torremans makes a similar point, see- PLC Torremans 'The Likelihood of Association of Trade Marks: An Assessment in the Light of the Recent Case Law of the Court of Justice' (1998) 3 Intellectual Property Q 307.

The danger of this scenario is that it provides a dilution principle within the framework of ordinary marks, because if non-origin association is actionable under section 10(2) then owners of ordinary marks could use it as the basis for protecting the exclusivity of their marks, as some scholars argue.[127] It has been argued that this is an evil in the context of well-known marks; thus this argument *a fortiori* includes the case of ordinary marks.

It seems essential to discuss the stand of the ECJ and UK courts in interpreting this ambiguous section. One of the leading cases tackling this issue was *Wagamama Ltd v City Centre Restaurants Plc.*[128] In this case, the plaintiff –the owner of the mark "Wagamama" used for a Japanese food restaurant– challenged the use of the sign "Raja Mama's" by the defendant for an Indian food restaurant. The plaintiff based his case on the grounds for infringement under section 10(2), claiming that such use would create an association between the two marks.[129] The defendant's defense was based on the interpretation of section 10(2) as being the "classic" type of infringement,[130] i.e. requiring confusion as to source and origin. The plaintiff opposed this approach and argued that confusion is no longer a requirement, as the introduction of association enlarged the basis of infringement to cover cases of mere "non-origin association" even when confusion is out of question.[131] The plaintiff contended that

> 'there will now be infringement if, on seeing the defendant's mark, the registered mark would be "called to mind" by a customer even if there is

[127] For example, see- AK Sanders 'Some Frequently Asked Questions about the 1994 UK Trade Marks Act' (1995) 17(2) EIPR 70, providing that 'section 10(2) incorporates both the source and the dilution doctrine and association must therefore be seen in this light.'

[128] [1995] FSR 713 (Ch).

[129] ibid 713-714.

[130] ibid 715.

[131] ibid 714. The plaintiff's argument was based on making a reference to the Directive, and argued that the reason for having this introduction in the UK TMA was in order to implement the Directive, where this was introduced on pressure by the Benelux countries, where likelihood of association is a substitute of confusion. However, the court did not accept this argument. See- ibid 723-724. This is the source of the argument that the Directive, as being the source of the UK TMA, is not of much assistance in defining a clear philosophical foundation as it has been the outcome of negotiations and compromise between member states. See *supra* pp 142-147.

no possibility of the customer being under any misapprehension as to the origin of the goods.'[132]

The court emphasized that the plaintiff's interpretation of association under this section is not valid. Rather, it provided that the rights of the owner under this section are limited to the "classic" type of infringement which includes *association as to origin*. In argument, Laddie J stated that:

> 'If the broader scope were to be adopted, the Directive and our Act would be creating a new type of monopoly not related to the proprietor's trade but in the trade mark itself. .... I can see nothing in the terms of the Directive (or our Act), or in any secondary material which I could legitimately take into account, which would lead me to assume that this was its objective. On the contrary, the preamble to the Directive seems to point in the opposite direction since it states:
> "Whereas the protection afforded by the registered trade mark, the function of which is in particular to guarantee the trade mark as an indication of origin ..." '[133]

Ultimately, the court ruled in favour of the plaintiff, but according to the "classic" confusion infringement.

The court's decision in the *Wagamama* case provided a good interpretation in terms of maintaining the requirement for confusion, which forms a reflection of the Economic-Social Planning theory's view in deploying the confusion concept as the ultimate test for trademark infringement. However, the decision in *Wagamama* was not free from criticism by scholars defending a wide scope of rights of monopolistic nature. For instance, Harris –who was acting for the Plaintiff in *Wagamama*– comments that this decision

> 'calls into question what function a trade mark serves and whether the modernizing legislation of both the Directive and the Trade Marks Act 1994 have really achieved all that was claimed in respect of them.'[134]

Sanders provides a more radical approach, arguing that this decision is 'a Pyrrhic victory for trade mark owners, as it reduces the scope of protection of the 1994 Act to the rigid confinements of the confusion rationale.'[135] He goes so far as to argue that 'the origin-based confusion

---

[132] ibid 721.
[133] ibid 730-731.
[134] P Harris 'UK Trade Mark Law: Are you Confused' (1995) 17(12) EIPR 603.
[135] Sanders (n124) 3.

rationale has not only been widened, but has also been appended by non-origin association, or the dilution doctrine.'[136] Sanders's main argument is based on the premise that if section 10(3) provides dilution protection 'where dissimilar products are concerned, the same must be true for similar products.'[137]

In response to this argument, it is not a matter of consensus that section 10(3) does not require confusion. For instance, Rahmatian argues that under the original version of section 10(3) which was in force until 2004,[138] '[t]here must be likely confusion (including association) as well to constitute an infringement, although this is not expressly stated in the Act.'[139] This is capable of reversing Sanders's argument, as it diminishes the premise on which it was based. Similarly, Prescott criticizes Sanders's argument and cites a number of pitfalls which prevent its validity. First, Prescott argues that:

> '[I]f legislators wish to introduce new monopolies, … incurring whatever degree of public odium as may arise, … they ought to say so sufficiently clearly. [They could have stated:] "confusion on the part of the public *or* the likelihood of association" ' (emphasis added).[140]

Second, and most importantly, he contends that section 10(3) is *sui generis*, and that as such 'it does not throw any further light on the meaning of section 10(2)',[141] rendering both sections incommensurable.[142]

Although clear and unequivocal arguments defend the approach that association is an instance and subset of confusion, –rather than a substitute

---

[136] AK Sanders 'The Return to Wagamama' (1996) 18(10) EIRR 521.
[137] ibid. See also, Sanders (n124) 5, arguing that '[n]ow that it is clear that expansion of the confusion rationale to the non-confusion rationale is applicable to the case of use of a sign on dissimilar goods, it is logically imperative that this is also true for similar goods, where the proximity of the products enhances the detrimental effect to the unique associative strength of the mark.' See also, P Torremans *Holyoak & Torremans Intellectual Property Law* (5th edn Oxford University Press Oxford 2008) 415, providing that many of the problems arising from section 10(3) would not even exist if it 'wa[s] to be … based on the public being confused.'
[138] See *infra* pp 175-176.
[139] A Rahmatian 'Infringement of Trade Marks in the United Kingdom and in Austria' (1999) 21(7) EIPR 358.
[140] P Prescott 'Think Before you Waga Finger' (1996) 18(6) EIPR 318.
[141] ibid 319.
[142] ibid.

of confusion, as expansionists argue– the ECJ's decision in the *Arsenal* case provides more support for this argument.[143] The court provided that:

> 'It should be borne in mind that, according to the case law of the Court of Justice, the concept of likelihood of association, used in Arts 4(1)(b) and 5(1)(b), *is not an alternative* to that of likelihood of confusion, but serves to define its scope' (emphasis added).[144]

In another decision, the ECJ clarified the emphasis of the confusion requirement under section 10(2). In *Davidoff v Gofkid Ltd*,[145] it was stressed that

> '[w]here goods or services are similar, the national court *must* examine … whether there exists a likelihood of confusion in accordance with Arts 4(1) [reflecting sections 5(1) and (2) of the UK TMA] or 5(1) [reflecting sections 10(1) and (2) of the UK TMA], as the case may be' (emphasis added).[146]

In conclusion, the UK TMA in relation to confusion-based protection for trademarks seems to be controversial. On the one hand, it deploys the concept of *likelihood* of confusion rather than *actual* confusion. The merit of this is to overcome the potential danger of the mark which shall affect both the owner and the consuming public equally. Courts have acknowledged a strict approach to the concept of identicality in section 10(1), which successfully defines definite boundaries for protection on this level, in that it does not allow the owners to benefit unduly from the presumption of confusion existence, which is ultimately of benefit to all parties in the trademark formula.[147] In section 10(2), a flexible approach was provided to include different cases up to the use of similar/similar marks and products. On the other hand, the problem with this section lies in a number of issues; first, it did not clarify the process of assessing the infringement, and this led courts to adopt the global appreciation approach, which resulted in an unjustifiable expansion of rights under this section because it considers that marks and products are similar if confusion is likely. Moreover, the drafting of section 10(2) was not successful in

[143] *Intellectual Property: Patents, Copyright, Trade Marks and Allied Rights* (n8) 717 (para 18-53), providing that '[t]he ECJ has accepted that "association" is one form of "confusion", not an independent concept.'
[144] *Arsenal Football Club Plc* (n11) 351. See also, *Sabel BV* (n111) 223.
[145] (Case C-292/00) [2003] 1 CMLR 35.
[146] ibid 1058.
[147] See ch 1 p 11.

providing: 'likelihood of confusion on the part of the public, which includes the likelihood of association with the trade mark.'[148] However, British legislators should not have given up the chance to clarify the ambiguity of this section, because this reflects the exact wording of the Directive; nonetheless, they could have provided more clarity to it.[149] This created an opportunity for the proponents of monopolistic rights in trademarks to argue that the dilution concept is included within the scope of this level of protection. However, unlike the unfortunate role of legislators in the drafting of section 10(2), the intervention of English courts and the ECJ was successful in denying this alleged notion and stressing that association is an instance of confusion and not a substitute to it. This approach is in keeping with the premises of the Economic-Social Planning theory in some aspects, and contradicts it in others. This shall be the matter of discussion below. However, it is essential first to tackle whether dilution exists under section 10(3) of the UK TMA.

- Dilution-based protection

Directive 2008/95/EC opened the way for a "semi-dilution"[150] concept under its ambit, it provides that:

> 'Any member state *may* … provide that the proprietor shall be entitled to prevent all third parties not having his consent from using in the course of

[148] Trade Marks Act 1994 (UK) c 26 s 10(2). Implementing Directive 2008/95/EC art 5(1)(b).

[149] Although some calls at the Parliament criticized the Directive, but they were unsuccessful. For example, in the House of Lords, Lord Peston provided that: 'I am not willing to believe that we should put into British law a directive which is not right in some sense or other.' See- Public Bill Committee on Trade Marks Bill HL (1994) 13 LA8/13 Job 2-8 Col 46.

[150] It is semi-dilution because although its content is equivalent to dilution but it did not use the word "dilution". Maniatis considers this type of infringement to be 'based on a rationale similar to the dilution rationale in the United States, even if this is not explicitly stated.' See- Maniatis (n119) 43-16. In *Premier Brands UK Ltd v Typhoon Europe Ltd*, the court provided that 'dilution is a useful concept to bear in mind when considering the application of section 10(3)[(the equivalent of art 5(2) of the Directive), but] it does not necessarily follow that every case of infringement under section 10(3) will necessarily involve dilution, nor does it follow that the proprietor of a mark will necessarily succeed in establishing infringement under Section 10(3) in every case where he establishes dilution. [Therefore,] one must be careful of applying it too blindly.' See- *Premier Brands UK Ltd v Typhoon Europe Ltd* [2000] ETMR 1071 (Ch) 1093, 1110.

trade any sign which is identical with, or similar to, the trade mark in relation to goods or services which are *not similar* to those for which the trade mark is registered, where the latter has a *reputation* in the Member State and where use of that sign *without due cause* takes unfair advantage of, or is detrimental to, the distinctive character or the repute of the mark' (emphasis added).[151]

The embodiment of this section under the legislations is by no means mandatory; the use of the word "*may*", in its beginning, clearly indicates that it is upon the discretion of member states to adopt this type of trademark protection. However, it could be inferred from the language of the Council Regulation (EC) No 207/2009 that this section is mandatory.[152]

Unfortunately however, in implementing this section, the UK TMA incorporated this type of trademark infringement in its section 10(3),[153] provides that:

'A person infringes a registered trade mark if he uses in the course of trade in relation to goods or services a sign which—
(a) is identical with or similar to the trade mark, […][154]
(b) […][155]

[151] Directive 2008/95/EC art 5(2).

[152] Council Regulation (EC) No 207/2009 art 9(1)(c), providing that: '1. A Community trade mark *shall* confer on the proprietor exclusive rights therein. The proprietor shall be entitled to prevent all third parties not having his consent from using in the course of trade: … (c) any sign which is identical with or similar to the Community trade mark in relation to goods or services which are *not similar* to those for which the Community trade mark is registered, where the latter has a reputation in the Community and where use of that sign without due cause takes unfair advantage of, or is detrimental to, the distinctive character or repute of the Community trade mark.' (emphasis added).

[153] Lord Strathclyde –the Parliamentary Under-Secretary of State, Department of Trade and Industry– provides that: 'There is some latitude in that some of the [Directive] provisions are cast as optional for member states, but we have taken the fullest advantage of those.' See- Public Bill Committee on Trade Marks Bill HL (1994) 6 LA8/6 Job 1-11 Col 31.

[154] Deleted word: [and]. Repealed by United Kingdom Statutory Instrument 2004/946 Reg 7.

[155] Deleted words: [(b) is used in relation to goods or services which are not similar to those for which the mark is registered]. Repealed by United Kingdom Statutory Instrument 2004/946 Reg 7.

where the trade mark has a reputation in the United Kingdom and the use of the sign, being without due cause, takes unfair advantage of, or is detrimental to, the distinctive character or the repute of the trade mark.'[156]

Although the adoption of the dilution concept is in itself a wide expansion, this section was amended in order to provide a further expansion in trademark owners' rights. Moreover, the conditions for dilution protection under this section also contribute to a widening of the scope of protection. The next section discusses these expansions, as well as the types of dilution available under section 10(3).

Expansion of scope

In 2004, this section was amended to its current draft provided above,[157] deleting the requirement that under this section the use should be on *dissimilar* goods and/or services, although the wording of Directive 2008/95/EC and Council Regulation (EC) No 207/2009 are clear in providing that the use should be on "not similar" products.[158] This shall lead to a wide scope for this section, and to overcome the requirement of likelihood of confusion when the use is regarding similar products. It is argued[159] that the amendment deleting the dissimilar requirement came in effect of the *Davidoff v Gofkid Ltd*,[160] and *Adidas-Salomon AG v Fitnessworld Trading Ltd.*[161]

In *Davidoff*, as has already been shown,[162] and despite the clear language of the Directive, the ECJ widened the scope of section 5(2) of the directive –the equivalent of section 10(3) of the UK TMA– to include the use of the mark over similar goods and/or services. The ECJ in the *Adidas-Salomon* case asserted the outcome of the *Davidoff* case, and ruled that likelihood of confusion is not a requirement in such a case.[163] Accordingly, confusion is out of question under section 10(3).

Regarding the requirement of confusion under section 10(3), English courts were at first glance intuitively ready to presume that confusion was

---

[156] Trade Marks Act 1994 (UK) c 26 s 10(3).
[157] See *supra* pp 175-176.
[158] See *supra* pp 174-175.
[159] *Intellectual Property: Patents, Copyright, Trade Marks and Allied Rights* (n8) 721-722 (para 18-57), 755 (para 18-101).
[160] (Case C-292/00) [2003] ETMR 42.
[161] (Case C-408/01) [2004] ETMR 10.
[162] See ch 3 pp 68-70.
[163] *Adidas-Salomon AG* (n161) 137.

a requirement.[164] Early case law after the introduction of the 1994 Act shows that although not expressly mentioned, confusion was a prerequisite for trademark infringement even under section 10(3). For example, in *BASF Plc v CEP (U.K.) Plc*,[165] Knox J stated: 'In my view, neither the distinctive character nor the repute of the plaintiff's mark is adversely affected when there is *no* risk of relevant confusion' (emphasis added).[166] Thus, the court held that

> 'the Trade Marks Act 1994 section 10(3) did not make the use of another's trade mark an infringement, in the circumstances stipulated by that provision, *in the absence of proof of risk of confusion*' (emphasis added).[167]

Similarly, in *Baywatch Production Co Inc v The Home Video Channel*,[168] it was stressed that:

> 'It would ... be illogical for section 10(3) to give a greater protection in relation to non-similar goods or services by dispensing with the ingredient of a likelihood of confusion than the protection afforded to similar goods under section 10(2).'[169]

The Court of Appeal in *British Telecommunications Plc v One In A Million Ltd*[170] addressed doubts as to whether confusion was a requirement under this type of trademark infringement. It provided that it was 'not satisfied that section 10(3) does require the use to be trade mark as use nor that it must be confusing use'.[171] However, the court provided that it was 'prepared to assume that it does.'[172] However, this matter was settled by the ECJ in *Sabel* case by providing that this type of protection

> 'permit[s] the proprietor of a trade mark which has a reputation to prohibit the use without due cause of signs identical with or similar to his mark and

[164] M Richardson 'Copyright in Trade Marks? On Understanding Trade Mark Dilution' (2000) 1 Intellectual Property Q 68, arguing that 'English courts [were] reluctant to find dilution in the absence of likelihood of confusion'.
[165] [1996] ETMR 51 (Ch).
[166] ibid 55.
[167] ibid 51.
[168] [1997] FSR 22 (Ch).
[169] ibid 30.
[170] [1999] FSR 1 (CA). Known as the "One in a million case".
[171] ibid 25.
[172] ibid.

do *not require proof of likelihood of confusion*, even where there is no similarity between the goods in question' (emphasis added).[173]

In effect, the court in *Pfizer Ltd v Eurofood Link (U.K.) Ltd*[174] provided that 'by the observations of the Court of Justice in Sabel[,] ... proof of likelihood of confusion is not a requirement of proving infringement pursuant to section 10(3).'[175] Accordingly, it has now been established that the likelihood of confusion does not form a part under section 10(3),[176] making fully a "semi-dilution" based protection.

Conditions for protection

Section 10(3) provides two conditions as to infringement under this section. First, marks eligible to protection should not be ordinary marks; rather they should be marks with "reputation". Second, the infringing use should be "without due cause". Both conditions seem to be problematic.

(i) Reputation in the UK

Thus far, three terms have been used in reference to marks other than ordinary marks, i.e. marks to which the public attribute a high degree of association. The US Lanham Act uses the term "famous", the UK TMA and Directive 2008/95/EC use the term "marks with reputation", while in this book the term "well-known marks" is used.[177]

---

[173] *Sabel BV* (n111) 223.
[174] [2001] FSR 3 (Ch).
[175] ibid 30.
[176] This is the approach currently followed by the UK Trade Marks Registry. See- *C. A. Sheimer (M.) Sdn Bhd's Trade Mark Application* [2000] RPC 484, 505, providing that 'it is unnecessary for an objector to establish a likelihood of confusion in order to substantiate an objection to registration under section 5(3).' See also, *Corgi Trade Mark Application* [1999] RPC 549, 557, providing that under section 5(3) 'the existence of a likelihood of confusion is neither necessary nor sufficient to sustain the relevant objection.' See also, *L'Oreal SA v Bellure NV* [2008] ETMR 1 (CA), 27, providing that '[t]he infringements referred to in [this] article ..., where they occur, are the consequence of a certain degree of similarity between the mark and the sign, by virtue of which the relevant section of the public makes a connection between the sign and the mark, that is to say, establishes a link between them *even though it does not confuse them*' (emphasis added).
[177] See ch 1 pp 9-10.

Relevant international treaties also use the term "well-known" to refer to such types of marks,[178] providing a clear interpretation of what might constitute a well-known trademark, and giving regard to the consuming public. However, this is not the case of "marks with reputation". The UK TMA and Directive 2008/95/EC did not define what constitutes reputation. In interpreting the condition of reputation, the ECJ provided that:

> 'Article 5(2) of the Directive [the equivalent of section 10(3) of the UK TMA] is to be interpreted as meaning that, in order to enjoy protection extending to non-similar products or services, a registered trade mark must be known by a significant part of the public concerned by the products or services which it covers.'[179]

Despite the ECJ's interpretation, '[t]he common view seems to be that the standards for reputation are below those for a "well-known trade mark" under article 6bis of the Paris Convention,' [180] because, '[a]ny genuine commercial use of a trade mark will generate at least some reputation'.[181] Kur argues that the 'criterion [of reputation] refer[s] to a

---

[178] Namely, the Paris Convention for the Protection of Industrial Property (adopted 20 March 1883) art 6bis(1), and the Agreement on Trade-Related Aspects of Intellectual Property Rights (15 April 1994) LT/UR/A-1C/IP/1 art 16(2). See also, the Joint Recommendation Concerning Provisions on the Protection of Well-Known Marks (adopted 20-29 September 1999) art 2(b).

[179] (Case C-375/97) *General Motors Corp v Yplon Sa* [2000] RPC 572, 578. McCarthy, who advocates a strict wide interpretation for famous marks, criticizes the ECJ approach citing a number of deficiencies in it; he argues that the court 'refused to define what is a "significant part" and refused to adopt a rule that there must be knowledge by a majority or, indeed, any given percentage of the public as being required.' He also argues that the ECJ did not require any direct evidence of the scope of usage of the mark, which could be achieved through survey evidence. See- JT McCarthy 'Dilution of a Trademark: European and United States Law Compared' (2004) 94 Trademark Reporter 1173-1174.

[180] S Casparie-Kerdel 'Dilution Disguised: Has the Concept of Trade Mark Dilution Made its Way into the Laws of Europe' (2001) 23(4) EIPR 192. See also, SM Maniatis and E Gredley 'Parody: A Fatal Attraction? Part 2: Trade Mark Parodies' (1997) 19(8) EIPR 419, arguing that 'the standard of "reputation" is unlikely to be as high as that required for "well-known" marks.' See also, *Intellectual Property: Patents, Copyright, Trade Marks and Allied Rights* (n8) 754 (para 18-101) providing that to sue under this type of infringement, the mark need to have "reputation", thus, 'it does not have to be "well-known" or "famous".'

[181] D Kitchin and others *Kerly's Law of Trade Marks and Trade Names* (14th edn Sweet & Maxwell London 2005) 384 (para 14-084).

certain quality of the mark[,] … it is precisely a trademark's "reputation" beyond its distinguishing function …'.[182]

Therefore, the concept of reputation aims to overcome trademarks' primary function as indicators of source and origin, and focuses on a utilitarian argument based on quality. Furthermore, such a concept undermines the role of the public in this type of marks and attributes the credit of the quality to the owner, and the assessment of the mark's reputation would focus solely on the owners' investment in the mark and the advertising he/she invests in it.

Contrary to this approach, the Economic-Social Planning theory holds that one aspect depends on such investment by owners, but the most crucial role lies in the high degree of association attributed by the public in the course of "co-authoring" such marks. It follows that in assessing the infringement to such marks, the public should be the cornerstone.

Consequently, the notion of reputation is wider than the requirement of well-known marks, and also wider than the requirement of fame under the US Lanham Act,[183] especially after the introduction of the TDRA which requires the mark to be famous across the entire public of the entire United States.[184] However, using the term "well-known" is more compelling, because it implies the public role and asserts its importance, whilst bringing with it a straightforward question: well-known by whom? The answer would be: certainly the public, whereas "reputation" suggests that the mark gained the repute only due to the investment of its owner, this view looks solely on one side of the coin and denies the role of the public in the creation of well-know marks as the Economic-Social Planning theory suggests. Moreover, in the light of the international legal framework, the term "well-known" to refer to marks with high public recognition is the appropriate terminology.

(ii) Use without due cause

There are no indications in the UK TMA and in the Directive 2008/95/EC as to the interpretation of this requirement; it is, indeed, not easy to identify what constitutes due cause.[185] Nonetheless, the

---

[182] A Kur 'Well-Known Marks, Highly Renown Marks and Marks Having a (High) Reputation – What's it All about?' (1992) 23 Intl Rev of Intellectual Property and Competition L 226.
[183] H Carty 'Do Marks with a Reputation Merit Special Protection' (1997) 19(12) EIPR 685.
[184] See ch 4 pp 134-136.
[185] *O2 Holdings Ltd v Hutchison 3G Ltd* [2006] RPC 29 (Ch) 745.

construction of this section itself seems to lead to an absurd conclusion, because it raises a question regarding the use of the words "without due cause" as to 'whether someone could take unfair advantage *with* due cause' (emphasis added).[186] It is submitted that the trademark owner does not bear the obligation of proving that the use was without due cause, but it falls to the defendant to prove that he/she had due cause to use the mark.[187]

Types of dilution

Taking unfair advantage or causing detriment to the distinctive character or repute of the mark leads to the presumption that the UK TMA and Directive 2008/95/EC do recognize both types of dilution: Blurring, and tarnishment, as in the case of the US Lanham Act. It is suggested that:

> '[D]etriment may take the form of making the earlier mark either less attractive (tarnishing) or less distinctive (blurring); unfair advantage may take the form of free-riding on the coattails of a famous mark or trading on it reputation.'[188]

The Act did not define what constitutes unfair advantage or detriment, and neither did the Directive 2008/95/EC. Martino considers that it '*is* surprising ... that the Act does not specify, with or without limitation, instances of conduct to be proscribed under this rubric.'[189]

Such types of dilution were previously discussed, and need not be discussed further for that reason.[190] Nevertheless, it should be noted that the ECJ in the *Adidas-Salomon* case provided that in this respect '[i]t is sufficient ... that the relevant section of the public establishes a link between the sign and the mark'.[191] However, the mere link in itself is not

[186] Public Bill Committee on Trade Marks Bill HL (1994) 8 LA7/8 Job 1-14 Col 16.

[187] Briggs (n114) 432. See also, *Premier Brands UK Ltd* (n150) 1099, providing that 'if an alleged infringer ... wishes to rely on those words, it is up to it to establish that it falls within the exception, rather than up to a proprietor of the mark to establish that the proviso does not apply.'

[188] *Kerly's Law of Trade Marks and Trade Names* (n181) 384 (para 14-088). See also, Griffiths (n110) 350-358.

[189] *Trademark Dilution* (n31) 104.

[190] See ch 4 pp 123-125.

[191] *Adidas-Salomon AG* (n161) 138.

sufficient, in *Premier Brands UK Ltd v Typhoon Europe Ltd,*[192] the court provided that:

> '[T]he mere fact that the way in which the sign is used by [the defendant] may give rise to an association between the sign and the mark in the minds of some members of the public is ... simply not enough on its own to enable the proprietor of the mark, however well known and valuable it may be, to invoke section 10(3).'[193]

The ECJ also provides that 'the national court must be satisfied by evidence of *actual* detriment, or of unfair advantage' (emphasis added).[194] Therefore, section 10(3) of the UK TMA and section 5(2) of Directive 2008/95/EC 'are not violated by a mere risk or likelihood of damage.'[195] This conclusion is also supported by the wording of the section itself, using the expression: "*takes* unfair advantage", not: "*likely to take*" unfair advantage.[196]

In conclusion, the UK TMA chose to adopt the non mandatory dilution-based article of Directive 2008/95/EC. Afterwards, despite the clear wordings of the directive, and as a result of ECJ decisions, it widened the scope of this type of protection to include similar marks. Both UK TMA and Directive 2008/95/EC widened the scope of marks eligible for protection under this section to "marks with reputation", with such marks bearing a lower degree than well-known or famous marks. The section includes both types of dilution: blurring and tarnishment. It does not require the proof of any likelihood of confusion, but requires the existence of actual damage. However, a recent decision of the ECJ decision in *Intel Corporation Inc v CPM United Kingdom Ltd*[197] might have its implications over the concept of dilution. This shall be discussed below.

---

[192] *Premier Brands UK Ltd* (n150).

[193] ibid 1109.

[194] (Case C-375/97) *General Motors Corp v Yplon Sa* [1999] 3 CMLR 427, 437.

[195] McCarthy (n179) 1170. This is distinct from the case of the US after the introduction of the Trademark Dilution Revision Act of 2005 (TDRA).

[196] *Kerly's Law of Trade Marks and Trade Names* (n181) 384 (para 14-089).

[197] (C-252/07) [2008] ECR 00.

Recent developments: Dilution after Intel

(i) History of the Intel case

The history of the *Intel* case dates back to when Intel Corporation Inc, the owner of the trademark "Intel", sought to invalidate the registration of the mark "Intelmark" owned by CPM United Kingdom Ltd.[198] The "Intel" mark carries with it a considerable reputation for computers and computer-linked products, while "Intelmark" was registered for marketing and telemarketing services. The Hearing Officer at the UK Trade Marks Registry dismissed the application of Intel Corporation, since the Officer was not convinced that CPM's use of "Intelmark" 'would entail any material damage to the distinctiveness or singularity of the Intel brand.'[199]

Afterwards, Intel appealed to the Court of Appeal. The court stated that the appellant's mark "Intel" has a huge reputation, the use of which by others is enough to *bring it to the minds* of consumers.[200] Intel Corporation Inc argued that, to satisfy the requirement of section 5(3) of the UK TMA it sufficed to show 'any kind of mental association between the later mark and the earlier mark.'[201] The court stayed the proceedings, and referred the following questions to the ECJ:

> '1. For the purposes of Art.4(4)(a) of the … Directive …, where: (a) the earlier mark has a huge reputation for certain specific types of goods or services; (b) those goods or services are dissimilar or dissimilar to a substantial degree to the goods or services of the later mark; (c) the earlier mark is unique in respect of any goods or services; (d) the earlier mark would be brought to mind by the average consumer when he or she encounters the later mark used for the services of the later mark; are those facts sufficient in themselves to establish (i) "a link" … and/or (ii) unfair advantage and/or detriment within the meaning of that Article?
> 2. If no, what factors is the national court to take into account in deciding whether such is sufficient? Specifically, in the global appreciation to determine whether there is a "link", what significance is to be attached to the goods or services in the specification of the later mark?

---

[198] On the basis of section 47 of the UK TMA.

[199] Trade mark decision, Application for Invalidation by Intel, 1 February 2006, available at
< http://www.ipo.gov.uk/types/tm/t-os/t-find/t-challenge-decision-results/t-challenge-decision-results-bl?BL_Number=O/037/06> (26 August 2009).

[200] *Intel Corp Inc v CPM UK Ltd* [2007] ETMR 59 (CA) 944.

[201] ibid 946. Intel Corporation Inc was relying of the ECJ's decision in *Adidas-Salomon AG* case. See *supra* p 181.

> 3. In the context of Art.4(4)(a) , what is required in order to satisfy the condition of detriment to distinctive character? Specifically: does (i) the earlier mark have to be unique; (ii) is a first conflicting use sufficient to establish detriment to distinctive character; and (iii) does the element of detriment to distinctive character of the earlier mark require an effect on the economic behaviour of the consumer?'[202]

The Court of Appeal provided its own vision as to the respective answers to the above questions. The court cited the expansion of trademark protection and the monopoly this embraces, and criticized the tendency of trademark owners to get more protection than is needed. As such, the court provided that "mere association" should not be enough to establish dilution.[203] The court also emphasised that

> 'it is very important that the harm or prospect of harm must be real and tangible. A mere possibility or assertion of damage is just too remote and would leave trade mark owners in too monopolistic a position.'[204]

(ii) The ECJ's decision

In November 2008, the ECJ issued its decision in the *Intel* case. As a starting point in the analysis of the *Intel* decision, it should be noted that the court did not introduce any change in the requirement of reputation. It stated that:

> 'The reputation of a trade mark must be assessed in relation to the relevant section of the public as regards the goods or services for which that mark was registered. That may be either the public at large or a more specialised public'.[205]

This accords with the previous approach of the court in the *General Motors Corp* case, which considered that fame amongst a significant part of the public concerned by the products is enough to enjoy protection of dilution.[206]

However, it seems that the court has established two new categories under dilution. Although this is not explicitly stated by the court, a thorough analysis of the court's decision leads to such a conclusion.

---

[202] *Intel Corp Inc* (n200) 948.
[203] ibid.
[204] ibid 950.
[205] *Intel Corp Inc* (197) para 47.
[206] See *supra* pp 176-178.

The first category includes marks whose reputation is *not* restricted to a certain class of goods and/or services. In relation to such marks, the court maintained the requirement established in *Adidas-Salomon AG*, which provides that the "link" between the two marks is enough.[207] In the words of the court:

> 'The fact that, for the average consumer, who is reasonably well informed and reasonably observant and circumspect, the later mark calls the earlier mark with a reputation to mind is tantamount to the existence of such a link, within the meaning of Adidas-Salomon and Adidas Benelux, between the conflicting marks'.[208]

Accordingly, it could be argued that if the consuming public attribute a high degree of association, and in relation to different classes of goods and/or services, then any subsequent use which calls to mind the senior mark is actionable. In this respect, the mere link would suffice. Still, however, actual dilution should be proved in this case.[209]

The second category relates to marks whose reputation is restricted to *a* certain class of goods and/or services for which it was registered. No matter how high this reputation is, as long as the reputation is restricted to this class. The "Intel" mark is an appropriate example for this category, since it holds huge reputation only in respect to a certain specific type of goods or services. It could be inferred from the court's decision that for this category, it is not sufficient for the latter use of the mark to call the senior mark to the minds of consumers. Rather, there should exist –at least a likelihood– of change in the economic behaviour of the average consumer. Again, in the words of the court:

> 'Proof that the use of the later mark is or would be detrimental to the distinctive character of the earlier mark requires evidence of a *change in the economic behaviour of the average consumer* of the goods or services for which the earlier mark was registered consequent on the use of the later mark, or a serious *likelihood* that such a change will occur in the future' (emphasis added).[210]

As such, in case of marks with reputation restricted to certain specific type of goods or services, the mere link in the minds of consumers in not

---

[207] See *supra* p 181.
[208] *Intel Corp Inc* (197) para 82.
[209] As the *General Motors Corp* case requires. See *supra* p 182.
[210] *Intel Corp Inc* (197) para 82.

enough. Owners of such marks should prove a serious *likelihood* of change in the economic behaviour of consumers.[211]

In sum, owners of marks with reputation restricted to certain class of goods and/or services should prove evidence of a serious *likelihood* of change in the economic behaviour of consumers,[212] while owners of marks with reputation in different classes of goods and/or services should prove an *actual* link or association. It could be argued that although, on its face, the court did not change the requirement for reputation, the court provided "preferential" treatment for marks with huge reputation in different classes of goods and/or services. In other words, the more the mark enjoys reputation in respect of different classes, the more it is likely to enjoy dilution protection. As Fhima argues:

> '[T]he fewer trade channels a senior user is active in, the narrower the scope of its protection and, perhaps more importantly, … it would not be enough to ask "does this mark have a reputation?" Rather, one would have to ask, "does this mark have a reputation? If so, what for?" Even if the mark is recognized by the entire consuming public, this approach would limit protection to goods or services that are in some way associated with the goods or services for which the senior user has a reputation.'[213]

Following this analysis of recent changes in dilution under both the US and the UK, it seems essential to provide an examination of these changes, to ascertain whether they might form an effective tool to provide boundaries to dilution.

---

[211] At least in the case of detriment to the distinctive character of the earlier mark (tarnishment).

[212] The court provided that: 'The proprietor of the earlier trade mark is not required, for that purpose, to demonstrate actual and present injury to its mark for the purposes of Article 4(4)(a) of the Directive. When it is foreseeable that such injury will ensue from the use which the proprietor of the later mark may be led to make of its mark, the proprietor of the earlier mark cannot be required to wait for it actually to occur in order to be able to prohibit that use. The proprietor of the earlier mark must, however, prove that there is a serious risk that such an injury will occur in the future.' See- *Intel Corp Inc* (197) para 38.

[213] IS Fhima 'The Fame Standard for Trademark Dilution in the United States and European Union Compared' (2008) 17 Transnational L and Contemporary Problems 664.

(iii) Effects of the Intel decision

In the light of the interpretation provided above, it is clear that the intentions of the ECJ aimed to bind the protection for marks with reputation limited to certain specific types of goods or services. To a large extent, this was in conformity with the premises of the Economic-Social Planning theory, and the view of the UK Court of Appeal in *Intel*, which took into account the monopolizing nature of dilution.[214]

The ECJ in *Intel*, kept a high standard of protection for marks with reputation in different classes of goods and/or services. In this type of marks, it is enough to prove that the latter use creates a "link" with the earlier mark. Clearly, this is not consistent with the premises of the Economic-Social Planning theory, mainly because it disregards the right of the public not to be confused, in addition to the possibility of curtailing their rights in using such marks in cultural and expressive uses. However, the case of the second category of marks under the *Intel* decision is different. It has been argued that a well-known trademark should enjoy broader protection over dissimilar goods and/or services, provided that such use is likely to create confusion in the minds of the public.[215] It seems that the ECJ adopted a similar approach. The court provided that marks with reputation limited to certain types of goods or services should prove a serious likelihood of change in the economic behaviour of consumers.

An important question is to be asked here: What else other than the "*likelihood of confusion*" could satisfy this requirement?

The court did not provide explicitly what proof would amount to the satisfaction of this burden. However, the court implied that this could be satisfied when the 'mark's ability to identify the goods or services for which it is registered and used as coming from the proprietor of that mark is weakened'.[216] It could, thus, be argued that the ECJ's decision was an attempt to limit dilution and only in respect of marks with reputation limited to certain types of goods or services.

In conclusion, this attempt by the ECJ to limit dilution could be a precious opportunity in the process of challenging the possible monopolies resulting from dilution. Nevertheless, the real implications of this decision depend on its application in national courts. After having discussed the current protection of trademarks under the UK TMA, the following discussion focuses on the application of this protection in view of the premises of the Economic-Social Planning theory.

---

[214] See the history of the *Intel* case above.

[215] See ch 3 pp 78-80.

[216] *Intel Corp Inc* (197) para 29.

Trademarks, "Marks with Reputation" under the UK TMA and Directive 2008/95/EC and the Economic-Social Planning Theory

The UK experience in the protection of trademarks should be assessed in the light of its consistency with the premises of the Economic-Social Planning theory. It shall be argued that certain aspects of the UK TMA are consistent with the Economic-Social Planning theory, whereas other aspects adhere to the utilitarian approach which reduces conformity with the Economic-Social Planning theory.

Aspects Consistent with the Economic-Social Planning Theory

As is now plain, the Economic-Social Planning theory considers the source and origin function as the only primary function of trademarks. Accordingly, with which, the definition of trademarks under the UK TMA, and Directive 2008/95/EC in determining what constitutes a trademark, requires that a mark should be able to perform this function in order to qualify for registration as a trademark. The Directive also stresses in its recitals the source identification function. Also, the ECJ initially adopted this function.

A major theme in the Economic-Social Planning theory considers that ordinary and well-known trademarks are the result of the "co-authorship" of the owner and the consuming public. In agreement with this approach, some aspects regarding the registrability of trademarks show the role of the public in the context of trademarks, such as the introduction of the doctrines of secondary meaning and genericness.

In implementing the source and origin function of trademarks, as being the only primary function of trademarks, the UK TMA did adopt the confusion rationale as the test of assessing trademark infringement in sections 10(1) and 10(2), and the same does the Directive. However, the use of an ambiguous language in section 10(2) created a problem as to the interpretation of the requirement of confusion, but the intervention of the English courts was beneficial in maintaining the requirement of confusion, and for preventing the use of association as a substitute of confusion. However, the protection under the confusion concept was still undermined by the deployment of the global appreciation approach, according to which the owner's burden of proof is simplified, in addition to other aspects which contradict the premises of the Economic-Social Planning theory. Such aspects are discussed below.

Aspects Contradicting the Economic-Social Planning Theory

The positive aspects of the UK TMA were undermined by adherence to utilitarian grounds. Therefore, the concept of dilution was introduced in section 10(3). This adoption of dilution, based as it is on the utilitarian and economic theory, forms a shift from considering the source and origin function to the adoption of the quality function as the rational basis for trademark protection. The ECJ expanded the scope of this type of protection to include even the case of similar marks, despite the clear language of Directive 2008/95/EC in this regard.

Moreover, the UK TMA did not take account of the role of the public in trademarks by considering that the rights in the mark should be enjoyed by the proprietor of the registered mark. It confers the rights solely to the owner, thereby disregarding the role of the public in the creation of marks, and especially in expanding the rights of the owner in the case of well-known marks at the expense of the public, especially that the public role in the case of well-known trademarks is more evident and clear. This expansion is not only achieved through the adoption of dilution, but also by deploying the notion of "marks with reputation" rather than the concept of "well-known marks", which resulted in expanding the scope of marks eligible for protection under the dilution section.

Another shortcoming derives from considering that the rights conferred to registrants as their sole "property rights". Contrary to the premises of the Economic-Social Planning theory, which consider that the entitlements in trademarks take the form of a bundle of rights to the registrant and the consuming public, the UK TMA and Council Regulation (EC) No 207/2009 confer "property rights" only to the registrant.[217] A stand which not only disqualifies the Economic-Social Planning theory, but also disregards the nature of trademarks, which are subject to revocation for non use and genericness.

In conclusion, it may readily be inferred that although there are some signs under the UK TMA that are consistent with the premises of the Economic-Social Planning theory, in general, the utilitarian grounds of this Act clearly show a departure from this theory, and bring about a decline in the public interest. At a European level, the position of the Directive 2008/95/EC is better, because it leaves the dilution section as a non mandatory one, a situation not justified, but understandable for two reasons. The first reason is that the Directive is a result of negotiations

---

[217] See *supra* pp 147-148.

between different parties, each having their own interests,[218] and the Directive came to compromise the needs of different parties. The second reason is that the non mandatory nature of this section leaves it to each member state to adopt the protection which is more suitable to its theoretical orientations. However, as shall be clarified, the ECJ's intervention did not leave any discretion to member states, and made the section regarding dilution a deal which was either to be taken or to be left.

Conclusion

The key conclusion of this chapter is that the UK TMA in particular, and generally the Directive 2008/95/EC are not grounded in a clear theoretical basis. However, utilitarian and economic grounds are sound in this jurisdiction. Therefore, they are out of the ambit of the Economic-Social Planning theory, as developed and envisioned by this book. In this concluding section, the role of different bodies will be summarized in order to be able to estimate their influence.

First, Directive 2008/95/EC –as already shown– is not based on a clear theoretical justification. It is, rather, the result of negotiations. In many of its mandatory sections, one could clearly cite its reference to the source and origin function and its test, as based on the confusion rationale. However, one major disadvantage is the embodiment of the non mandatory dilution-based protection. A more radical approach is clear in Council Regulation (EC) No 207/2009, which refers to the proprietary nature of the owners rights, and indicates that the dilution section is mandatory. Unfortunately however, British legislators chose to adopt a wide interpretation of owners' rights and in considering them to be their property rights, in addition to the embodiment of the dilution protection.

Second, looking at the role of the UK government and courts, the UK government –in some instances such as in the *Davidoff* case[219]– defended a narrow interpretation for trademark owners. UK courts provided good efforts in the course of defining and limiting the scope of rights. For example, English courts overcame the arguments which aimed to make association a substitute of confusion under section 10(2),[220] which aimed to simplify the owner's burden of proof. Moreover, English courts struggled to embody a requirement of confusion under section 10(3),[221]

---

[218] Namely, the influence of Benelux countries.
[219] *Davidoff* (n160).
[220] For example, see- *Wagamama Ltd* (n128).
[221] For example, see- *BASF Plc* (n165).

but unfortunately failed to maintain this requirement. The same was true of the destiny of the judicial efforts which aimed to provide a sequential test for protection under section 10(2).[222] Fortunately however, they were successful in mitigating the effects of the dilution action, by requiring the proof of actual damage rather than the likelihood of damage.[223]

Third, from the Economic-Social Planning theory point of view, the ECJ had a negative influence in the course of interpreting the Directive.[224] It opened the gate for considering the quality function as a subset of the origin function,[225] although the Directive was clear in its recognition of the source and origin function as the primary function of trademarks. Furthermore, it extended the scope of section 10(3) to include similar products,[226] contradicting the explicit wording of the Directive. In this respect, the ECJ provided that the Directive does include similar marks, and member states –although this section in not mandatory– can only take this section as it is, and cannot alter its content. This forced the UK to delete the reference to dissimilar marks in this section, in order to include in its scope similar marks. However, the UK TMA could simply have deleted this section totally. This does not mean that the extension of protection of well-known marks is contrary to the Economic-Social Planning theory. Rather, the merit of this theory is that it recognizes the need for such extension over dissimilar marks, but only if this shall affect the well-known marks' ability to denote the source and origin of the products in question. This interpretation shall remunerate the owner, though extending the protection of his/her well-known mark over dissimilar products, and it protects the consuming public by prohibiting any use by others which shall alter the high degree of association they attribute to the mark. It shall also de-monopolize the rights in trademarks by allowing other traders to use the mark if no confusion is likely to occur. In the light of this interpretation, and since English courts were keen to embody confusion in the context of section 10(3), the UK could have deleted this section and left the role of protection well-known marks to courts. However, it has been shown that the ECJ's decision in the *Intel* case is vital in terms of narrowing the boundaries of dilution.[227]

---

[222] For example, see- *British Sugar Plc* (n106).
[223] For example, see- *Premier Brands UK Ltd* (n150).
[224] This does not mean that all ECJ decision has negative impact, but the results of some decision caused negative impact on key issues.
[225] For example, see- *Arsenal Football Club Plc* (n11).
[226] For example, see- *Adidas-Salomon AG* (n161).
[227] See *supra* p 187.

Generally, the UK experience shows in clear evidence that the philosophical foundation of well-known marks should, indeed, be revisited. Thus far, it has been proved that the right of the public in not being confused is not fully regarded;[228] this is concluded from the adoption of the dilution concept in the UK and US. In addition, the scope of the confusion rationale has been unjustifiably expanded. As such, it is important to turn to the second type of protection which should be accorded to the public, which is the right of using trademarks in cultural and expressive contexts. To this end, the case of parody as a particularly instructive example of the relevance of the Economic-Social Planning theory will be discussed.

[228] See ch 2 pp 57-59. See also, ch 3 p 81.

CHAPTER SIX

PARODY AS AN EXAMPLE OF THE RELEVANCE OF THE ECONOMIC-SOCIAL PLANNING THEORY FOR TRADEMARKS

'Where trademarks come to carry so much communicative freight, allowing the trademark holder to restrict their use implicates our collective interest in free and open communication.'[1]

Introduction

The previous chapters have demonstrated that current trademark systems in the US and the UK are not consistent with the first right of the consuming public, namely not to be confused.[2] It has been shown that the shortcomings of the current concept of confusion, in addition to the adoption of the dilution doctrine, have proved that such systems are in need of having their theoretical basis revisited. This should, however, be in accordance with the premises of the suggested theoretical approach. In this chapter, the second aspect of the rights of the pubic will form the main subject of discussions, in the light of the Economic-Social Planning theory; that is, the right of cultural and expressive uses of trademarks.[3]

People have the right to freedom of expression; this is often considered an important aspect of today's modern world. Indeed, many calls have been made to consider such rights as part of fundamental human rights,[4]

---

[1] A Kozinski 'Trademarks Unplugged' (1994) 84 Trademark Reporter 454. See also, K Levy 'Trademark Parody: A Conflict between Constitutional and Intellectual Property Interests' (2001) 69 The George Washington L Rev 426.

[2] See ch 2 pp 57-59. See also, ch 3 p 81.

[3] ibid.

[4] See, for example, the Universal Declaration of Human Rights (adopted 10 December 1948) (UDHR) arts 19 and 27(1). See also, the Convention for the

with legislation ensuring that such rights are highly regarded and maintained. In the process of formulating legislations, legislators should make sure that they do not affect this fundamental human right. The US Constitution provides that 'Congress shall make no law ... abridging the freedom of speech ...'.[5] Similarly, in the UK, the Human Rights Act recognizes the right of freedom of expression.[6]

Thus, trademark systems should be formulated in a manner which regards the rights of all the parties, as stated in the trademark formula,[7] in order to accord with the rights of free expression. Accordingly, the public should enjoy the right to parody, criticism and satire, amongst others, while other traders should also enjoy the right of comparative advertising. However, the argument of this chapter will only be restricted to parody as a sound example of the relevance of the Economic-Social Planning theory. The reason for choosing this example in particular is because the right of the public is more crucial than in other forms of expression. In the case of parody, the public should enjoy the right to communicate and receive the parodistic message.[8] This is less clear in other forms such as comparative advertising, where the protection is directed towards other traders and rivals.[9] As such, parody could be used by the public, individual speakers, and other traders and rivals; therefore, it serves as an ideal form of expression to be studied for the purposes of this book.

The Economic-Social Planning presumes that the granting of rights to trademark owners should not hinder the ability of the public to express themselves. In particular, ordinary trademarks and well-known trademarks are legal and social icons, as has been maintained throughout this book. It is thus vital to consider whether current trademark legislation in the US and UK, where they stand today, are capable of ensuring that trademark protection not only affects freedom of expression, but may enhance the freedom and rights of the public in this regard.

Firstly, a discussion will be provided regarding the rights to freedom of speech, as perceived by the Economic-Social Planning theory. It shall be argued that the confusion rationale is the most suitable form of protection, and that this opens the gates for cultural and expressive uses of trademarks, without affecting the rights of the owner. No less important is the need to

---

Protection of Human Rights and Fundamental Freedoms (European Convention on Human Rights) (ECHR) art 10.

[5] The United States Constitution Amendment I.

[6] Human Rights Act 1998 (UK) c 42 s 12.

[7] See ch 1 p 11.

[8] ibid.

[9] ibid.

differentiate between the different types of cultural uses, and whether a particular use is commercial, non-commercial, or mixed. It also seems crucial to assess whether the US Trademarks Act of 1946 (Lanham Act) and the UK Trade Marks Act (TMA) of 1994 do, in fact, recognize the right of the public in using marks for cultural and expressive uses. Finally, it is important to discuss the different types of uses and the treatment of commercial speech as one of the forms of expression. In its attempt to support and prove the need of reform in current trademark systems, this chapter shall argue in favour of the merits of the Economic-Social Planning theory in sustaining the rights of the public in regards to free speech.

Freedom of Speech under the Economic-Social Planning Theory

We “author” trademarks. This statement clearly aims to emphasize the joint authorship of trademarks by both owners and the consuming public. In chapters four and five above, only one aspect of the public protection has been shown. That is, protecting the public by ensuring that the association they attribute to the mark and the products is not altered and by maintaining their ability to identify the source and origin of products. Therefore, the confusion rationale should be regarded as the test for trademark infringement. However, the role of the public is not limited to attributing an association between marks and products; nor is it confined to attributing higher levels of certain marks to render them well-known. The consuming public are, rather, the creators of the cultural meanings of marks. The Economic-Social Planning theory does not consider the rights of the public as exceptions to the owner’s rights. Rather, ‘the trademark holder’s proprietary claims … are limited *ab initio* because of the public contribution in creating the mark’;[10] this creates competing interests in favour of the public.[11] Therefore, it is important to discuss the meaning-making of marks in the light of the Economic-Social Planning theory premises. It is of no less importance to tackle the types of expressive uses, as well as the effects of dilution over the freedom of speech, as perceived by this theory.

---

[10] S Wilf ‘Who Authors Trademarks?’ (1999) 17 Cardozo Arts & Entertainment L J 5.

[11] ibid 3-4.

The Meaning-Making of Trademarks

The consuming public play an essential role in the life of a mark. They can attribute a low degree of association, which classifies the mark as an ordinary one, while in other instances, where the association granted is high, the mark may turn into a well-known one. What is surprising, however, is the fact that such well-known marks are worth a considerable sum of money, to the direct benefit of owners, while the role of the public is underestimated.

More importantly, the consuming public, in certain instances, tend to attribute a cultural meaning to the mark; this is the process of meaning-making of trademarks, which is a vital component and means of democratic dialogue;[12] for instance, where marks are used in the context of criticism,[13] parodies, or to convey social and political messages. The meaning-making of marks is, thus, an aspect of the role of the public in trademarks. Indeed,

> 'a trademark has no meaning on its own. Whatever meaning it does have takes it cues … from the context in which it sits and the interpretation of that mark in context by consumers. [As such, t]he meaning of any trademark depends not on the intent of its creator'.[14]

Consequently, due to the role of the public in attributing meanings to trademarks,

> 'speech should be free, whether because free speech is thought necessary to the discernment of truth, to citizen participation in a democracy or to speaker or listener autonomy.'[15]

It is, thus, essential that trademark systems recognize the rights of the public in this regard, and seek to enhance such dialogue, which might assist in the advent of the culture. This is mainly because using

---

[12] RJ Coombe 'Objects of Property and Subjects of Politics: Intellectual Property Laws and Democratic Dialogue' (1990-1991) 69 Texas L Rev 1866.

[13] M Barrett 'Domain Names, Trademarks and the First Amendment: Searching for Meaningful Boundaries' (2007) 39 Connecticut L Rev 981, arguing that 'suppressing unauthorized use of marks may seriously undermine the public's ability to discuss or criticize the mark owner and its products.'

[14] LA Heymann 'The Birth of the Authornym: Authorship, Pseudonymity, and Trademark Law' (2005) 80 Notre Dame L Rev 1423.

[15] M Spence 'Intellectual Property and the Problem of Parody' (1998) 114 L Q Rev 608.

'trademark[s] for criticism, social commentary, parody, or other speech-related purposes can have positive social benefits that outweigh the harm to the trademark holder.'[16] This, in turn, fulfils the general aim and purpose of the Economic-Social Planning theory in achieving a just, attractive culture out of our trademark systems. The safeguarding of the right to free speech shall therefore benefit those conveying the message, and the other parts of the public to whom the message is conveyed, and consequently, benefits the society at large. It shall benefit the trademark owner as well, due to the free advertisement such uses would offer, because the parodistic use shall convey a non-confusing message to consumers.

The Economic-Social Planning theory argues in favour of more access to the public over trademarks, because of their role in their creation. The application of this theory also suggests that the public is entitled to use the mark for cultural and expressive purposes, even if the owner claims that such use would create an unwanted association. Such claims by trademark owners are misplaced. If the consuming public attribute an association between the mark and the products, then it could not be upheld that the public's own cultural use would create in their own minds an "unwanted association". Besides, it seems illogical 'to allow[…] a trademark owner to come to "own" as private property a set of meanings that are literally public'.[17] After all, any association in a trademark is attributed by the public, and they might alter or even withdraw this association. Therefore, trademark legislations should not discredit the rights of the public in the expressive use of trademarks. Additionally, the public should enjoy the right to use the mark in a cultural context in order to clarify their low degree of association between the mark and the products, and in certain cases, to express disapproval of the characteristics of the owner's products.

On this basis, it should be inferred from the adoption of the confusion rationale that cultural or expressive uses of the mark are *prima facie* non-confusing uses. That is to say, it should be assumed that using a trademark for parody purposes is not a use which might cause, or result in, the likelihood of confusion.

Prior to the introduction of the dilution concept, a number of US cases clarified this point, stressing that since the latter use was for the purposes of parody, confusion is unfounded. For example, in *Jordache Enterprises*

[16] C Long 'Dilution' (2006) 106 Columbia L Rev 1057.

[17] K Aoki 'Authors, Inventors, and Trademark Owners: Private Intellectual Property and the Public Domain Part 2' (1993-1994) 18 Columbia-VLA J of L & the Arts 249.

Inc v Hogg Wyld Ltd,[18] the appellant contested the appellees' use of the mark "Lardashe" with the head of a pig, which was claimed to infringe the appellant's mark "Jordache", used with the head of a horse.[19] The court referred to the parodistic nature of the appellees' use, and stated that using the mark for the purpose of parody aimed to amuse the public, and the appellees' use focused on the humorous differences between their mark and the appellant's mark. Thus, the court provided that the finding of parody exempts any confusion by the public.[20] Similarly, in *Universal City Studios Inc v Nintendo Co Ltd*,[21] the court held that 'the fact that [the defendants-appellees's mark] so obviously parodies the [plaintiff-appellant's mark] strongly contributes to dispelling confusion on the part of consumers.'[22]

However, the lack of any express statutory protection to the parodic uses of trademarks, in the context of the confusion concept, led other courts in the US to adopt a different approach. This has been shown in *Dallas Cowboys Cheerleaders Inc v Pussycat Cinema Ltd.*[23] Confusion was relied upon by the court, because of its view that the mark was used in a "depraved" manner.[24] Other cases clarify the negative treatment by some US courts even before the introduction of dilution. In *Coca-Cola Co v Gemini Rising Inc*,[25] the defendant produced posters reading "Enjoy Cocaine", which the plaintiff claimed to be a reproduction of its familiar mark "Coca-Cola". The plaintiff's use of its mark was associated with the word "Enjoy", usually written before the mark "Coca-Cola".[26] The defendant's use of the poster intended to make an association with the plaintiff's mark, and argued that its use ' "... was intended to be a spoof, satirical, [and] funny ..." '.[27]

In its decision, the court was driven by the proposition that the plaintiff's mark is a 'widely known trademark ... [which] ... is valid and

---

[18] 828 F.2d 1482 (1987).
[19] ibid 1484-1485.
[20] ibid 1485-1487.
[21] 746 F.2d 112 (1984).
[22] ibid 116. See also, *Black Dog Tavern Co Inc v Hall* 823 F.Supp. 48 (1993) 57, providing that the defendant's use of the plaintiff's marks 'allow[s] an ordinarily prudent consumer to appreciate the point of the parody, thereby diminishing the risk of confusion.'
[23] 604 F.2d 200 (1979). See ch 4 pp 107-108.
[24] See ch 4 pp 107-108.
[25] 346 F.Supp. 1183 (1972).
[26] ibid 1186.
[27] ibid 1187.

worthy of protection'.[28] Clearly, the proposition of the court devalued the role of the public in rendering the plaintiff's mark well-known, and disregarded the high degree of association they provided. The court also disqualified the defendant's argument that there was no possibility of likelihood of confusion between their posters and the plaintiff's mark. Accordingly, the court 'overlooked, or perhaps simply didn't care about, Coca-Cola's very real historical usage of cocaine',[29] and found that

> 'defendant's imitation of plaintiff's registered mark is *likely to cause confusion* or mistake as to the source or sponsorship of the poster and constitutes trademark infringement under the Lanham Act' (emphasis added).[30]

On the contrary, in *Girl Scouts of the US of America v Personality Posters Mfg Co*,[31] a case similar in facts to the *Coca-Cola* case, it was held that ' "[t]o enjoin any publication, no matter how libelous, would be repugnant to the First Amendment to the Constitution …".'[32]

It is thus evident that the lack of explicit protection entitling the public to use trademarks in cultural and expressive contexts results in confusion within the courts as to whether this should fall under the classification of infringing uses.[33] This is the case under systems adopting the confusion test –as was the situation in the US before the introduction of dilution– and thus, the situation is even worse if trademark dilution is adopted. However, from the above cases, it seems essential to address the types of expressive uses of marks.

Types of Expressive Uses of Trademarks

Using a trademark in cultural and expressive contexts seems to involve three types of uses. The first use occurs when it is completely parodistic in

---

[28] ibid 1188.

[29] K Aoki 'How the World Dreams of Itself to be American: Reflections on the Relationship Between the Expanding Scope of Trademark Protection and Free Speech Norms' (1996-1997) 17 Loyola of Los Angeles Entertainment L J 534.

[30] *Coca-Cola Co* (n25) 1190.

[31] 304 F.Supp. 1228 (1969).

[32] ibid 1234.

[33] A Rahmatian 'Trade Marks and Human Rights' in PLC Torremans (ed) *Intellectual Property and Human Rights* (1st edn Kluwer Law International BV Netherlands 2008) 352, arguing that '[t]he US cases show inconsistency in the application of trade mark laws to parodies.'

nature.[34] The second occurs when the use is partially parodistic and partially commercial. The third involves completely commercial use. Therefore, it should be clarified that the claim that the protection of cultural and expressive uses of trademarks is confined to non-commercial uses[35] is not accurate. These types of parodistic uses will be discussed in the light of the premises of the Economic-Social Planning theory.

The totally parodistic uses of trademarks occur when the public use the mark for the *sole* purpose of expressing themselves, without any commercial benefits resulting from such a use.[36] In the light of the premises of the Economic-Social Planning theory, such types of use should be entirely protected in favour of the public, because they are the natural right of the consuming public in return of their "co-authorship" of marks. Thus, it should be presumed that wholly parodistic uses shall not result in consumer confusion; rather, the aim is to freely communicate ideas and to practice rights within the framework of democratic dialogue.

As regards the second type of use, this is concerned with the mixed uses of parodistic and commercial natures. This type of use is the most common in trademark parody. In such cases, parodists aim to focus on the differences between their use and the use of the owner in a humorous manner. Thus, as the courts concluded in the *Jordache Enterprises* case and *Universal City Studios* case, using the mark for parody is a proof of the non-confusing nature of the mark, because parody 'by its very nature … aims to imitate without confusing.'[37] In the UK, the court in *Alan Kenneth McKenzie Clark v Associated Newspapers Ltd*[38] provided that '[w]hether a customer is confused is the ultimate question. If the

---

[34] Also known as non-commercial speech.

[35] *Mutual of Omaha Ins Co v Novak* 836 F.2d 397 (1987) 403, providing that the defendant 'is prohibited from using the [mark] only in the specific commercial ways mentioned in the injunction. His right to use the design in other ways … is not restricted in any manner whatsoever.'

[36] See for example, *Stop the Olympic Prison v US Olympic Committee* 489 F.Supp. 1112 (1980). Another example of this use is the *Gay Olympic* case, where the use of the Olympic symbol was intended to express the equal rights of the gays. See- *San Francisco Arts & Athletics Inc v US Olympic Committee* 483 US 522, 107 S Ct 2971 (1987). See also, ch 2 pp 52-56. Coombe provides a similar example in Canada, where a gay rights group used the trademark "Air Canada" to deliver their message: "Lesbians Fly Air Canada". The purpose of this use was 'to remind people of the similarities between lesbians and all other people.' See- Coombe (n12) 1865.

[37] SM Maniatis and E Gredley 'Parody: A Fatal Attraction? Part 2: Trade Mark Parodies' (1997) 19(8) EIPR 412.

[38] [1998] RPC 261 (Ch).

defendant employs a successful parody, the customer would *not* be confused, but amused' (emphasis added).[39] Therefore, emphasis should be directed towards the question of whether the parody was successful, i.e. that the parody was clear, rather than whether the use causes confusion, because a clear parody use shall diminish any possibility of confusion.[40] As Keller and Bernstein comment:

> 'If the parody is sufficiently outlandish, any … confusion would be unlikely because reasonable consumers will recognize the product or service as a parody, and will not believe that it originated from or was approved by the trademark owner.'[41]

Therefore, if this is the case with ordinary marks, then the more the mark is famous and well-known, the more confusion is unlikely to occur. '[I]t is precisely because of the mark's fame and popularity that confusion is avoided, and it is this lack of confusion that a parodist depends upon to achieve the parody.'[42] In its recent decision, the US Court of Appeals in *Louis Vuitton Malletier v Haute Diggity Dog*[43] affirmed this outcome. The court considered that: '[I]t [is] apparent that an effective parody will actually diminish the likelihood of confusion, while an ineffective parody does not.'[44]

---

[39] ibid 272. (Citing *Nike Inc v Just Did It Enterprises* 6 F.3d 1225 (1993) 1227-1228).

[40] MK Cantwell 'Confusion, Dilution and Speech: First Amendment Limitations on the Trademark Estate: An Update' (2004) 94 Trademark Reporter 559, arguing that 'when the joke is made clear to viewers, confusion is unlikely, notwithstanding a similarity between the marks.'

[41] BP Keller and DH Bernstein 'As Satiric As They Wanna Be: Parody Lawsuits Under Copyright, Trademark, Dilution and Publicity Laws' (1995) 85 Trademark Reporter 250. See also, RJ Shaughnessy 'Trademarks Parody: A Fair Use and First Amendment Analysis' (1986) 72 Virginia L Rev 1093, arguing that 'no competently executed parody is likely to be attributed to the trademark owner, because the parodist uses the mark in a different manner than its owner.' See also, RC Denicola 'Trademarks as Speech: Constitutional Implications of the Emerging Rationales for the Protection of Trade Symbols' (1982) 1982 Wisconsin L Rev 188-189, arguing that 'the joke itself reinforces the public's association of the mark with the [owner].'

[42] *Tommy Hilfiger Licensing Inc v Nature Labs LLC* 221 F.Supp.2d 410 (2002) 416.

[43] 507 F.3d 252 (2007).

[44] ibid 261.

Moreover, even if parodists gain substantial revenue from their use of marks, this should not affect their rights in terms of using marks. '[T]he test is whether the defendant has used the plaintiff's mark to express an idea rather than simply to propose a commercial transaction',[45] and less emphasis should be directed towards the parodists' commercial benefits. As such, the court in the *Coca-Cola* case erred on the side of considering that the defendant's substantial revenue is a factor to be taken into consideration in determining trademark infringement.[46] Such a finding is likely to hinder the promotion of fair and free competition in order to achieve the desired just and attractive culture, which is the main goal of the Economic-Social Planning theory.

It follows that parodists should have their right to freedom of speech protected, regardless of the merits of the message conveyed. Protection in this regard should be similar to copyright protection, which does not depend upon the value and merits of the work. Accordingly, it is not reasonable to argue that in the *Coca-Cola* case, for example, the defendant's poster 'conveyed no social message',[47] or that in the *Dallas Cowboys Cheerleaders* case the defendant's 'movie [was] devoid of any social message.'[48] This is because, as the US Court of Appeals found in *L.L. Bean Inc v Drake Pub Inc*,[49] '[t]rademark parodies, even when offensive, do convey a message.'[50]

The last type of parodistic uses is totally commercial use. However, in certain cases, the use might have some message to convey to the public, although the commercial nature is dominant and clearer than the parodistic nature of the use, which is minimal.[51] In such cases, in deploying the premises of the Economic-Social Planning theory, this category should adhere to the confusion test, and assess whether this use might confuse the public as to the source and origin of the products. This is, though, unlikely to happen if the use is for dissimilar products, given that the parodistic use,

---

[45] EB Staffin 'The Dilution Doctrine: Towards a Reconciliation With the Lanham Act' (1995-1996) 6:105 Fordham Intellectual Property Media & Entertainment L J 170.
[46] *Coca-Cola Co* (n25) 1187.
[47] Staffin (n45) 175.
[48] ibid.
[49] 811 F.2d 26 (1987).
[50] ibid 34.
[51] In some instances, it is difficult to distinguish between parodistic and commercial uses. See for example, *Deere & Co v MTD Products Inc* 41 F.3d 39 (1994).

in addition to the use for other type of goods, would diminish any possibility or likelihood of confusion.

Another issue intuitively follows from this argument. It is questionable whether cultural and expressive uses should be available to the public if other means of conveying their message are available. In *Mutual of Omaha Ins Co v Novak*,[52] the court provided that the defendant's use – which included a mix of parodistic and commercial uses– should be prohibited, and this does not violate the defendant's constitutional right to freedom of expression. The court reasoned that

> '[o]ther avenues for [the defendant] to express his views exist and are unrestricted by the injunction; for example, it in no way infringes upon the constitutional protection the First Amendment would provide were [the defendant] to present an editorial parody in a book, magazine, or film. Because the injunction leaves open many such avenues of expression, it deprives neither [the defendant] nor the public of the benefits of his ideas.'[53]

However, this judgment is unjust in terms of its approach towards the right of the public. The public should be free to use whatever means they find suitable to express themselves. As Tasker argues, 'due to the unique nature of parody, the parodist will probably not be able to find an equally satisfactory substitute for its form of expression.'[54] Thus, it is not accurate to deprive the public of the exercising of their right to use the mark when other means are available. In particular, the public might decide to use several means and would not wish to confine themselves to a certain tool in practicing their freedom of expression. As such, the court's approach in the *Mutual of Omaha* case seems impractical and illogical.

Consequently, from the application of the premises of the Economic-Social Planning theory in this manner,[55] it is clear that the cultural and

---

[52] *Mutual of Omaha Ins Co* (n35).

[53] ibid 402. See also, *Elvis Presley Enterprises Inc v Capece* 141 F.3d 188 (1998), 200, providing that '[t]he [d]efendants' parody of the faddish bars of the sixties does not require the use of [the plaintiff's] marks[.] … [T]herefore, the necessity to use the marks significantly decreases and does not justify the use.' Michael Spence provides a similar approach, and argues that there are two situations in which intellectual property rights and free speech might be incompatible[. One of which is when] adequate alternative means of expression do not exist.' See- Spence (n15) 610.

[54] T Tasker 'Parody or Satire as a Defense to Trademark Infringement' (1987) 77 Trademark Reporter 237.

[55] See *infra* pp 214-216.

expressive uses of trademarks, and those well-known in particular, should be regarded as a genuine right. As such, it should not be looked at as an exception to the owner's right, or as something being taken from trademark owners and given to the public. Such a right is granted to the public not only as the natural consequence of their "co-authorship" of the mark, but also due to their role in the meaning-making of such marks.

One last issue should be discussed in order to perceive the whole image as regards the approach of the Economic-Social Planning theory: that is, to assess whether the dilution concept is in any way of compatible with the premises of the Economic-Social Planning theory as regards the rights of the public in parodistic uses of trademarks.

Dilution, Freedom of Speech and Economic-Social Planning

The use of a trademark for the purposes of expressing ideas and conveying messages obviously requires the parodist to use the mark. This focuses upon using the mark in a manner which aims to make an association with the owner's mark, so as to convey a message by stressing the difference between the parodist's use and the owner's use. Thus, the mark forms an essential tool for the parodist to freely express his/her views and to create a humorous image, whether through the mark or in relation to the owner's use of the mark.

Clearly, the Economic-Social Planning theory considers that the consuming public, being "co-authors" of marks, should enjoy the inherent right to use them for expressive purposes. Therefore, this approach by the Economic-Social Planning theory *ab initio* contradicts the dilution theory, and there is little or no possibility of their co-existence. As one scholar argues, '[i]f trademark holders were allowed to shut down parodic or critical speech involving the mark, dilution law may prove to create a net social loss.'[56] Such social losses are, in particular, what the Economic-Social Planning theory argues against.

While the use of the mark for parodistic purposes necessitates the use of the mark, the dilution concept considers such use as blurring the owner's mark and as harming and eroding the distinctive character of the mark. The parodist use might be for goods and/or services which the owner might classify as being of inferior quality, and from the dilution concept perspective, this shall tarnish the owner's mark. This is especially the case when the parodist's use is directed towards mocking and ridiculing the owner's use. However, the damage that the dilution rationale

---

[56] Long (n16) 1066.

suggests is ill-defined and, as Farley argues, such harm lacks any supportable theorization.[57]

Consequently, as Shaughnessy puts it: '[U]nder the dilution theory … the rights of the trademark owner seriously *conflict* with the parodist's first amendment rights' (emphasis added).[58] Hence, the dilution concept forms an unconstitutional means, which is responsible for hindering the ability of the public to express themselves.[59] Indeed, as Aoki argues,

> '[s]trong anti-dilution laws grant trademark owners increasingly strong veto power over downstream uses of such a trademark for purposes of social commentary and expression critically of or radically alternative to a trademark owner's practices and products.'[60]

All in all, the Economic-Social Planning theory considers that the public, in addition to their role as "co-authors" of trademarks, are the creators of the meaning of the mark. As such, this requires the use of the confusion doctrine, which is unlikely to occur because the parodistic nature of the use excludes any possibility of confusion. However, it has been shown that the lack of any explicit statutory recognition of this right has affected the enjoyment of the public of their rights in this respect. It also been argued that the dilution doctrine, in addition to its inherent shortcomings already discussed in the previous chapters, is a tool which extinguishes the right of the public to freely express and communicate their ideas.

After setting out the approach of the Economic-Social Planning theory as regards the cultural and expressive uses of marks, it seems crucial to shed light on the two jurisdictions of this book, and their treatment of expressive uses of trademarks. This is vital in order to be able to assess whether trademark legislation in US and UK, as it stands today, provides an equitable approach to parodistic uses of trademarks. Ultimately, this benefits in proving the need of revisiting the foundations of current trademark systems.

---

[57] CH Farley 'Why we are Confused about the Trademark Dilution Law' (2006) 16 Fordham Intellectual Property Media & Entertainment L J 1184.

[58] Shaughnessy (n41) 1113.

[59] This shall be clearly outlined in discussing the application of the dilution concept over the rights of the public. See *infra* pp 214-216.

[60] Aoki (n17) 247-248.

Current Approach to Parody

From the ongoing argument, it is clear that courts were not treating the rights of the public in the parodistic use of trademarks in a consistent manner. Therefore, the theoretical shortages of legislations in protecting expressive uses are the cause of such shortcomings. As has already been argued, trademark legislations should provide clear protection to such rights as a competing and genuine right, and should make sure that a consistent treatment of parody is granted.

Legislations in both jurisdictions of this book have adopted dilution protection, favouring trademark owners over the rights of the consuming public. It is a common argument that dilution is harmful to the rights of freedom of expression. Gulasekaram points out that

> '[t]rademark law threatens to exceed its proper boundary only when it leaves the realm of confusion and meanders into the quagmire of reputational harms alleged in dilution claims.'[61]

Therefore, it is vital to discuss the effects of current dilution claims under both the UK TMA and the Lanham Act. This shall clarify the real harm caused by dilution to the right of the public to free speech.

Freedom of Speech under the UK TMA

In the UK, there are no articles providing an exception to the fair use of trademarks in cultural and expressive contexts. The legislative history of the UK TMA shows support towards comparative advertising,[62] whereas there is no mention of the case of the right of the public to use trademarks in parodistic contexts. However, scholarly arguments provide that a defence against dilution could be inferred under section 10(3). This section, as previously indicated, provides a semi-dilution protection to owners of marks with reputation against any use that takes unfair advantage or causes detriment to the mark's distinctive character without *due cause*.[63] Maniatis and Gredley argue that: ' "Due cause" is not defined in the Act … and might provide a public interest based defence for parody'.[64]

---

[61] P Gulasekaram 'Policing the Border between Trademarks and Free Speech: Protecting Unauthorized Trademark Use in Expressive Works' (2005) 80 Washington L Rev 926.

[62] Public Bill Committee on Trade Marks Bill HL (1994) 10 LA8/ Job 2-2 Col 39.

[63] Trade Marks Act 1994 (UK) c 26 s 10(3).

[64] Maniatis and Gredley (n37) 419.

However, they contend that ' "[d]ue case" is more likely to be interpreted as commercial necessity.'[65] Also, it has been argued that even within the boundaries of the confusion doctrine, there is an emerging need for explicit protection for the public in uses of a cultural and expressive nature. Moreover, parody is indeed a due cause to use a trademark, but the dilution protection in itself is an elusive doctrine, which provides monopolistic rights;[66] hence, it 'is not at all clear when a parody of a trade mark would amount to dilution.'[67] From the US experience with dilution, as shall be argued, the effects of dilution were destructive of the claims of parodistic uses even in the light of the limitation regarding non-commercial use. Therefore, the reliance on "due cause" is of little assistance, and, consequently, it could be argued that the UK TMA, as well as Directive 2008/95/EC, have been silent as regards the rights of the public in cultural and expressive uses.

Although '[i]n the U.K. case law, trade mark parodies have been conspicuous by their absence',[68] one may still find few instances which are related to freedom of expression. For example, in the recent case of *Miss World Ltd v Channel Four Television Corp*,[69] the defendant intended to transmit a beauty show for transvestites and transsexuals under the title "Mr Miss World". This title was similar to the plaintiff's well-known mark "Miss World".[70] It was not disputed that the defendant's use was parodistic and aimed to stress the equal rights of transsexuals, and as such, was protected under the Human Rights Act and the European Convention on Human Rights as a form of free speech.[71] However, the court eventually considered that this case fell under section 10(3) of the UK TMA, and that 'the principal function of the [defendant's] mark is indeed to take unfair advantage of the distinctive character and the repute of the Miss World mark.'[72]

However, although '[t]here is no freedom of expression defence in U.K.',[73] the Human Rights Act provides that 'particular regard to the importance of the ... right to freedom of expression [should be ensured]'.[74]

[65] ibid.
[66] Shaughnessy (n41) 1087.
[67] Spence (n15) 600.
[68] Maniatis and Gredley (n37) 418.
[69] [2007] ETMR 66.
[70] ibid 1046.
[71] ibid 1050-1051.
[72] ibid 1055.
[73] Maniatis and Gredley (n37) 420.
[74] Human Rights Act 1998 (UK) c 42 s 12(4).

Accordingly, in certain instances the right of freedom of expression was regarded in the course of deciding the registrability of trademarks.[75] For example, in the *Basic Trademark SA's Application*,[76] the right of free expression was taken into consideration[77] although it was eventually considered that the mark "Jesus" was not registrable because of it was considered 'contrary to public policy [and] to accepted priniciples of morality',[78] particularly due to the religious connotations of this mark.[79] However, in *French Connection Ltd's Trade Mark Application*,[80] the opposition to the registration of the mark "Fcuk" failed and French Connection Ltd was successful in registering the "Fcuk" mark.

As such, it could be inferred that the lack of express protection to the expressive uses have an adverse effect on freedom of expression,[81] because it causes confusion in terms of determining whether such types of expression could be protected. However, the implications of the US case should be instructive to the UK in enabling it to benefit from and to overcome the resulting negative effects.

Freedom of Speech under the Lanham Act

Concerns regarding the First Amendment's right of freedom of expression were addressed in the House Report's discussions of the Federal Trademark Dilution Act (FTDA 1995). It was provided that

> '[t]he proposal adequately addresses legitimate First Amendment concerns espoused by the broadcasting industry and the media. The bill will not prohibit or threaten "non-commercial" expression …'.[82]

---

[75] Rahmatian (n33) 348.
[76] [2006] ETMR 24.
[77] ibid 301, providing that the 'it is necessary to interpret and apply the prohibition in s.3(3)(a) of the Act consistently with the provisions of the [ECHR and the Human Rights Act]'.
[78] Trade Marks Act 1994 (UK) c 26 s 3(3)(a).
[79] *Basic Trademark SA's Application* (n76) 310.
[80] [2007] ETMR 8.
[81] C Geiger 'Trade Marks and Freedom of Expression – The Proportionality of Criticism' (2007) 38 Intl Rev of Intellectual Property and Competition L 319, arguing that 'the absence of express limits allows the rightholder to forbid *any* use of the protected sign.'
[82] House Rep No 104-374 (1996 U.S.C.C.A.N. 1029) 1031.

As such, the Lanham Act considers that '[n]oncommercial use of a mark'[83] is not actionable under section 43(C) of the Act. The recent Trademark Dilution Revision Act (TDRA 2005) provides that:

> 'The following shall not be actionable as dilution by blurring or dilution by tarnishment under this subsection:
> ''(A) Any fair use, including a nominative or descriptive fair use, or facilitation of such fair use, of a famous mark by another person other than as a designation of source for the person's own goods or services, including use in connection with—
> ...
> ''(ii) *identifying and parodying, criticizing, or commenting upon the famous mark owner or the goods or services of the famous mark owner*' (emphasis added).[84]

- Effects of FTDA and TDRA

From the outset, it could be inferred that the protection of the FTDA of non-commercial uses of the mark, and the addition provided by the TDRA in protecting expressive uses of the mark could form the basis for ensuring the public theirs right in terms of freedom of speech. However, it will be argued that this is far from true. There is much evidence which leads to the contrary.

First, under the FTDA, the exclusion is only confined to cases where the use is *non-commercial.* The amendment provided by the TDRA was of little help in solving this problem; it states that "fair use" of the trademark could be any use 'other than as a designation of source for the person's own goods or services'.[85] As such, a scrutinized analysis of the TDRA means that it provides protection to expressive uses of the famous mark, provided that such uses are not directed towards identifying the source and origin of the junior users. This means that the owner of the famous mark can prohibit the uses when they are directed towards commercial and expressive uses. Clearly, it is surprising that the TDRA refers to the "designation of source". Interpreting such reference suggests that mixed use shall cause confusion to the public and should therefore be prohibited. This is ironic, because it uses confusion to protect the trademark owner in

---

[83] Trademarks Act 1946- Lanham Act (USA) 15 U.S.C. § 1125 (Section 43(c) (4) (b)).
[84] Trademark Dilution Revision Act 2005 (USA) § 2 – Trademarks Act 1946- Lanham Act (USA) 15 U.S.C. § 1125 (Section 43(c) (3) (a)).
[85] ibid.

the dilution context which claims that the presence or absence of confusion is irrelevant. It also undermines the effects of dilution over the rights of the public. As a result, the alleged protection to speech under the TDRA is more formal than real.

The second problem is that the nature of the dilution doctrine contradicts the freedom of speech. Under the dilution rationale, as perceived by the TDRA, any use of the mark for parodistic purposes which is *likely* to create an association between the two marks shall blur and erode the distinctive character of the mark. Also, if the use of the mark creates an unwholesome association, which is *likely* to tarnish the reputation of the mark, it is hard to imagine that the public could still enjoy protection for their expressive and cultural uses of the mark. This is the case because a number of court decisions, even under the FTDA, were sensitive to the "unwholesome" or "unsavoury" uses of trademarks. Thus, after the TDRA, which explicitly regarded the notion of likelihood of tarnishment, it seems that such uses would be treated too harsh. In support of this argument, Hofrichter holds that the TDRA

> 'threaten[s] free speech … by expanding liability through the acceptance of a "likelihood" standard of proof, enshrinement of "dilution by tarnishment" and a free speech exception that does not unambiguously provide a sufficient safeguard for protected speech. … [B]y allowing such expansion, the "chilling effects" on speech will be exacerbated and that federal trademark law liability will be taken to its most expansive point in history.'[86]

In *Kraft Foods Holdings Inc v Helm*,[87] the plaintiff was the owner of the trademark "Velveeta". The defendant used for seventeen years the sign "King VelVeeda" as his nickname and as a sign to his artwork; this use was on his website which contained adult materials. Also, the site offered for sale tee-shirts, coffee mugs and custom artwork designed by the defendant.[88] While the plaintiff argued that such use tarnished its mark, the defendant referred to the parodistic nature of his use, which fell under the constitutionally protected right of freedom of speech. The court ruled in favour of the plaintiff, finding that the defendant's use tarnished the

[86] JA Hofrichter 'Tool of the Trademark: Brand Criticism and Free Speech Problems with the Trademark Dilution Revision Act of 2006' (2007) 28 Cardozo L Rev 1930. See also, Gulasekaram (n61) 926-927, arguing that 'dilution laws … have the potential to extend trademark law into areas it was never intended to reach.'

[87] 205 F.Supp.2d 942 (2002).

[88] ibid 944.

plaintiff's mark because the defendant's 'website contains items of a sexually explicit nature'.[89] Most importantly, the court provided that: 'A First Amendment defense fails "where the trademark functions to connote the source of the product or message, rather than being used in a communicative message." '[90] This latter part of the court's decision was indicative in terms of the interpretation of the TDRA. Mixed uses under the TDRA will be prevented because of its reference to the "designation of source". As the court held in the *Kraft Foods Holdings* case, the parodistic nature of the use shall be overlooked, thereby halting the ability of the public to express themselves. These are not, however, the only shortcomings within the TDRA. It did not consider other means of free expression such as satire. This was due to the fact that satire contradicts the rationale behind the dilution concept, namely tarnishment.[91]

It has already been argued that the Economic-Social Planning theory considers the protection of the rights of the public in cultural and expressive uses to be a major aspect, in addition to their right not to be confused. However, in the light of this shortcoming of both the FTDA and the TDRA, and the courts' unwillingness to protect commercial speech (mixed uses of marks for expressive purposes), it is thus essential to assess whether the prohibition of such speech contradicts the right to free speech.

- Commercial speech and freedom of speech

This book is not about the constitutionality of trademark protection. However, because 'trademark protection is [not] delimited by the confusion rationale, recourse to constitutional principles is

---

[89] ibid 953.

[90] ibid 954. It is apparent that the court totally disregarded the fact that products 'such as T-shirts, posters, and Coffee mugs, frequently are purchased not for their utility but for the messages they express.' See- M LaFrance 'No Reason to Live: Dilution Laws as Unconstitutional Restrictions on Commercial Speech' (2007) 58 South Carolina L Rev 712.

[91] The importance of the lack of reference to satire lies in the distinction provided by courts between parody and satire. Although court's referred to this distinction in the context of copyrights, this might constitute an escape root to trademark owners to rely upon in their tarnishment cases. For example, in *Dr. Seuss Enterprises L.P. v Penguin Books USA Inc*, the court provided that fair use and free speech protection is available to true parodies, but not to satire. See- *Dr. Seuss Enterprises L.P. v Penguin Books USA Inc* 924 F.Supp. 1559 (1996) 1567.

[…]necessary.'[92] This would be beneficial in weighing up whether such protection fosters the right of the public to freedom of speech. '[T]he essence of the first amendment claim is that there are instances in which the loss of vocabulary is, effectively, the loss of the ability to communicate.'[93] The standard test for assessing the constitutionality of limiting commercial speech has been discussed by the US Supreme Court in *Central Hudson Gas & Elec Corp v Public Service Commission of New York*.[94]

The Central Hudson Gas test

In the *Central Hudson Gas* case, the Supreme Court has set out four conditions which need to be fulfilled in order to legitimize the regulation of commercial speech. The court provided that governmental interest in regulating commercial speech would be constrained if the speech were 'neither misleading nor related to unlawful activity'.[95] Also, the government 'must assert a substantial interest to be achieved by restrictions on commercial speech.'[96] In addition, the court also emphasized that 'the regulatory technique must be in proportion to that interest[, and t]he limitation on expression must be designed carefully to achieve the [government's] goal.'[97] Therefore, in order for dilution to legitimately restrict commercial speech, it must comply with the Supreme Court's requirements. Thus, the court's conditions, as applied to the dilution concept, shall be duly analysed.

As per the first condition, the expressive use should be neither misleading nor unlawful. This condition should be looked at from one perspective, that is, the confusion test. In the case of trademarks, the use would be misleading and unlawful if such use were likely to cause confusion to the public as to the source and origin of the products. This clearly lies within the main proposition and practical application of the Economic-Social Planning theory; such confusion is the corner-stone in

---

[92] Denicola (n41) 190. See also, Kozinski (n1) 454, arguing that '[s]o long as trademark law limits itself to its traditional role of avoiding confusion in the market place, there's little likelihood that free expression will be hindered.'

[93] RC Dreyfuss 'Expressive Genericity: Trademarks as Language in the Pepsi Generation' (1989-1990) 65 Notre Dame L Rev 412.

[94] 447 U.S. 557, 100 S.Ct. 2343 (1980).

[95] ibid 564.

[96] ibid.

[97] ibid.

the protection of trademarks. Hence, as already pointed out,[98] this condition is not present in the case of parodistic use, since parody focuses on making a non-confusing connection with the senior mark. It has also been argued[99] that if the parody is successful, confusion is *not* likely, and thus, focus should be directed, in such cases, on whether the parody is successful or not. As such, parodistic uses –by their very nature– are neither misleading, nor unlawful. Consequently, the first condition is not met.

The court also required that the government should have substantial interest in restricting commercial speech. Needless to say, substantial interest on the part of the government is far from dilution. Dilution in essence is about providing means to maintain "*uniqueness*" of marks. This was Schechter's main proposition,[100] and was meant to provide proper incentives to trademarks owners. Thus, the individualistic nature of the dilution concept leads to a simple conclusion; restricting commercial speech lacks any interest whatsoever, whether "substantial" or not.

Subsequently, the third and fourth conditions shall not be considered. The proportion of the regulation with the governmental interest and limiting the restriction over the governmental goal are illogical. This is because there is no governmental "interest" or "goal" in the first place in restricting commercial speech in trademarks.

Many scholarly arguments have opposed the dilution concept on the basis of its contradiction with first amendment freedom of speech.[101] LaFrance argues that '[d]ilution laws fail the *Central Hudson* test[, because] the types of speech that are actionable under dilution laws concern lawful, non-misleading activities.'[102] More crucially, LaFrance contends that there is no substantial governmental interest underlying dilution which could justify restriction of commercial speech. She, correctly, reasons that:

> 'The supposed harms that dilution laws prevent or remedy are either nonexistent, insubstantial, or relevant only to the ability of businesses to

---

[98] See *supra* pp 196-199.

[99] See *supra* pp 199-204.

[100] FI Schechter 'The Rational Basis of Trademark Protection' (Reprint in 1970 of the 1927 text) 60 Trademark Reporter 342. See also, ch 3 pp 64-70.

[101] For example, see- MJ Kaplan 'Antidilution Statutes and the First Amendment' (1992) 21 Southwestern U L Rev 1165-1166, arguing that dilution is 'an unconstitutional regulation of free speech.'

[102] LaFrance (n90) 716.

derive profits from consumers without bestowing any commensurate public benefits …'.[103]

Similarly, Barrett argues that under the dilution concept,

'the speech the mark owner is able to enjoin is nonmisleading speech[.] … In addition, there is significantly less public benefit arising from dilution protection to counteract and justify imposing restrictions on expressive speech.'[104]

In sum, the restriction of commercial speech by means of the dilution concept fails to fulfil the *Central Hudson Gas* test. Hence, dilution should be treated as a piece of legislation which contravenes the Constitution, due to its unjustified restriction of speech, which is entitled to First Amendment protection. Needless to say, Congress has thus exceeded its power by enacting a legislation (dilution) which abridged the fundamental right of the public to freely express and communicate their ideas, seriously curtailing the free flow of ideas. This outcome leads to the conclusions of this chapter.

Conclusion

After having discussed the current treatment of cultural and expressive uses in both jurisdictions of this book, it is imperative to outline the implications of applying the premises of the suggested Economic-Social Planning theory over the present state of art.

Economic-Social Planning as Applied to Freedom of Speech

Important questions call for an answer. Does the current approach in the jurisdictions of this book help to foster a just and attractive culture? Is the dilution concept appropriate in seeking to protect the public as regards their right to freely express their ideas and to communicate their thoughts? More precisely, can dilution, based on its utilitarian grounds, fulfil the goals which the Economic-Social Planning theory aims to achieve?

The foregoing arguments show that the dilution concept is *individualistic* in nature, and *absolute* in its granting of rights solely to the owner. Therefore, the application of the Economic-Social Planning theory to current protection shall lead to a number of outcomes.

---

[103] ibid.

[104] Barrett (n13) 1002-1003.

Firstly, attempts to provide a fair use exception within the dilution rationale do not have a practical effect. Such attempts fail because the goals and purposes of dilution contradict the fair use doctrine.[105] It is impossible to reconcile the two concepts. Dilution looks at trademarks as the sole right of their owners, and systems for their protection should focus on providing incentives to the owners to produce products of high quality, the tool of which is to use utilitarian arguments to protect the uniqueness of the mark. The overwhelming majority of expressive uses aim to mock, ridicule or criticize using the mark. In many instances, the use of a mark might be directed against the trademark owner. Such uses are the typical "evils" which dilution fights against, and is designed to prohibit. As such, fair use under dilution laws seems to be an unsuccessful "plastic surgery" to legitimize the concept of dilution, and to overcome a major hurdle which jeopardizes the whole concept of dilution. For this reason, the current protection of trademarks, even with the alleged exception of fair use, fails to fulfil the main goal of the Economic-Social Planning theory in achieving a just and attractive culture.

Secondly, the Economic-Social Planning theory is based on the premise of the "co-authorship" of marks. It also considers the cultural and expressive uses as the gateway to the process in which the public engage in the meaning-making of marks. This requires full protection of the public as genuine contributors in the creation of marks and their cultural meanings. 'Therefore, [it is] not suggested that a capacious fair use doctrine should be extended to trademarks',[106] because 'even if trademark included a more robust fair use exception, it might not provide an answer to the problem of public domain.'[107] In contrast, the dilution concept, in addition to its inherent shortcomings, considers the owners as the only party to enjoy protection. This explains why this concept tends to deal with the rights of the public as exception to the owners' protection. This clearly contradicts the Economic-Social Planning theory's perception in treating all the parties in the trademark formula[108] equally.

Third, even when looking at the right of the public as exceptions, the current orientations of such exceptions are not successful. It has been shown that under the FTDA, the only exception concerned non-

---

[105] In support of this argument, recent scholarly arguments call for the need to amend the Lanham Act, even after the introduction of the TDRA, in order to provide specific protection to parody and satire which ensures protection of free speech. See for example, Rahmatian (n33) 353.

[106] Wilf (n10) 3.

[107] ibid.

[108] See ch 1 p 11.

commercial uses of the mark. It has also been argued that the TDRA was unhelpful, because it constrained the fair use exception when the mark was used as a designation of the source. Therefore, commercial speech faces real dangers under the dilution concept. This latter defect, as regards commercial speech, leads to another hurdle. The Economic-Social Planning theory calls for an environment of free and fair competition in order to achieve the just and attractive culture it calls for. Apparently, the lack of protection as to commercial speech shall prevent the existence of the suggested competition.

All in all, the current dilution protection favouring trademark owners fails the standards of the Economic-Social Planning theory. The exceptions provided by the TDRA fall short of protecting the right of the public in freedom of expression. As a result, dilution threats to curtail the cultural advent of societies.

Summarizing Remarks

The conclusion to this chapter focuses on three aspects. The first relates to the current confusion protection, while the second is directed to dilution, under the Lanham Act. The final word goes to the UK TMA.

Throughout this book, it has been shown that the confusion concept is the real rational basis for trademark protection in the context of maintaining product differentiation. In this chapter, it has been explained that this is no less true in the context of cultural and expressive uses. However, it has been clarified that the lack of explicit mention of the right of the public to such uses has led to the courts misusing this concept. Courts have usually used the confusion concept to prevent parodistic or satiric uses, especially when they are discontent with the nature of such uses. For this reason, it is essential to refer plainly to the rights of the public to overcome any possibility of negative treatment of expressive uses, on the grounds of confusion. This should, however, be regarded as a genuine right to be enjoyed by the public as being "co-authors" of the marks. It has also been shown that in the case of non-commercial use, there should be a *prima facie* assumption that confusion is not likely to occur. In contrast, in the case of mixed uses, the focus should be directed towards assessing whether the parodist was successful in addressing his/her message, rather than looking to the existence of confusion. This is due to the fact that a successful parody excludes any likelihood of confusion. As such, the confusion concept forms a comprehensive manifestation of the premises of the Economic-Social Planning theory.

As regards the dilution concept and its impact on freedom of speech, it has been clearly shown that this concept is not suitable to protect free speech; rather, it restrains such a right. Furthermore, this chapter argues that the distinction between commercial speech and non-commercial speech is not useful. Therefore, it lacks justification in arguing that commercial speech deserves less protection, due to the conditions provided by the *Central Hudson Gas* case. This book holds that commercial and non-commercial speech should enjoy equal protection, on the basis that the *Central Hudson Gas* case requires the commercial speech to be non-misleading for it to be protected. This should be the case for both cases of speech, whether commercial or not. This could be achieved by adherence to the confusion rationale, as provided above, i.e. that the conveyance of a clear and successful message prevents any doubts of confusion, as such the use shall indeed be non-misleading.

Finally, in the UK, it is fortunate that the dilemma of cultural and expressive uses of marks has not yet emerged. What is unfortunate, though, is that the UK TMA leaves the dilution protection open, without any kind of restrictions, even if formal more than real, as is the case under the Lanham Act. Legislators in the UK should take a lesson from the US experience and from the distortive effects of dilution over freedom of expression, and safeguard the public against any possible harm as to their right in free speech. They need not wait until the public bear the huge cost of suppressing their right of speech.

Dilution was not, and will never be, a solution to the problem of protection of the genuine right of the public in using marks for the purpose of expression. The appropriate solution lies in the Economic-Social Planning theory and its deployment of the confusion concept.

CHAPTER SEVEN

CONCLUSIONS

The Argument

This book has argued that current trademark systems have diverted from protecting the consuming public and trademark owners[1] to the sole protection of trademark owners. The rights of trademark owners have been expanded;[2] such an expansion was at the expense of other parties in the trademark formula,[3] namely the consuming public.

In the US, the Trademarks Act of 1946 (Lanham Act) in its current format disregards the dual purpose on which its protection was initially based.[4] The confusion doctrine under this Act has been widened to include types of confusion such as "subliminal confusion" which occurs on a subconscious level.[5] This was the natural outcome of removing the requirement that confusion should be as to the source and origin of goods and/or services.[6] The Lanham Act also incorporated the dilution concept. Currently, owners of famous marks are able to contest uses that blur or tarnish their marks, to which the proof of likelihood of damage would suffice.[7]

Similarly, the UK Trade Marks Act of 1994 (UK TMA) expanded the rights of trademark owners. It considered trademarks as the property rights of trademark owners.[8] The confusion doctrine under the UK TMA does not specify a standard to assess infringement; therefore, the global

---

[1] See ch 1 pp 4-5.
[2] ibid.
[3] See ch 1 p 11.
[4] Namely to protect trademark owners and the consuming public. See ch 4 pp 85-89.
[5] ibid pp 102-104.
[6] See the current format of section 32(a), previously requiring confusion to be as to source of origin of products. See- Trademarks Act 1946- Lanham Act (USA) 15 U.S.C. § 1114 (Section 32(a)). See also, ch 4 pp 102-104.
[7] ibid pp 132-134.
[8] See ch 5 pp 147-155.

appreciation test was deployed.[9] This in turn widened the scope of owners' rights. In addition, dilution was incorporated under the UK TMA, although this was a non-mandatory section under Directive 2008/95/EC.[10] This section requires a low standard of reputation for marks eligible for dilution protection.[11] Moreover, the dilution protection under the UK TMA has also been widened, to include uses of the mark with reputation on similar as well as dissimilar goods and/or services.[12]

The expansion of the confusion doctrine undermines the right of the consuming public to have their state of mind (confusion) as the sole test for trademark infringement.[13] This expansion also threatens the right of the public to use trademarks in cultural and expressive contexts.[14] In the US, this right has been considered as an exception to the rights of trademark owners.[15] In addition, these exceptions do not cover cases of commercial speech, even if the use is not likely to cause confusion as to the source and origin of the goods and/or services in question.[16] The case of the UK TMA is different; it completely ignores the rights of the public in this regard.[17] This threatens the fundamental human right in free speech.

In dealing with the troubles of current trademark systems, this book has developed the Economic-Social Planning theory, which provides a practical solution to such troubles.

Economic-Social Planning of Trademarks

The above-mentioned troubles with trademarks prove the need to revisit the philosophical foundations of current trademark systems. In an attempt to provide a proper justification for trademark systems, this book proves that the utilitarian justification, the Lockean theory and the Hegelian approach fail to provide a satisfactory justification for trademark systems.

---

[9] ibid pp 165-168.

[10] Directive 2008/95/EC of the European Parliament and of the Council of 22 October 2008 to approximate the laws of the Member States relating to trade marks, OJ L 299, 08/11/2008.

[11] See ch 5 pp 178-180.

[12] ibid pp 176-178.

[13] ibid pp 190-192.

[14] See ch 2 pp 57-59. See also, ch 3 p 81.

[15] See ch 6 pp 208-209.

[16] ibid pp 211-214.

[17] ibid pp 206-208.

It has been argued that the utilitarian model fails to justify trademarks. This theory considers that the uniqueness of trademarks should be preserved, and therefore, trademark owners should be ensured maximum protection in order to provide them with the incentive to produce high quality goods and/or services.[18] However, this argument is an artificial argument, because it is based on economic principles which are distinct from, and fail to justify, trademark systems.[19] In addition, it has been shown that the incentive argument is subjective, and differs in individual cases.[20]

Locke's labour theory was not intended to justify trademarks, and it is not of much assistance when applied to trademarks. Applying his treatise over trademarks fails to justify the high amount of rights enjoyed by trademark owners. The application of Locke's justification over trademarks would simply over-compensate trademark owners.[21] Locke insisted on the enough and as good condition. In this sense, it has been shown that the amount of rights conferred to trademark owners –if Locke's labour theory is applied– will not leave enough and as good to others, because the commons of signs is not infinite.[22] Thus, this theory is individualistic, and does not consider the rights of all the parties in the trademark formula,[23] and falls short in forming a valid justification to trademarks. It has also been shown that Hegel's personhood approach is not satisfactory. In addition to being individualistic, as in the case of Locke's labour theory, this theory fails to justify the alienability of rights in trademarks. This also exempts it from the ability to provide a proper justification.

It is suggested that the Economic-Social Planning theory provides an equitable approach for the justification of trademarks. This theory considers that trademarks reduce consumer search costs.[24] In order to define the boundaries for the rights of the parties involved in the trademark formula,[25] the Economic-Social Planning theory considers that trademarks should be shaped in a manner which helps fostering the achievement of a "just and attractive culture",[26] whereby monopoly is prohibited and a free

[18] See ch 2 pp 17-23.
[19] ibid pp 25-27.
[20] ibid pp 23-24.
[21] ibid pp 34-38.
[22] ibid pp 38-40.
[23] See ch 1 p 11.
[24] See ch 2 pp 27-30.
[25] See ch 1 p 11.
[26] ibid.

and fair competition is promoted. This theory considers that trademarks are created when an undertaking affixes a sign over his/her products, and the public attribute an association between the sign and the products. This is the process of "co-authorship" of trademarks.[27]

Practical Solution

The Economic-Social Planning theory develops a new argument in relation to the functions of trademarks. It considers the source and origin function as the only *primary* function of trademarks, upon which protection should be based. This approach opens the way for other secondary functions of trademarks, but these could not form the basis for protection.[28]

The significance of the argument developed by this book is that it develops a clear vision as regards the rights of the public as "co-authors" of trademarks. It is suggested that the public should enjoy the right of having their state of mind (confusion) as the only test for trademark infringement.[29] This book has also advocated more public access to trademarks, according to which the consuming public should enjoy the right of using trademarks in cultural and expressive contexts.

The aim of the Economic-Social Planning theory is not to undermine the rights of trademark owners. Rather, owners of trademarks should enjoy the right to use their marks, and prevent others from using them when such uses are likely to confuse the public as to the source and origin of goods and/or services. In addition, owners of well-known trademarks should enjoy extra protection which extends to using these marks by others on dissimilar products, provided that such use is likely to cause confusion.[30]

Additionally, the Economic-Social Planning theory recognizes the rights of other traders as a party in the trademark formula.[31] This protection derives from adopting confusion as the test for trademark infringement, an opens the gate for other traders to use trademarks in cases where the use is not likely to confuse the public.

---

[27] ibid p 10. See also, ch 2 pp 57-59.
[28] Such as the quality, advertising and informative functions. See- ch 3 pp 75-78.
[29] See ch 2 pp 57-59. See also, ch 3 p 81.
[30] See ch 3 pp 78-80.
[31] See ch 1 pp 9-10.

The Future of Trademark Protection

In the light of the premises of the Economic-Social Planning theory and the practical solution it developed, this final section provides the recommendations which form the fruits of this book.

Policy-makers, judges, legislators, scholars and courts should reconsider the deployment of utilitarian justification that dominates current trademark systems, which is responsible for the current expansion of trademark owners' rights. This reconsideration should take into account the possible threats to the expanding rights of trademark owners to the detriment of the consuming public and other traders and rivals. Thus, trademarks should not consider trademarks as the sole property rights of trademark owners.

It is also recommended that the source and origin function should be considered as the only primary function of trademarks, and protection should be based on this function. Accordingly, current trademark systems should not be based on the quality function which is subjective and differs amongst individuals.

The most crucial recommendation relates to the right of the consuming public not to be confused. Thus, confusion should be regarded as the corner-stone and the sole test for trademark infringement. Trademark systems should also recognize the rights of the public to use trademarks in cultural and expressive uses. In addition, it is recommended that other traders and rivals should be able to use trademarks when such uses are not likely to cause confusion.

Finally, this book considers that the recent change in the standard of "fame" under the Trademark Dilution Revision Act of 2005 (TDRA),[32] and the recent decision of the European Court of Justice (ECJ) in *Intel Corporation Inc v CPM United Kingdom Ltd*,[33] could be an important step towards limiting the scope of the dilution concept, which might lead the way towards the recommendations of this book.

---

[32] Trademark Dilution Revision Act 2005 (USA) § 2 – Trademarks Act 1946-Lanham Act (USA) 15 U.S.C. § 1125 (Section 43(c) (2) (a). See also, ch 4 pp 120-122.

[33] [2008] ECR 00. See also, ch 5 pp 183-187.

BIBLIOGRAPHY

Abdel-khalik J 'To Live in in-"Fame"-Y: Reconceiving Scandalous Marks as Analogous to Famous Marks' (2007) 25 Cardozo Arts & Entertainment L J (173-236).

Akazaki L 'Source Theory and Guarantee Theory in Anglo-American Trade Mark Policy: A Critical Legal Study' (1990) 72 J of the Patent & Trademark Office Society (255-278).

Akerlof GA 'The Market for "Lemons": Quality Uncertainty and the Market Mechanism' (1970) 84 Q J of Economics (488-500).

Alexander MJ and Coil JH 'Geographic Rights in Trademarks and Service Marks' (1978) 68 Trademark Reporter (101-120).

Allen MJ 'The Scope of Confusion Actionable under Federal Trademark Law: Who Must be Confused and When?' (1991) 26 Wake Forest L Rev (209-254).

Aoki K 'Authors, Inventors, and Trademark Owners: Private Intellectual Property and the Public Domain Part 2' (1993-1994) 18 Columbia-VLA J of L & the Arts (193-267).

—. 'How the World Dreams of Itself to be American: Reflections on the Relationship Between the Expanding Scope of Trademark Protection and Free Speech Norms' (1996-1997)17 Loyola of Los Angeles Entertainment L J (523-548).

Assaf K 'The Dilution of Culture and the Law of Trademarks' (2008) 49 IDEA: The Intellectual Property L Rev (1-83).

Barendt E *Freedom of Speech* (2nd edn Oxford University Press Oxford 2005).

Barrett DS 'The Future of the Concurrent Use of Trademarks Doctrine in the Information Age' (2000-2001) 23 Hastings Comm/Ent L J (687-722).

Barrett M 'Domain Names, Trademarks and the First Amendment: Searching for Meaningful Boundaries' (2007) 39 Connecticut L Rev (973-1050).

Barthes R 'The Death of the Author' in Roland Barthes, *Image, Music, Text, Essays selected and translated by Stephen Heath* (Fontana Press London 1977) (142-148).

Bartow A 'Likelihood of Confusion' (2004) 41 San Diego L Rev (721-818).

Beebe B 'A Defence of the New Federal Trademark Antidilution Law' (2006) 16 Fordham Intellectual Property Media & Entertainment L J (1143-1174).

—. 'The Continuing Debacle of U.S. Antidilution Law: Evidence from the First Year of Trademark Dilution Revision Act Case Law' (2007-2008) 24 Santa Clara Computer & High Technology L J (449-467).

Beerline JF 'Anti-Dilution Law, New and Improved: The Trademark Dilution Revision Act of 2006' (2008) 23 Berkeley Technology L J (511-535).

Beier F 'Basic Features of Anglo-American, French and German Trademark Law' (1975) 3 Intl Rev of Industrial Property and Competition L (285-303).

Bell A and Parchomovsky G 'A Theory of Property' (2005) Vol 90 No 3 Cornell L Rev (531-615).

Bently L and Sherman B *Intellectual Property Law* (2nd edn Oxford University Press Oxford 2004).

Blakeney M 'Trade Marks and the Promotion of Trade' (1999) 5(6) Intl Trade L & Regulation (140-146).

Blerman MH and Wexler JD 'Toward a Reformulation of the Test for Determining Trademark Infringement' (1990) 80 Trademark Reporter (1-35).

Bone RG 'A Skeptical view of the Trademark Dilution Revision Act' (2007) 11 Intellectual Property L Bulletin (187-198).

Bosland J 'The Culture of Trade Marks: An Alternative Cultural Theory Perspective' (2005) Vol 10 No 2 Media & Arts L Rev (1-33), available at <http://www.ipria.org/publications/workingpapers/WP13.05.pdf>

Bouckaert B 'What is Property?' (1990) 13 Harvard J of L & Public Policy (775-816).

Briggs N 'Infringement under Section 10(2) and 10(3) of the 1994 Trade Marks Act in Perspective' (2000) 22(9) EIPR (429-434).

Brown C 'A Dilution Delusion: The Unjustifiable Protection of Similar Marks' (2003-2004) 72 U of Cincinnati L Rev (1023-1042).

Burstein SL 'Dilution by Tarnishment: The New Cause of Action' (2008) 98 Trademark Reporter (1189-1252).

Byrne DM 'Locke, Property, and Progressive Taxes' (1999) 78 Nebraska L Rev (700-743).

Callmann R 'Unfair Competition without Competition?' (1946-1947) 95 U of Pennsylvania L Rev (443-467).

Cantwell MK 'Confusion, Dilution and Speech: First Amendment Limitations on the Trademark Estate: An Update' (2004) 94 Trademark Reporter (547-584).

Carboni A 'Distinctive Character Acquired Through Use: Establishing the Facts' in J Phillips and I Simon (eds) Trade Mark Use (1st edn Oxford University Press Oxford 2005) (71-92).

Carter SL 'Owning What Doesn't Exist' (1990) Vol 13 No 1 Harvard J of L & Public Policy (99-107).

—. 'The Trouble with Trademark' (1989-1990) 99 Yale L J (759-800).

Carty H 'Dilution and Passing off: Cause for Concern' (1996) 112 L Q Rev (632-666).

—. 'Do Marks with a Reputation Merit Special Protection' (1997) 19(12) EIPR (684-688).

—. 'The Common Law and the Quest for the IP Effect' (2007) 3 Intellectual Property Q (237-266).

Casparie-Kerdel S 'Dilution Disguised: Has the Concept of Dilution Made its Way into the Laws of Europe' (2001) 23(4) EIPR (185-195).

Cendali DM Matorin CM and Maltby J 'Moseley v. V Secret Catalogue, Inc.: One Answer, Many Questions' (2003) 93 Trademark Reporter (833-841).

Chalk PC 'The True Value of Trademarks: Influencing who we are and who we Want to be' (2001-2002) 12 J of Contemporary Legal Issues (20-25).

Chicoine C and Visintine J 'The Role of State Trademark Dilution Statutes in the Light of the Trademark Dilution Revision Act of 2006' (2006) 96 Trademark Reporter (1155-1181).

Chong S 'Protection of Famous Trademarks Against Use for Unrelated Goods and Services: A Comparative Analysis of the Law in the United States, the United Kingdom and Canada and Recommendations for the Canadian Law Reform' (2005) 95 Trademark Reporter (642-704).

Clark ES 'Finding Likelihood of Confusion with Actual Confusion: A Critical Analysis of the Federal Courts' Approach' (1992) 22 Golden Gate U L Rev (393-412).

Cody JA 'Initial Interest Confusion: What Ever Happened to Traditional Likelihood of Confusion Analysis?' (2002-2003) 12 The Federal Circuit Bar J (643-686).

Coombe RJ 'Objects of Property and Subjects of Politics: Intellectual Property Laws and Democratic Dialogue' (1990-1991) 69 Texas L Rev (1853-1880).

—. *The Cultural Life of Intellectual Properties* (1st edn Duke University Press Durham and London 1998).

Cornish W and Llewelyn D *Intellectual Property: Patents, Copyright, Trade Marks and Allied Rights* (6th edn Sweet & Maxwell London 2007).

Cornish W *Intellectual Property Omnipresent, Distracting, Irrelevant?* (1st edn Oxford University Press Oxford 2004).

Cornish WR and Phillips J 'The Economic Function of Trade Marks: An Analysis with Special Reference to Developing Countries' (1982) Vol 13 No 1 Intl Rev of Industrial Property and Copyright L (41-64).

Craig CJ 'Locke, Labour and Limiting the Author's Right: A Warning Against a Lockean Approach to Copyright Law' (2002-2003) 28 Queen's L J (1-60).

Creasman WS 'Establishing Geographic Rights in Trademarks Based on Internet Use' (2005) 95 Trademark Reporter (1016-1033).

Davis J 'European Trade Mark Law and the Enclosure of the Commons' (2002) 4 Intellectual Property Q (342-367).

—. 'To Protect or Serve? European Trade Mark Law and the Decline of the Public Interest' (2003) 25(4) EIPR (180-187).

Dawson N 'Famous and Well-Known Trade Marks – "Usurping a Corner of the Giant's Robe" ' (1998) 4 Intellectual Property Q (350-382).

Delflache ML, Silbert S and Hillson C 'Life After Moseley: The Trademark Dilution Revision Act' (2007) 16 Texas Intellectual Property L J (125-150).

Denicola RC 'Some Thoughts on the Dynamics of Federal Trademark Legislation and the Trademark Dilution Act of 1995' (1996) 59 L and Contemporary Problems (75-92).

—. 'Trademarks as Speech: Constitutional Implications of the Emerging Rationales for the Protection of Trade Symbols' (1982) 1982 Wisconsin L Rev (158-207).

Derenberg WJ 'The Problem of Trademark Dilution and the Antidilution Statutes' (1956) 44 California L Rev (439-488).

Diamond SA 'The Historical Development of Trademarks' (1983) 73 Trademark Reporter (222-247).

—. 'The Public Interest and the Trademark System' (1980) 62 J of the Patent Office Society (528-545).

Diamond SS 'Trademark Dilution: of Fame, Blurring, and Sealing Wax, with a Touch of Judicial Wisdom' (2007-2008) 24 Santa Clara Computer & High Technology L J (521-540).

Dinwoodie GB 'The Rational Limits of Trademark Law' in H Hansen (ed) *U.S. Intellectual Property Law and Policy* (1st edn Edward Elgar Cheltenham 2006) (59-84).

Doellinger CJ 'A New Theory of Trademarks' (2007) 111 Penn State L Rev (823-862).

Domenico DD 'Mark Madness: How Brent Musburger and the Miracle Bra May Have Led to a More Equitable and Efficient Understanding of the Reverse Confusion Doctrine in Trademark Law' (2000) 86 Virginia L Rev (597-648).

Dougherty T 'Group Rights to Cultural Survival: Intellectual Property Rights in Native American Cultural Symbols' (1998) 29 Columbia Human Rights L Rev (355-400).

Drahos P *A Philosophy of Intellectual Property* (1st edn Dartmouth England 1996).

Dreyfuss RC 'Expressive Genericity: Trademarks as Language in the Pepsi Generation' (1989-1990) 65 Notre Dame L Rev (397-424).

Duvall SA 'The Trademark Dilution Revision Act of 2006: Balanced Protection for Famous Brands' (2007) 97 Trademark Reporter (1252-1285).

Economides N 'The Economics of Trademarks' (1988) 78 Trademark Reporter (523-539).

Farley CH 'Why we are Confused about the Trademark Dilution Law' (2006) 16 Fordham Intellectual Property Media & Entertainment L J (1175-1187).

Farmany T 'Dallas Cowboys Cheerleaders v. Pussycat Cinema' (2001-2002) 12 J of Contemporary Legal Issues (275-279).

Fhima IS 'The Fame Standard for Trademark Dilution in the United States and European Union Compared' (2008) 17 Transnational L and Contemporary Problems (631-666).

Fisher W 'Property and Contract on the Internet' (1997-1998) 73 Chicago-Kent L Rev (1203-1256).

—. 'Theories of Intellectual Property' in S Munzer (ed) *New Essays in the Legal and Political Theory of Property* (1st edn Cambridge University Press Cambridge 2001) (168-199).

Fletcher PK 'Joint Registration of Trademarks and the Economic Value of a Trademark System' (1981-1982) 36 U of Miami L Rev (297-336).

Folsom RH and Teply LL 'Trademarked Generic Words' (1979-1980) 89 Yale L J (206-242).

Geiger C 'Trade Marks and Freedom of Expression – The Proportionality of Criticism' (2007) 38 Intl Rev of Intellectual Property and Competition L (317-327).

—. 'Harmonisation of Trade Mark Law in Europe: The First Trade Mark Harmonisation' (1992) 14(8) EIPR (262-269).

Gilson J 'A Federal Dilution Statute: Is it Time?' (1993) 83 Trademark Reporter (108-121).

Goodberlet K 'The Trademark Dilution Revision Act of 2006: Prospective Changes to Dilution Definition, Claim Analyses, and Standard of Harm' (2006) 6 J of High Tech L (249-279).

Gordon WJ 'On Owning Information: Intellectual Property and the Restitutionary Impulse' (1992) Virginia L Rev (1533-1610).

Greenberg AS 'The Ancient Lineage of Trade-Marks' (1951) 33 J of the Patent Office Society (876-887).

Griffiths A 'The Impact of the Global Appreciation Approach on the Boundaries of Trade Mark Protection' (2001) 4 Intellectual Property Q (326-360).

Grotius H *De Jure Belli Ac Pacis Libri Tres* (Vol 2 Oceana Publications New York and Wildy & Sons Ltd London FW Kelsey Translation Reprinted 1964).

Gulasekaram P 'Policing the Border between Trademarks and Free Speech: Protecting Unauthorized Trademark Use in Expressive Works' (2005) 80 Washington L Rev (887-942).

Hacking JF 'Trademark Dilution: Setting the Dilution Standard under the Federal Trademark Dilution Act' (2003) 5 Tulane J of Technology & Intellectual Property (115-130).

Hamilton WH 'Property- According to Locke' (1931-1932) 41 Yale L J (864-880).

Handler MW 'Are the State Antidilution Laws Compatible with the National Protection of Trademarks?' (1998) Trademark Reporter (419-439).

Harris P 'UK Trade Mark Law: Are you Confused' (1995) 17(12) EIPR (601-606).

Hegel GWF *Philosophy of Right* (1st edn Oxford University Press Oxford T M Knox Translation 1952).

Hein C 'Confused About the Federal Trademark Dilution?' (1997) 87 Trademark Reporter (370-417).

Hettinger EC 'Justifying Intellectual Property' (1989) Vol 18 No 1 Philosophy and Public Affairs (31-52).

Heymann LA 'The Birth of the Authornym: Authorship, Pseudonymity, and Trademark Law' (2005) 80 Notre Dame L Rev (1377-1450).

Higgins DM and James TJ 'The Economic Importance of Trade Marks in the UK (1973-1992) A Preliminary Investigation' (1996) The Intellectual Property Institute (1-27).

Higgins JR and Duvall SA 'The FTDA after Moseley v. V Secret' (2003) 93 Trademark Reporter (813-832).

Hofrichter JA 'Tool of the Trademark: Brand Criticism and Free Speech Problems with the Trademark Dilution Revision Act of 2006' (2007) 28 Cardozo L Rev (1923-1960).

Horwitz JA 'Conflicting Marks: Embracing the Consequences of the European Community and its Unitary Trademark Regime' (2001) 18 Arizona J Intl & Comparative L (245-278).

Howell C 'A Loaded Question: On Section 5(3) of the Trade Marks Act 1994' 2002 13(3) Intl Company and Commercial L Rev (118-125).

Hughes J 'The Philosophy of Intellectual Property' (1988-1989) 77 The Georgetown L J (287-366).

Hughes JR 'The Federal Trademark Dilution Act of 1995 and the Evolution of the Dilution Doctrine – Is it Truly a Rational Basis for the Protection of Trademarks?' (1998) Vol 1998 Issue 3 Detroit College L Rev (759-806).

Jacoby J 'Considering the Who, What, When, Where and How of Measuring Dilution' (2007-2008) 24 Santa Clara Computer & High Technology L J (601-639).

—. 'The Psychological Foundations of Trademark Law: Secondary Meaning, Genericism, Fame, Confusion and Dilution' (2001) 91 Trademark Reporter (1013-1071).

Kaplan MJ 'Antidilution Statutes and the First Amendment' (1992) 21 Southwestern U L Rev (1139-1168).

Kaufmann D 'How to Prevent Your Mark Becoming Generic' (2007) 168 Managing Intellectual Property (125-127).

Kaul DA 'Concurrent Use and Registration of Trademarks' (1972) 62 Trademark Reporter (581-600).

Keller BP and Bernstein DH 'As Satiric As They Wanna Be: Parody Lawsuits Under Copyright, Trademark, Dilution and Publicity Laws' (1995) 85 Trademark Reporter (239-262).

Khoury AH 'Ancient and Islamic Sources of Intellectual Property Protection in the Middle East: A Focus on Trademarks' (2003) 43 The J of L and Technology (151-206).

Kinkade CR 'Is Trademark Dilution Law Diluting Rights? A Survey of the Trademark Dilution Revision Act of 2006' (2007) 31 Seton Hall Legislative J (433-461).

Kinsella NS 'Against Intellectual Property' (2001) Vol 15 No 2 J of Libertarian Studies (1-53), available at <http://www.mises.org/journals/jls/15_2/15_2_1.pdf>

Kitchin D and others *Kerly's Law of Trade Marks and Trade Names* (14th edn Sweet & Maxwell London 2005).

Klieger RN 'Trademark Dilution: The Whittling Away of the Rational Basis for Trademark Protection' (1997) 58 U of Pittsburgh L Rev (789-866).

Kozinski A 'Trademarks Unplugged' (1994) 84 Trademark Reporter (441-459).

Krafte-Jacobs L 'Judicial Interpretation of the Federal Trademark Dilution Act of 1995' (1998) 66 U of Cincinnati L Rev (659-696).

Kur A 'Well-Known Marks, Highly Renown Marks and Marks Having a (High) Reputation – What's it All about?' (1992) 23 Intl Rev of Intellectual Property and Competition L (218-231).

Ladas SP 'Trademark Licensing and the Antitrust Law' (1973) 63 Trademark Reporter (245-266).

LaFrance M 'No Reason to Live: Dilution Laws as Unconstitutional Restrictions on Commercial Speech' (2007) 58 South Carolina L Rev (709-724).

Landes W and Posner R 'An Economic Analysis of Copyright Law' (1989) 18 J of Legal Studies (325-363).

Landes WM and Posner RA 'The Economics of Trademark Law' (1988) 78 Trademark Reporter (523-539).

Leaffer M 'Fifty Years of the Lanham Act: The Decline and Demise of Monopoly Phobia' in HC Hansen (ed) *International Intellectual Property Law & Policy* (Volume 7 Juris Publishing Inc Huntington NY 2001) (38–1 - 38–34).

—. 'Sixty Years of the Lanham Act: The Decline and Demise of Monopoly Phobia' in H Hansen (ed) *U.S. Intellectual Property Law and Policy* (1st edn Edward Elgar Cheltenham 2006) (85-133).

Lefkowitz S 'A Concurrent Use Registration as a Reflection of Established Territorial Rights; Fact or Fiction?' (1975) 65 Trademark Reporter (71-82).

Lessig L 'The Creative Commons' (2004) 65 Montana L Rev (1-13).

Levine JK 'Contesting the Incontestable: Reforming Trademark's Descriptive Mark Protection Scheme' (2005-2006) 41 Gonzaga L Rev (29-80).

Levy K 'Trademark Parody: A Conflict between Constitutional and Intellectual Property Interests' (2001) 69 The George Washington L Rev (425-452).

Levy PA 'The Trademark Dilution Revision Act – A Consumer Perspective' (2006) 16 Fordham Intellectual Property, Media & Entertainment L J (1189-1221).

Liddy SJ 'The Lanham Act- An Analysis' (1996) 86 Trademark Reporter (421-441).

Litman J 'The Public Domain' (1990) 39 Emory L J (965-1024).

Lobur J 'Trademarks – Likelihood of Confusion and the Public Interest' (1973-1974) 20 Wayne L Rev (1205-1214).

Locke J *Two Treatises of Government, a Critical Edition with an Introduction and Apparatus Criticus by Peter Laslett* (1st edn Cambridge University Press Cambridge 1964).

Long C 'Dilution' (2006) 106 Columbia L Rev (1029-1078).

Loon NLW 'Time to Re-think the Ever Expanding Concept of Trade Marks? Re-calibrating Singapore's Trade Mark Law after the Controversial US-Singapore FTA' (2008) 30(4) EIPR (151-161).

Luepke MHH 'Taking Unfair Advantage or Diluting a Famous Mark – A 20/20 Perspective on the Blurred Differences Between U.S. and E.U. Dilution Law' (2008) 98 Trademark Reporter (789-833).

Lunsford JR 'Trademark Infringement and Confusion of Source: Need for Supreme Court Action' (1949) 35 Virginia L Rev (214-234).

Mahaffey-Dowd B 'Famous Trademarks: Ordinary Inquiry by the Courts of Marks Entitled to an Extraordinary Remedy' (1998) 64 Brook L Rev (423-455).

Maniatis S 'Dilution in Europe?' in HC Hansen (ed) *International Intellectual Property Law & Policy* (Volume 7 Juris Publishing Inc Huntington NY 2001) (43–1 - 43–17).

—. *Trade Marks in Europe: A Practical Jurisprudence* (1st edn Sweet & Maxwell London 2006).

Maniatis SM 'Trade Mark Rights– A Justification Based on Property' (2002) 2 Intellectual Property Q (123-171).

Maniatis SM and Gredley E 'Parody: A Fatal Attraction? Part 2: Trade Mark Parodies' (1997) 19(8) EIPR (412-420).

Maniatis SM *The Communicative Aspects of Trade Marks: A Legal, Functional and Economic Analysis* (PhD Thesis University of London 1998).

Martino T *Trademark Dilution* (1st edn Clarendon Press Oxford 1996).

McCabe KB 'Dilution-by-Blurring: A Theory Caught in the Shadow of Trademark Infringement' (2000) 68 Fordham L Rev (1827-1876).

McCarthy JT 'Dilution of a Trademark: European and United States Law Compared' (2004) 94 Trademark Reporter (1163-1181).

—. 'Proving a Trademark has been Diluted: Theories or Facts?' (2004) 41 Houston L Rev (713-748).

—. 'The 1996 Federal Anti-Dilution Statute' (1998) 16 Cardozo Arts & Entertainment L J (587-600).

—. *Trademarks and Unfair Competition* (2nd edn The Lawyers Co-operative Publishing Co. New York 1984).

McClure DM 'Trademarks and Unfair Competition: A Critical History of Legal Thought' (1979) 69 Trademark Reporter (305-356).

McKenna MP 'The Normative Foundations of Trademark Law' (2006-2007) 82 Notre Dame L Rev (1839-1916).

Menell PS 'Intellectual Property: General Theories' in B Bouckaert and G de Geest (eds) *Encyclopedia of Law & economics* (Edward Elgar Cheltenham UK 2000) Vol 2 (129-188).

Michaels A 'Confusion in and about Sections 5(3) and 10(3) of the Trade Marks Act 1994' (2000) 22(7) EIPR (335-339).

Moffat VR 'Mutant Copyrights and Backdoor Patents: The Problem of Overlapping Intellectual Property Protection' (2004) 19 Berkeley Technology L J (1473-1532).

Moore A 'A Lockean Theory of Intellectual property' (1997-1998) 21 Hamline L Rev (65-108).

Moore AD 'Intellectual property, Innovation, and Social Progress: The Case Against Incentive Based Arguments' (2003) Vol 26:3 Hamline L Rev (602-630).

Moskin JE 'Dilution or Delusion: The Rational Limits of Trademark Protection' (1993) 83 Trademark Reporter (122-148).

Mossoff A 'What is Property? Putting the Pieces Back Together' (2003) 45 Arizona L Rev (371-443).

Moulds H 'Private Property in John Locke's State of Nature' (1964) 23(2) The American J of Economics and Sociology (179-188).

Nozick R *Anarchy, State, and Utopia* (1st edn Blackwell Oxford 1974).

Oppenheim SC 'The Public Interest in Legal Protection of Industrial and Intellectual Property' (1950) 32 J of the Patent Office Society (903-935).

Palladino VN 'Assessing Trademark Significance: Genericness, Secondary Meaning and Surveys' (2002) 92 Trademark Reporter (857-889).

Palmer TG 'Are Patents and Copyrights Morally Justified? The Philosophy of Property Rights and Ideal Objects' (1990) 13 Harvard J of L & Public Policy (817-866).

—. 'Intellectual Property: A Non-Posnerian Law and Economics Approach' (1988-1989) 12 Hamline L Rev (261-304).

Park DK 'Trademark Infringement – Lanham Act § 43(a) – Source Confusion' (1980-1981) 48 Tennessee L Rev (182-195).

Pattishall BW 'Trade-Marks and the Monopoly Phobia' (1951-1952) 50 Michigan L Rev (967-990).

Phillips J and Simon I 'Going Down in History: Does History Have Anything to Offer Today's Intellectual Property Lawyer' (2005) 3 Intellectual Property Q (225-235).

Pickering CDG *Trade Marks in Theory and Practice* (1st edn Hart Publishing Oxford 1998)

Port K 'The "Unnatural" Expansion of Trademark Rights: Is a Federal Dilution Statute Necessary?' (1995) 85 Trademark Reporter (525-575).

Port KL 'Foreword: Symposium on Intellectual Property Law Theory' (1992-1993) 68 Chicago-Kent L Rev (585-608).

—. 'Judging Dilution in the United States and Japan' (2008) 17 Transnational Law and Contemporary Problems (667-687).

—. 'The Congressional Expansion of American Trademark Law: A Civil Law System in the Making' (2000) 35 Wake Forest L Rev (827-914).

Prescott P 'Think Before you Waga Finger' (1996) 18(6) EIPR (317-321).

Pretnar B 'Use and Non-Use in Trade Mark Law' in J Phillips and I Simon (eds) *Trade Mark Use* (1st edn Oxford University Press Oxford 2005) (11-27).

Pulliam AE 'Raising the Bar Too High: *Moseley V. V Secret Catalogue, Inc.* and Relief under the Federal Trademark Dilution Act' (2004) 53 Catholic U L Rev (887-912).

Radin MG 'Property and Personhood' (1981-1982) 34 Stanford L Rev (957-1016).

Rahmatian A 'Copyright and Commodification' (2005) 27(10) EIPR (371-378).

—. 'Infringement of Trade Marks in the United Kingdom and in Austria' (1999) 21(7) EIPR (354-363).

—. 'Trade Mark Infringement as a Criminal Offence' (2004) 67(4) MLR (670-683).

—. 'Trade Marks and Human Rights' in PLC Torremans (ed) *Intellectual Property and Human Rights* (1st edn Kluwer Law International BV Netherlands 2008) (335-357).

Rangel T 'What's the Secret? – Proving Actual Harm in Trademark Dilution' (2005-2006) 47 South Texas L Rev (131-156).

Raz J 'On the Nature of Rights' (1984) 93 Mind (194-214).

Richardson M 'Copyright in Trade Marks? On Understanding Trade Mark Dilution' (2000) 1 Intellectual Property Q (66-83).

Rogers ES 'Excerpts from the Lanham Act and the Social Function of Trade-Marks' (1972) 62 Trademark Reporter (255-261).

Roncaglia PL 'Should We Use Guns and Missiles to Protect Famous Trademarks in Europe?' (1998) 88 Trademark Reporter (551-563).

Ruwe K 'The Federal Trademark Dilution Act: "Actual Harm" or "Likelihood of Dilution"?' (2001-2002) 70 U of Cincinnati L Rev (1175-1200).

Sanders AK 'Some Frequently Asked Questions about the 1994 UK Trade Marks Act' (1995) 17(2) EIPR (67-74).

—. 'The Return to Wagamama' (1996) 18(10) EIRR (521-525).

—. 'The Wagamama Decision: Back to the Dark Ages of Trade Mark Law' (1996) 18(1) EIPR (3-5).

Schechter FI 'Fog and Fiction in Trade-Mark protection' (1936) 36 Columbia L Rev (60-87).

—. 'The Rational Basis of Trademark Protection' (Reprinted in 1970) 60 Trademark Reporter (334-352). FI Schechter 'The Rational Basis of Trademark Protection' (1926-1927) 40 Harvard L Rev (813-833).

Shanahan D 'The Trademark Right: Consumer Protection or Monopoly?' (1982) 72 Trademark Reporter (233-250).

Shaughnessy RJ 'Trademark Parody: A Fair Use and First Amendment Analysis' (1986) 72 Virginia L Rev (1079-1117).

Shiffrin SV 'Lockean Arguments for Private Intellectual Property' in S Munzer (ed) *New Essays in the Legal and Political Theory of Property* (1st edn Cambridge University Press Cambridge 2001) (138-167).

Smith PW 'Trademarks, Parody, and Consumer Confusion: A Workable Lanham Act Infringement Standard' (1990-1991) 12 Cardozo L Rev (1525-1582).

Spector HM 'An Outline of a Theory Justifying Intellectual and Industrial Property Rights' (1989) 11 EIPR (270-273).

Spence M 'Intellectual Property and the Problem of Parody' (1998) 114 L Q Rev (594-620).

Sreenivasan G *The Limits of Lockean Rights in Property* (1st edn Oxford University Press Oxford 1995).

Staffin EB 'The Dilution Doctrine: Towards a Reconciliation With the Lanham Act' (1995-1996) 6:105 Fordham Intellectual Property Media & Entertainment (105-178).

Stillman PG 'Hegel's Analysis of Property in the Philosophy of Right' (1988-1989) 10 Cardozo L Rev (129-188).

Strasser M 'The Rational Basis of Trademark Protection Revisited: Putting the Dilution Doctrine into Context' (1999-2000) 10 Fordham Intellectual Property, Media & Entertainment L J (375-432).

Tasker T 'Parody or Satire as a Defense to Trademark Infringement' (1987) 77 Trademark Reporter (216-247).

Thomas JS 'Likelihood of Confusion Under the Lanham Act: A Question of Fact, a Question of Law, or Both?'(1984-1985) 73 Kentucky L J (235-254).

Tichane DM 'The Maturing Trademark Doctrine of Post-Sales Confusion' (1995) 85 Trademark Reporter (399-423).

Torremans P *Holyoak & Torremans Intellectual Property Law* (5th edn Oxford University Press Oxford 2008).

Torremans PLC 'The Likelihood of Association of Trade Marks: An Assessment in the Light of the Recent Case Law of the Court of Justice' (1998) 3 Intellectual Property Q (295-310).

Ullah W and Martino TR 'The Quality Guarantee Function of Trade Marks: An Economic Viewpoint' (1989) 11(8) EIPR (267-269).

Waldron J 'What is Private Property?' (1985) 5 Oxford J of Legal Studies (313-349).

—. 'When Justice Replaces Affection: The Need for Rights' (1988) 11 Harvard J of L & Public Policy (625-648).

—. *The Right to Private Property* (1st edn Clarendon Press Oxford 1988).

Walker A 'The Burden of Actual Dilution: In the Wake of *Moseley v. Victoria Secret Catalogue*' (2003) Volume 8 Number 2 Intellectual Property L Bulletin (23-26).

Weber SR 'Trademarks and Genericness: Loss of a Mark to the Public Domain Through its Transformation into a Generic Term' (1989-1990) 17 Western State U L Rev (415-428).

Welkowitz DS 'State of the State: Is There a Future for State Dilution Laws?' (2007-2008) 24 Santa Clara Computer & High Technology L J (681-713).

—. DS *Trademark Dilution Federal, State, and International Law* (1st edn The Bureau of National Affairs Washington 2002).

Wilf S 'Who Authors Trademarks?' (1999) 17 Cardozo Arts & Entertainment L J (1-46).

Zekos GI 'Trademarks and Cyberspace' (2006) 9(5) The J of World Intellectual Property (496-547).

Zemer L 'On the Value of Copyright Theory' (2006) 1 Intellectual Property Q (55-71).

—. *The Idea of Authorship in Copyright* (1st edn Ashgate Publishing Limited England 2007).

INDEX